ONE HUNDRED AND FIFTY YEARS OF COLLECTING
BY THE HISTORICAL SOCIETY OF PENNSYLVANIA

George Washington by Joseph Wright

ONE HUNDRED AND FIFTY YEARS OF COLLECTING

by the

HISTORICAL SOCIETY OF PENNSYLVANIA 1824–1974

by

NICHOLAS B. WAINWRIGHT

HISTORICAL SOCIETY OF PENNSYLVANIA
PHILADELPHIA PENNSYLVANIA 1974

*Copyright © 1974 by the Historical Society of Pennsylvania
Library of Congress Catalog Card No. 74-24334
ISBN: 0-910732-09-4*

*Manufactured in the United States of America
by The Winchell Company of Philadelphia*

TABLE OF CONTENTS

Preface by Boies Penrose	vii
Author's Introduction	ix
Relics of the Penns	3
Poor Richard	15
Washingtoniana	25
Munificent Collectors	35
Colonial Days	45
Dawn of a New Nation	59
Nineteenth Century from 1800 to 1860	71
Civil War to Twentieth Century	85
Twentieth Century	99

PREFACE

This year the Historical Society of Pennsylvania passes an important milestone—its sesquicentennial (not to be confused with the civic disaster of 1926). Although our Society was not founded by Benjamin Franklin, yet its history is venerable and its accomplishments of great importance. Many of its manuscripts are of national value, while its holdings of early Pennsylvania printing are unique, and its service to scholars and researchers through a century and a half has been absolutely inestimable. Thus, it has seemed fitting, on our hundred-and-fiftieth anniversary, to publish a description of our more significant possessions.

It is not always realized that historical societies are more than mere repositories of books and manuscripts of local interest; many of them contain much material of an artistic nature, while a few have picture galleries of enviable quality. And, of course, every historical society that is sufficiently well established issues a magazine in addition to other publications. In consequence, therefore, of our sesquicentennial, the Historical Society of Pennsylvania is publishing an anniversary volume which we hope will be a lasting memorial to our collections.

We have in our building at 1300 Locust Street, Philadelphia, one of the greatest of all collections of early American paintings (a splendid catalogue of which has just been published by the Society); we also possess a fine selection of colonial Philadelphia silver, along with some highly important pieces of English silver of Philadelphia interest; some outstanding examples of Philadelphia Chippendale furniture; the most complete assemblage known of prints and drawings of Philadelphia and southeastern Pennsylvania; a wonderful cabinet of early maps and atlases, especially of those concerning Pennsylvania; a mass of other works of art and virtu, and other decorative memorabilia (I refuse to use the dirty word "artifacts"), much of which is described herein; and a manuscript collection magnificent beyond description.

It is especially appropriate that this volume should appear in the year of the retirement of our popular and accomplished Director, Nicholas Biddle Wainwright, who has controlled the fortunes of the Society since the retirement of his predecessor, Richard Norris Williams II, in 1965. As his name implies, Nick (as he is known to all the officers of the Society) is a true-born Philadelphian to the bone, or at least since the Biddles descended on us like manna from Heaven. He received the groundings of an education at St. George's School at Newport, that nursery of many Philadelphians. There he was taught to read and write at the feet of Arthur Roberts, the one original Mr. Chips who also mentored Ogden Nash and the present writer. Thence he matriculated at Princeton, where he studied American history and literature, graduating with distinction in 1936. Three years later he signed on with the Historical Society as Research Librarian, and, with the exception of five years service with the colors (1941-1946), he has been with us ever since. In 1952 Mr. Wainwright became the editor of our quarterly, *The Pennsylvania Magazine of History and Biography*, which he has constantly maintained as the "front-runner" of all historical society journals, a place it has held throughout its long life and which Julian P. Boyd so well sustained during his editorship four decades ago. Besides this, he has written five books of outstanding merit published by the Historical Society, as well as half a dozen other volumes of Philadelphia interest published outside our walls. His Historical Society books are: *Philadelphia in the Romantic Age of Lithography* (1958 and reissued in 1970); *Colonial Grandeur in Philadelphia: The House and Furniture of General John Cadwalader* (1964); *The Irvine Story* (1964); *A Philadelphia Perspective: The Diary of Sidney George Fisher* (1967); and *Paintings and Miniatures at the Historical Society of Pennsylvania* (1974). Among his other books on local subjects, two deserve special mention: *A Philadelphia Story: 1752-1952. The Philadelphia Contributionship* (1952), a beautifully illustrated volume which gained him The Athenaeum Literary Award that year and which was subsequently republished in Japanese; and, as principal author, *The History of the First Troop, Philadelphia City Cavalry* (1948), in which vigorous but ancient organization Mr. Wainwright served as an officer.

In addition to his literary work and his brilliant editorship of the *Pennsylvania Magazine*, as well as his routine administrative duties, Mr. Wainwright has been extremely successful in gaining for the Society some of its most valuable and most valued treasures, while his ability to wheedle money from foundations for divers projects has been absolutely magnetic. The Society does well to honor him.

To his place as Director has recently been named James E. Mooney, a Harvard graduate who did his apprenticeship at the American Antiquarian Society at Worcester, and who in his own right is a qualified historian of the American Tories in the Revolution. Mr. Mooney has been with us over a year now, and has "settled in." We all hope that his tenure as Director will be a long one. Meanwhile, Director Emeritus Wainwright will remain with us and will continue to edit the *Magazine* from the upper reaches of our building. He may even have several more books in the stocks as well.

And so the Historical Society of Pennsylvania enters its fourth half-century with pride in its past and high hopes for its future.

Boies Penrose
President

INTRODUCTION

To mark the centennial of the Historical Society of Pennsylvania in 1924, its President, Hampton L. Carson, composed a two-volume history of the institution. Various vicissitudes delayed publication and it was not until 1940 that the work appeared in print, eleven years after its author's death. Now, in 1974, another anniversary year is at hand which the Board of the Society has decided should be noticed by yet another commemorative publication.

Mr. Carson's volumes give a complete account of the Society for its first hundred years. In addition to dwelling on accessions, he devoted extended coverage to biographies of officers and prominent members. The Society's various homes, programs, and publications are all presented in detail.

The present volume does not carry on by bringing Mr. Carson's history up to date. Instead, its scope is restricted to a discussion of the Society's holdings, with emphasis on the most significant. At that, its collections are so numerous, so various, so vast that only a synopsis is possible. Still, it is the author's hope that this illustrated narrative will sufficiently suggest to the reader the wealth of the overall collections, and that he will be able to surmise from what has been revealed the extent of that part of the iceberg which remains submerged.

Mr. James E. Mooney, my successor as Director, is the designer and editor of this volume. What it contains in artistry in printing and layout is due to him. Two of the Society's department heads, Peter J. Parker and John H. Platt, Jr., have been helpful in their readings of the manuscript. Finally, I tip my hat to Sarah B. Pomerantz, the efficient Assistant to the Treasurer, who typed the manuscript, to Louis W. Meehan, the Society's talented photographer, who supplied most of the illustrations, and to Assistant Librarian Anthony A. Roth, to whom I confidently turned when in need of obscure facts.

Nicholas B. Wainwright
Director Emeritus

ONE HUNDRED AND FIFTY YEARS OF COLLECTING
BY THE HISTORICAL SOCIETY OF PENNSYLVANIA

Relics of the Penns

From its start the Historical Society conceived its major role to be that of a collector. Not long after its founding, its somewhat indiscriminate approach to acquiring possessions was set forth in a circular which began, "As it is the intention of the Society to form an ample library and cabinet, it will gratefully receive all donations of books, pamphlets, or manuscripts, on any subject or of any date; medals, coins, or any other article deriving value from historical or biographical affinities. . . ." As it chanced, its first gift, presented by Joseph Sansom on May 13, 1825, was a silver medal, a most appropriate initial acquisition, for the medal honored William Penn.

Made in London about 1731 for the Barclay family, it commemorates the settlement of Pennsylvania. On one side of the medal are figures of Penn and an Indian shaking hands, and the legend, "By Deeds of Peace. Pensylvania Setled 1681"; the other side displays a portrait of Penn after Silvanus Bevan's ivory bas-relief, and is inscribed with Penn's name and dates.

Bevan, a talented London apothecary who had known Penn, carved the likeness from memory about 1720, two years after the Quaker's death. His portrait, of which Bevan made three copies—medallion busts 2⅞ by 2

FURNISHINGS OF PENNSBURY

inches in size—shows Penn in portly old age. Unfortunately, all three of the original carvings are lost, but the Society owns a cast taken from one of them in 1893 as well as an eighteenth-century replica in wax, and, in addition to the silver medal given by Sansom, has one in copper, a gift from the celebrated London physician Dr. John Fothergill to James Logan, long Penn's representative in Philadelphia. The starting point in the Historical Society's collection is thus the likeness of Penn after Bevan, as captured in the silver medal. It was the foundation on which the Society was to concentrate much of its energy in accumulating records of the Proprietors of Pennsylvania.

Upon Penn's return to England in 1701 quite a number of his possessions remained in the colony, some of them furnishings of his manor house, Pennsbury. A large Jacobean chest, a

SILVER MEDAL HONORING PENN

3

PENN IN ARMOR

cradle, and several chairs, gifts to the Society, have this provenance. From other backgrounds have come Penn's shaving basin and ewer, a donation in 1827 by Thomas I. Wharton, one of the Society's founders, and such varied items of

PENN'S PARAPHERNALIA

Penn's as a brass pocket compass, a razor, and the blue sash he wore in 1682 at an Indian treaty. A quaint reminder of the past is the 1864 gift of the weather vane which crowned the first mill on Chester Creek, built in 1699 by Penn in partnership with Samuel Carpenter and Caleb Pusey. The craftsman who forged the vane included on it the 1699 date and the initials of the three partners.

In its early days, the Society was fortunate in gaining a patron in Granville Penn, the Founder's grandson. He presented in 1833 the portrait in armor which has been so extensively reproduced. This painting, inscribed with the date October 14, 1666, shows Penn at the age of twenty-two. However, it was actually not painted until a century after that time, being one of three identical copies ordered possibly by Penn's son and Granville's father, Thomas Penn, evidently taken from an original which has not survived. Of its authenticity, Granville Penn had no doubt. He declared that it was "a very perfect portrait of William Penn," and, moreover, the only one taken of him from life. Of the two other armor copies, one was last located in 1916, and the third is still owned by a Penn descendant. The Society's copy has always been accorded the place of honor in its hall.

GRAVE OF PENN BY DE CORT

Stimulated by his 1833 generosity, Granville Penn sent more paintings the following year. One of these was a landscape commissioned by his brother John and executed by Hendrik Frans De Cort of Antwerp. It portrays a view of the Quaker meeting house at Jordan's. To give the scene an historical character, "it supposes Montesquieu visiting William Penn's grave." The painting was subsequently given a more local flavor when copied in primitive

PENN, CARPENTER, AND PUSEY VANE

style by Edward Hicks. Also included in the 1834 gift was a portrait of Patrick Gordon, Governor of Pennsylvania from 1726 to 1736, painted by Gustavus Hesselius, and two great prizes—Gustavus Hesselius' magnificent Delaware Indians, Tishcohan and Lapowinsa, painted for the Founder's son, John Penn, in 1735. Finally, Granville Penn sent over a gold ring made by John Lamb of London in 1792. It contains a lock of William Penn's hair cut in 1715 by his wife Hannah, and has been worn on state occasions by the President of the Historical Society. The last of the Penn benefactions came from the hands of Granville's son. In 1857, Granville John Penn called at the Society to present the great wampum belt given to William Penn by the Indians at the fabled peace meeting at Shackamaxon, held in the shade of the ancient Kensington elm, known thereafter as the Treaty Tree.

Portraits of members of the Penn family continued to arrive, enriching the collection. The Society was given paintings of Penn's wife Hannah and daughter Margaret, both by John Hesselius, son of Gustavus, and two large portraits of Penn's sons John and Richard, taken in the early 1740s by Joseph Highmore. Highmore also painted their brother Thomas at the same time, and this likeness is represented at the Society by a copy commissioned in the 1890s shortly before the original was destroyed by fire. Other portraits include an enormous one of Granville Penn, painted by Robert McInnes in 1837, and a pair of colored crayon portraits of William and Hannah Penn by Francis Place, acquired at auction in London

TISHCOHAN AND LAPOWINSA BY GUSTAVUS HESSELIUS

PENN'S WAMPUM BELT RECEIVED AT SHACKAMAXON

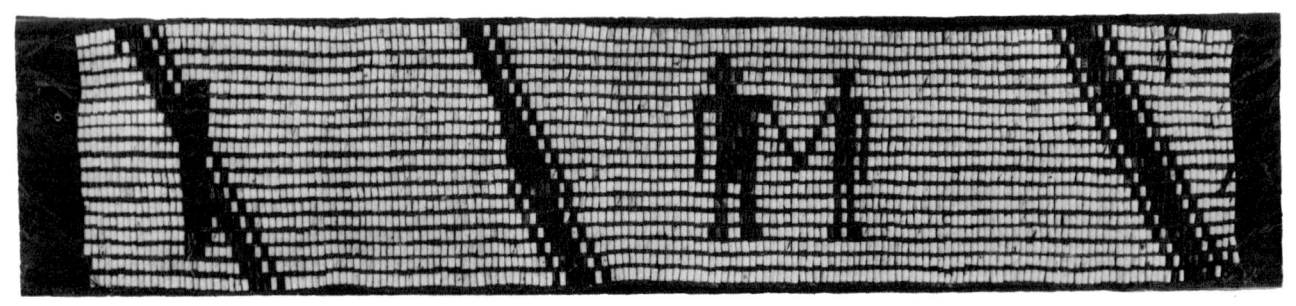

PENN AND HIS WIFE BY FRANCIS PLACE

MRS. PENN AND MARGARET PENN BY JOHN HESSELIUS

in 1957. These are both signed by the artist and have a lengthy provenance, although they were not described in print as Penn portraits until 1840.

The circular previously mentioned on the Society's collecting ambitions stressed the intention to form an "ample library." Such a hope has been fulfilled, and careful attention to William Penn has resulted in the amassing of a major number of his religious, political, and promotional works, many of them in numerous editions. These include an early tract, printed in London in 1668, *The Guide Mistaken, And Temporizing rebuked*; a 1669 edition of his celebrated *No Cross, no Crown: or several Sober Reasons Against Hat-Honour, Titular-Respects, You to a single Person, with the*

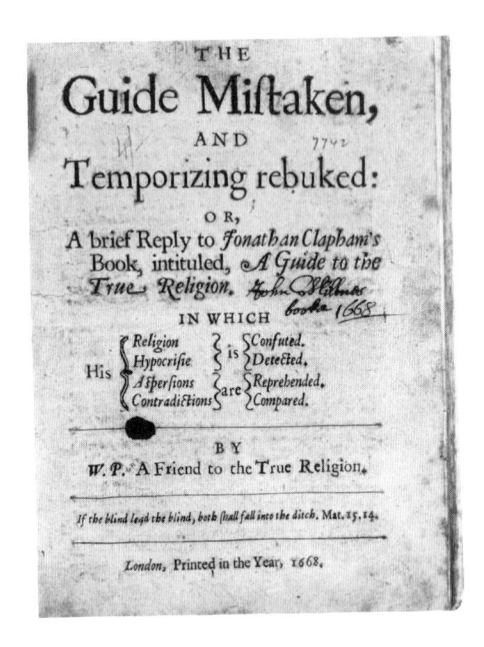

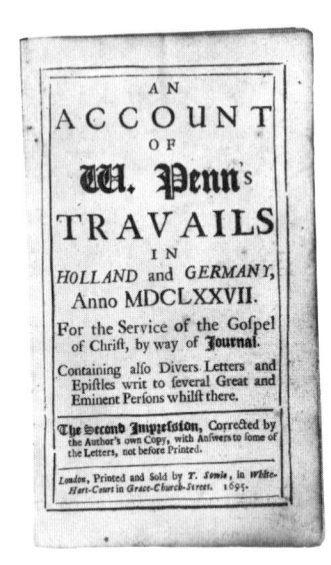

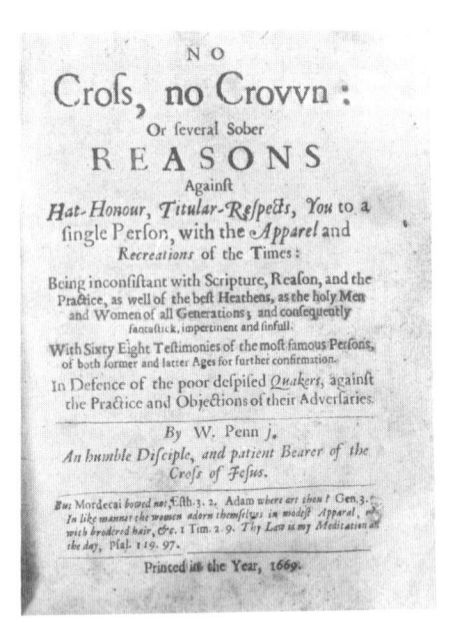

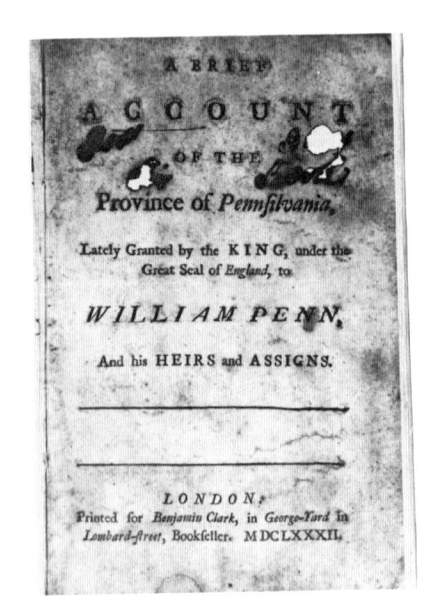

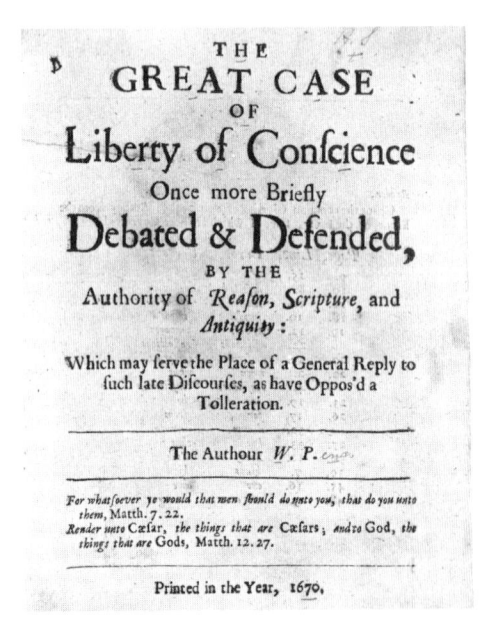

SOME OF PENN'S PUBLISHED WORKS

Apparel and Recreations of the Times... In Defence of the poor despised Quakers (also a 1702 edition that belonged to Hannah Penn); and a 1670 printing of *The Great Case of Liberty of Conscience Once more Briefly Debated & Defended... a General Reply to such late Discourses, as have Oppos'd a Tolleration.*

Of sentimental interest is *An Account of W. Penn's Travails in Holland and Germany, Anno MDCLXXVII* (London, 1695). In this the author inscribed "For my Deare ffriend Hannah Callowhill junr. W.P." Shortly afterwards she became his second wife. The Society owns not only their marriage certificate but the original manuscript of Penn's travel book. Yet another 1695 printing of a Penn tract, *Tender Counsel and Advice*, is inscribed on its inside cover "For my Deare Daughtr Laetitia Penn. W.P." Of further association interest is Penn's Bible which contains his 1703 book plate. It was presented in 1874, by the subscribers to the Penn Papers.

The Founder's writings on Pennsylvania, present in the collection in various languages, are of special historical interest. Upon obtaining the royal grant for his province in March, 1681, Penn issued *A Brief Account of the Province of Pensilvania, Lately Granted by the King, under the Great Seal of England, to William Penn, And his Heirs and Assigns.* At about the same time there appeared a broadsheet, *A Brief Account of the Province of Pennsylvania in America, Lately Granted under the Great Seal of England, to William Penn.* Both of these accounts bear Penn's printed signature; the broadsheet is a unique copy.

The next year Penn revealed his liberal constitution for his province, printed in England by William Bradford. Titled *The Frame of the Government of the Province of Pennsylvania in America: Together with certain Laws Agreed upon in England By the Governour and Divers Free-Men of the aforesaid Province,* the Society's copy, acquired by purchase in 1881, is enhanced by Penn's bookplate.

In 1683, Penn described his province and gave an account of Philadelphia and its advantages in *A Letter from William Penn, Proprietary and Governor of Pennsylvania in America to the Committee of the Free Society*

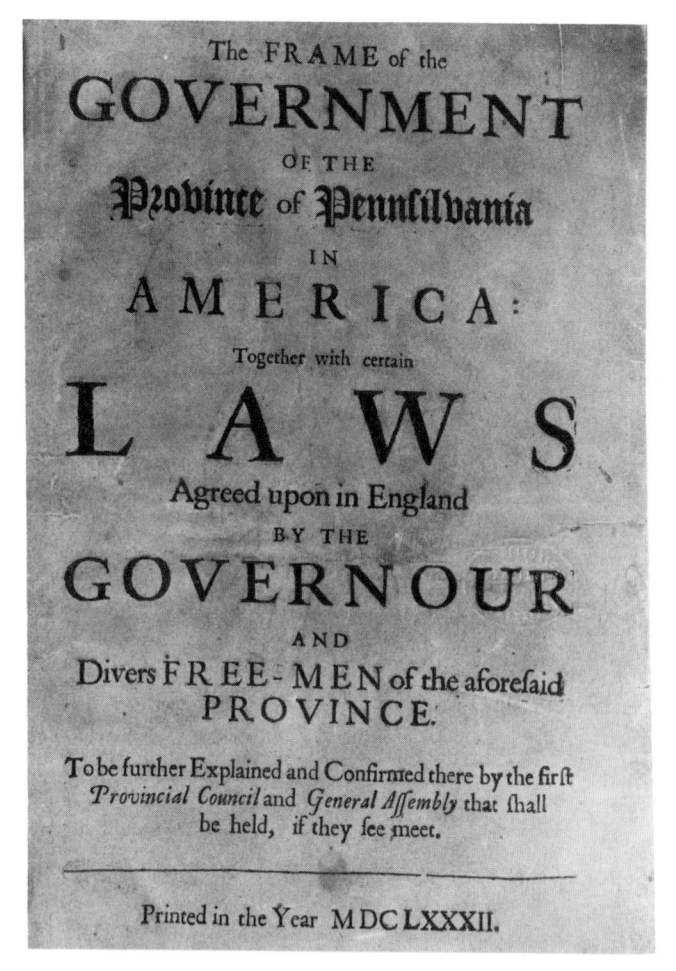

PENN'S FRAME OF GOVERNMENT

of Traders of that Province Residing in London. This pamphlet was accompanied by the first map of Philadelphia, and it is gratifying to note that the Society owns the original copper plate from which the map was printed. Of the

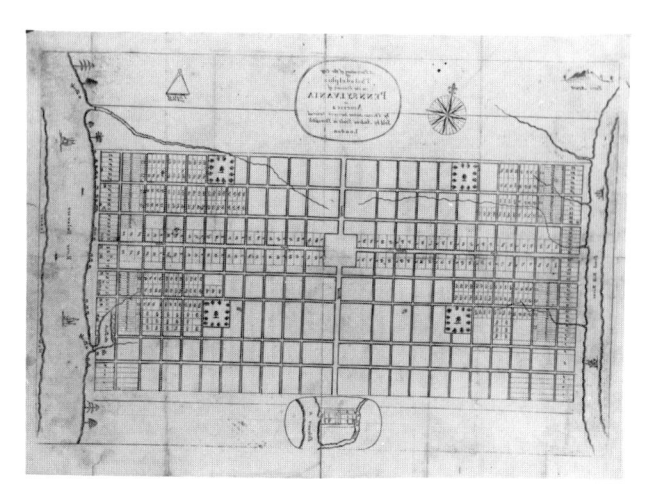

COPPER PLATE OF FIRST PHILADELPHIA MAP

Society's several copies of Penn's *Letter* to the Free Society of Traders, one was owned by Benjamin Franklin. Mention of Penn's promotional literature is limited here to these rare printings of 1681, 1682, and 1683, for it would take a catalogue to do justice to the others within the collection.

To revert a second time to the Society's circular of 1825, we note the desire to collect manuscripts "on any subject or of any date." It is fair to say that no subject for manuscript collecting proved more impelling than that of William Penn and his family. From the Society's inception down to the present day, Penn manuscripts have held priority interest and have been gathered in from a wide variety of sources. As an example, William Penn's correspondence is to be found in 157 locations in the Society's Manuscript Department. Important Penn collections have been received in the papers of Penn agents and officers, notably James Logan, Richard Peters, James Hamilton, Edmund Physick, the Cadwaladers and Rawles. Autograph collectors assembled an almost unbelievable wealth of Penn material and gave it to the Society. And there have been important purchases, highlighted by sales in the 1870s.

In 1869 the last of William Penn's descendants to bear the family name died and changes took place in estate arrangements. During the course of this an effort was made to destroy the family papers, carefully preserved in storage in London. That disaster was largely thwarted and before long an immense number of manuscripts, dating back to the career of Admiral Sir William Penn, father of the Founder, came on the market. It was an opportunity not to be missed. Money was hastily raised by subscription and most of the Penn archives were secured. Portions that the Society failed to obtain at the time were acquired later. So it was that the Society gained the most important collection of historical Pennsylvania records to come into its possession. Included in the 20,000 documents purchased were letters of all the Penns, petitions, charters, constitutions, frames of government, political and business records of the province, vast amounts of paper to do with the lengthy Penn-Baltimore boundary question, Indian affairs, correspondence of William Penn, two of his letter books, his Irish Journal, his love letters to Hannah Callowhill, Thomas Penn's vitally important letter books covering decades of proprietarial control of Pennsylvania, and a great deal more of the stuff from which history is made. While the purchases of the 1870s were not to be rivalled, other accessions, great and small, garnered in the past century and a half, have added significantly to the corpus of the Penn archive which now totals more than 30,000 items. In terms of size in one category of high interest—William Penn's original surviving letters—the Society owns the majority; in terms of specifics, many of the Penn manuscripts are spectacular.

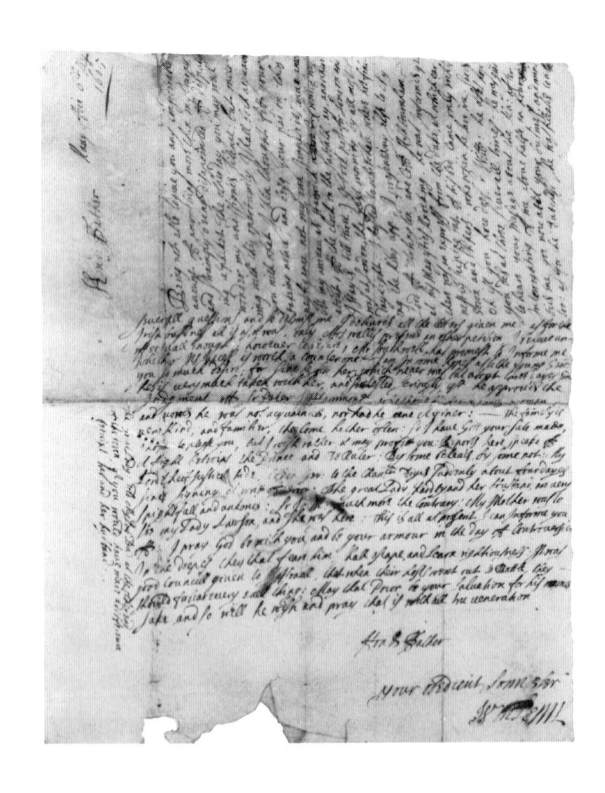

PENN'S EARLIEST LETTER

The Society has, for example, William Penn's earliest letter, written to his father from France on May 5, 1665, and it also owns Penn's last letter, addressed to James Logan, August 15, 1712. There is another letter to James Logan at the Society in Penn's hand of later date, October 4, 1712, but, sorely enfeebled by a stroke, he was unable to complete it, and it is signed by his wife.

Acquired only a few years ago is the original 1670 will of Admiral Penn. Without this instru-

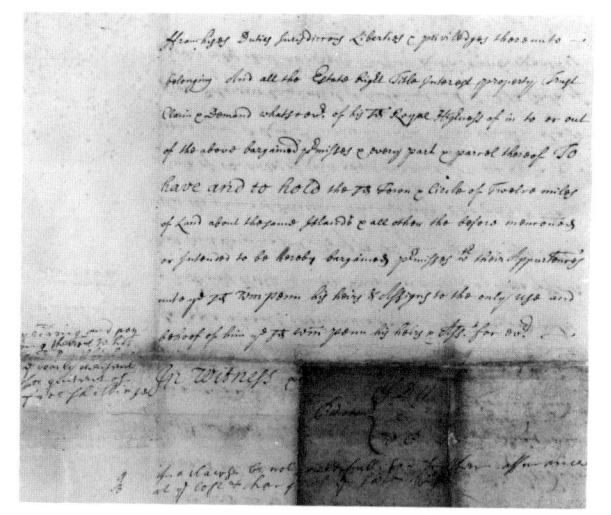

CONTRACT BETWEEN PENN AND DUKE OF YORK

ment there would have been no Pennsylvania, for in his will the Admiral appointed his son William his sole executor and chief heir, and it was on that basis that Penn sued for a grant of land in America in exchange for debts owed by the Crown to his father's estate. Also in the collection is the original draft of the terms of the grant, with corrections in Penn's hand, which served as the basis for the Royal Charter.

Having achieved his goal, Penn next persuaded Charles II to issue a directive to the inhabitants of Pennsylvania, ordering them to recognize Penn's proprietarial powers. Two copies of this document of April 2, 1681, are at the Society, each one endorsed by Penn. Six days later Penn wrote on his own behalf a three-page letter "To the Inhabitants of Pennsylvania," informing them of what had transpired, and this, too, is at the Society. By "inhabitants" only white people were intended. Penn sent a special letter, his signed retained copy of which is in the Society's Penn archive, to the "King or Kings of the Indians in Pennsylvania," telling them that he would soon come to America, but that in the meantime they were to treat with his commissioners "about Land and a firm League of Peace."

Penn's commissioners were soon at work. One evidence at the Society of their activity is a deed of sale signed by a dozen sachems who made their marks on parchment. In return for a large consignment of wampum, blankets, needles, fish hooks, axes, shot, tobacco, rum, beer and other goods, the Indians sold an

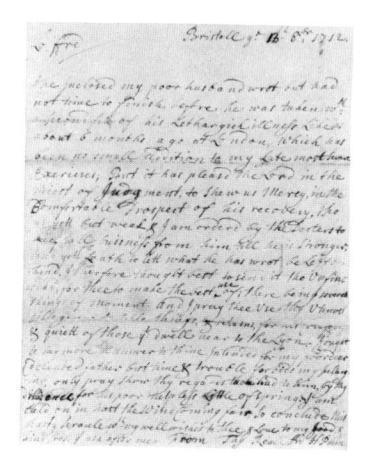

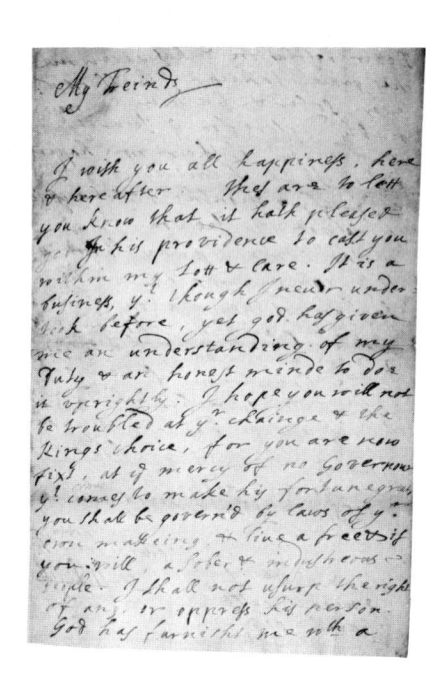

PART OF PENN'S WIFE'S LETTER

PENN'S LETTER TO THE INHABITANTS

extensive tract of land on the Delaware River that was later to constitute much of Bucks County.

A deed of earlier date, and perhaps greater interest, is dated July 10, 1680, when John Moll, agent for the Duke of York, obtained the signatures of seven chiefs to their sale of what was to become the greater part of New Castle County, Delaware, including the site of Wilmington. Receipts at the Society show that the Duke did not value this large purchase greatly. Before releasing it to William Penn he rented it to him for six shillings a year. Upon Penn's arrival at New Castle in October, 1682, he demanded possession of the Indian purchase through his right from the Duke. Moll endorsed the deed over to him, to which Penn added an identifying comment: "Jo Moll Indian Purchase to me. W.P." Considered one of the prizes of the 1870 sale, this document was too expensive for the Society at that time, but was finally acquired in 1936.

In August, 1684, Penn was obliged to return to England. His commission to Thomas Lloyd and others to take charge of his government has survived at the Society as has his letter of August 12 from on board the ketch *Endeavor*, again addressed to Lloyd and his associates, which, together with his final instructions, contains Penn's well-known prayer for Philadelphia. Upon his departure he gave Lloyd his silver snuff box, marked "W.P." It remained in the possession of Lloyd descendants until 1973, when it was bequeathed to the Society.

While in England Penn continued to direct his provincial officers and much of this correspondence is in the Society's collection, letters such as one of 1685 ordering the Philadelphia magistrates to reduce the number of drinking houses and to purge the caves in the river bank, where nocturnal activities had become notorious. Among documents of state, engrossed on huge sheets of parchment, are the original Charter of Germantown, signed by Penn on August 12, 1689, and the second Charter of Philadelphia, which he signed on May 20, 1691.

In 1699 Penn returned to Philadelphia, but in 1701 was forced to hasten back to London to protect his interests against Lord Baltimore. With him he took an address to the Crown "signed" by six Susquehanna and Shawnee Indians, and witnessed by five of the principal colonists. The Indians commended Penn's behavior, expressed grief at his departure and thanks for his generosity, "besides what he has paid us for our Lands, which no Governr.

PENN'S LETTER FROM THE INDIANS

PENN'S LAST LETTER

ever did before him." They recorded the hope that he would always govern "these parts." Penn evidently did not use this piece of propaganda aimed at Lord Baltimore's land claims, for it remained with the family archives in England until coming to Philadelphia. Other 1701 documents with a similar history, dating from just before Penn sailed from "New Castle on Delaware," were his departing commission to the Provincial Council and his seven-page will, each page of which bears his autograph.

This will was superseded by another in the collection dated 1705, the year Penn wrote a recently acquired letter to Governor John Evans, mentioning that he had been attacked with "some swimming in my head." Poor Penn's last years were ones of trouble and ill-health.

While the emphasis in this account of the Society's Penn family records has been on the Founder, the bulk of the record pertains to the running of the province after his death. More manuscripts have survived for this much longer period. During the proprietorship of Thomas Penn, Philadelphia became the largest and richest city in the colonies, inland towns were laid out, the frontiers were pushed back by more Indian purchases, a French and Indian war was won, Pittsburgh came into being. A meticulous and hard-working man, Thomas Penn's correspondence deals closely with all developments in the colony from about 1740 to 1770. The Society has published his correspondence in a microfilm edition of ten reels accompanied by a printed guide. Steps are now in progress at the Society which will lead to a similar publication of his father's papers.

PENN'S 1703 BOOKPLATE WITH COAT OF ARMS

A PAGE OF FRANKLIN'S PRINTING ACCOUNTS

Poor Richard

Pennsylvania has had its share of prominent sons and daughters, but none has equalled the fame of Benjamin Franklin. His story, part folklore, often controversial, always interesting, bulks large in the nation's historical annals. In part, it rests on the holdings at the Society, for, to begin with, Franklin was a printer, and the Society owns the largest number of works from his press.

The forerunner of these was the first Philadelphia pamphlet for which Franklin set the type. Printed with Samuel Keimer's imprint in 1725, it was the work of Pennsylvania's first political economist, Francis Rawle—*Ways and Means for the Inhabitants of Delaware to become Rich*. For Franklin, a major means to wealth was the publishing of a newspaper. On October 2, 1729, he began to issue *The Pennsylvania Gazette*, which he had purchased from Keimer. The Society owns the most complete run of this important paper, the first two volumes of which (including Franklin's initial number known in only three copies) may have been Franklin's otherwise missing file copy, for it was purchased from the Brinley library which contained books procured from a Franklin source. As a service to scholars, the Society has reproduced the *Gazette* on microfilm and in a facsimile edition. The industrious printer also published a German newspaper in 1755-1757, the *Philadelphische Zeitung*, the only known copies of which are at the Society.

Franklin's printing of Ralph Sandiford's antislavery essay, *A Brief Examination of the Times*, published January-February, 1729, was the first pamphlet to bear his imprint. The Society's copy is one of six known. Rarer yet is Franklin's second pamphlet, a treatise on the paper currency, written by Franklin and dated April 13, 1729. The Society's copy of *A Modest*

FRANKLIN'S ENGLISH-LANGUAGE AND GERMAN-LANGUAGE NEWSPAPERS

Enquiry into the Nature and Necessity of a Paper-Currency (Printed and sold at the New-Printing Office, near the Market) is inscribed "To Springet Penn Esqr," a grandson of William Penn, and is one of three known copies.

Prospering as a printer, Franklin was drawn inevitably to almanacs. Filled with all sorts of information, almanacs were popular and therefore profitable. They were issued in the autumn and forecast the weather for the following year. Franklin's first *Poor Richard, 1733*, appeared late in 1732 and was an instant success. Despite the three impressions of it which were prepared, only two variant copies have survived. Fortunately, the Society has one of them as well as the most complete run of *Poor Richard*, lacking only four years through 1775, and complete from 1778 through 1800 except for four years. In addition, its run of the minute miniature version of *Poor Richard*, the pocket almanacs, wants only two years between 1742 and 1769.

Franklin's interests were never limited to the needs of the print shop. His friendship with James Logan led to his printing two translations by that noted scholar. The first was *Cato's Moral Disticks, Englished in Couplets*, printed in 1735. The Society's copy may have belonged to Logan since written on its title page in the

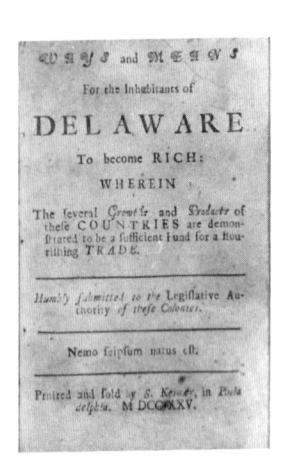

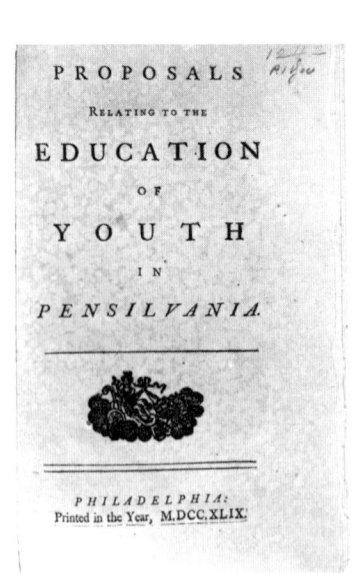

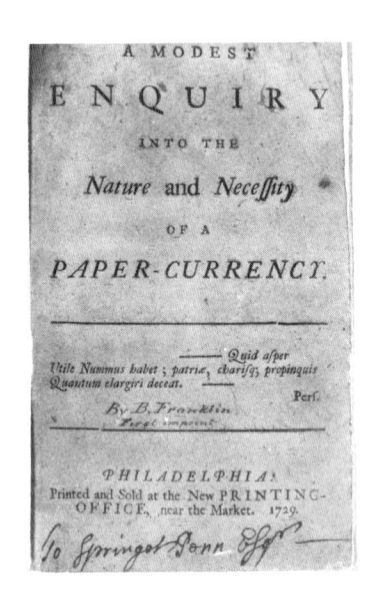

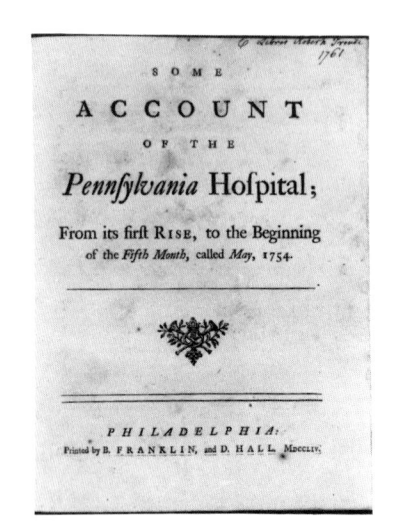

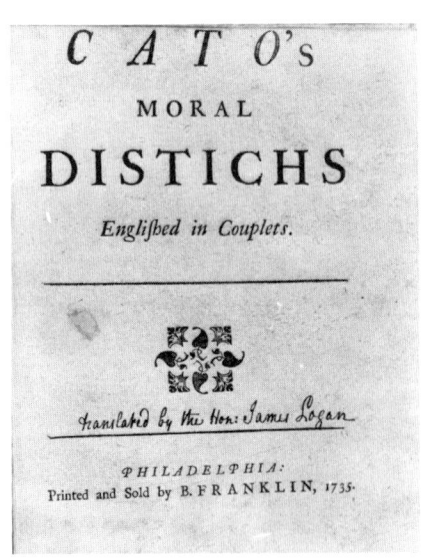

EXAMPLES OF FRANKLIN AS TYPE-SETTER, AUTHOR, AND PRINTER

hand of his grandson's wife is "translated by the Hon: James Logan." Logan's second work was *M. T. Cicero's Cato Major, or His Discourse of Old-Age*. Printed in 1744, its title in both red ink and black, this has been acclaimed the best specimen of printing from Franklin's press. Among the Society's copies is one of the first state with "ony" for "only" on line five, page twenty-seven, and, preserved in its original leather binding, this is one of the finest copies in existence. It was formerly owned by A. Edward Newton, noted Philadelphia bookman.

Among other Franklin printings which have aroused the enthusiasm of collectors is his *An Account of the New Invented Pennsylvanian Fire-Places* (1744). Here, in promoting the comfort of his fellow man, we see the many-sided genius—inventor, author, printer and publisher. The engraved plate of this comparatively scarce pamphlet, some twenty-one copies have been located, was drawn by Franklin's friend Lewis Evans and may be the first piece of his to be engraved. Evans was to achieve renown as the leading American cartographer of his day. The Society's copy belonged to John Dickinson.

Between 1736 and 1762, Franklin printed thirteen Indian treaties. These stately folios represented a new form of literature, recording in the quaint language of the forest the tenuous Indian relations of colonial times. The Society owns ten of these treaties, including the first and rarest (only two copies known), *A Treaty of Friendship Held with the Chiefs of the Six Nations, at Philadelphia, in September and October, 1736*. In 1938, all thirteen of Franklin's

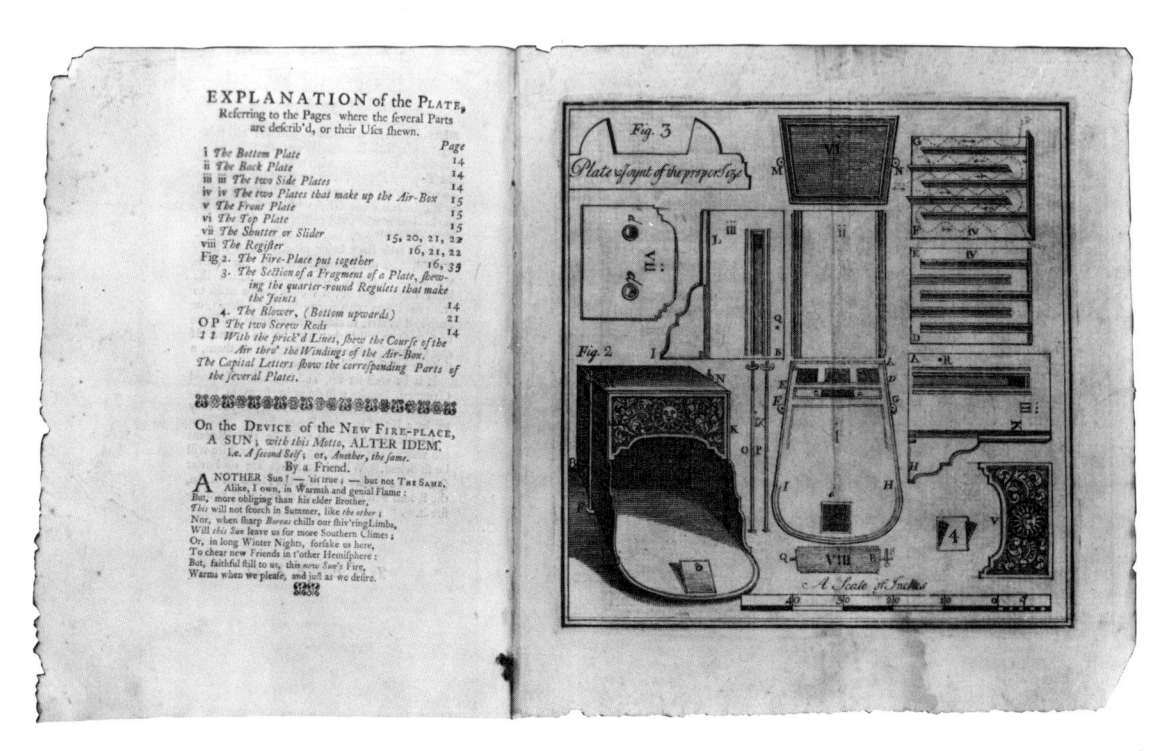

FRANKLIN'S TANKARD, TOOLS, AND BOOK

LAST PAGE AND PLATE OF FRANKLIN'S ACCOUNT OF HIS FIREPLACE

treaties were reproduced in facsimile under the editorship of Julian P. Boyd and were published by the Society in the handsomest volume it has yet sponsored.

One of Franklin's rare unsuccessful ventures was his attempt to establish a periodical in imitation of *The Gentleman's Magazine*, which had been founded in London in 1731. His *General Magazine, and Historical Chronicle For all the British Plantations in America* ran for only the first six months of 1741. On the title page of the Society's copy appears the signature of our first female historian, Deborah Logan.

Franklin's genius lay in his ability to rise to the occasion. In 1747 with Great Britain at war with both France and Spain, Philadelphians feared an attack by privateers. The Quaker province offered no defense against such a threat. In his customary practical way, Franklin sought a solution through a voluntary military organization and published a pamphlet in which he called for an association for defense. *Plain Truth: or Serious Considerations On the Present State of the City of Philadelphia and Province of Pennsylvania*, of which the Society owns a first edition, was a rousing success, and the Association it promoted spread throughout the colony, creating an impressive militia, the offshoots of which have continued to the present day.

The printer's many interests are to be seen in a variety of his works at the Society. In 1741 he issued *A Catalogue of Books Belonging to the Library Company of Philadelphia*, of which Franklin was a founder. The Society's copy is autographed by Charles Norris, Deborah Logan's father. To promote the establishment of a college, Franklin in 1749 wrote and published *Proposals Relating to the Education of Youth in Pennsylvania*, which led to his recognition as the founder of the University of Pennsylvania. When the institution opened in 1751, he printed the Rev. Richard Peters' inaugural sermon. That same year the basis of his international reputation was established with the printing in London of *Franklin's Experiments And Observations on Electricity, Made at Philadelphia*.

Franklin excelled in matters of a practical nature. His wholehearted support for the proposal to found a hospital led him to write and print in 1754 *Some Account of the Pennsylvania Hospital*. Its cornerstone was laid the next year and Franklin was elected president of its board. The Society has several copies of *Some Account*, one of them signed in 1761 by the teacher and historian Robert Proud. On the flyleaf of

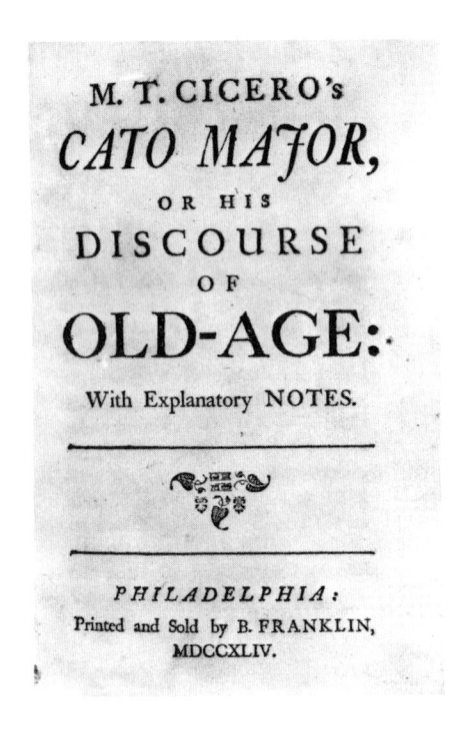

FRANKLIN'S FINEST PRINTING

FRANKLIN'S UNSUCCESSFUL MAGAZINE

another copy, a gift to the Society in 1872, is inscribed "This was a presentation copy from the Contributors to the Pennsylvania Hospital to William Bingham Esquire Speaker of the House of Representatives of Pennsylvania 1792."

Not all of the Society's Franklin-associated books were the product of his press. *An Essay Upon Money and Coins* bears a London, 1757, imprint and his inscription, "From B. F. for Isaac Norris Esq." Another example is his authorship while in London in 1761 of an argument to persuade the British to retain Canada, rather than to release it in favor of keeping sugar-rich Guadaloupe, which the British had also captured from the French. The Society's copy of his *The Interest of Great Britain Considered With Regard to Her Colonies and the Acquisitions of Canada and Guadaloupe* contains Franklin's inscription, "To the Revd. Dr. Mayhew from his humble Servt. The Author."

The Society's Frankliniana is enhanced not only by books printed or written by Franklin but by books owned by him. In 1822 the Athenaeum of Philadelphia acquired from William

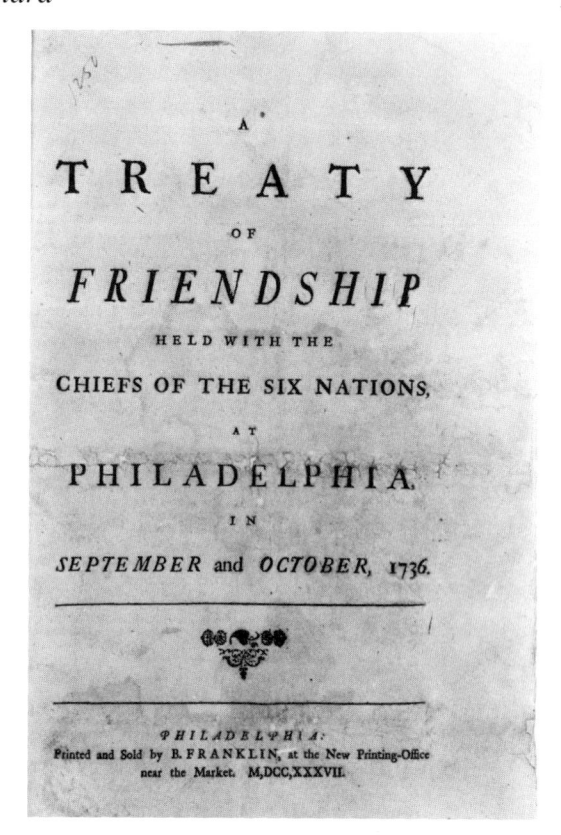

AN INDIAN TREATY BY FRANKLIN

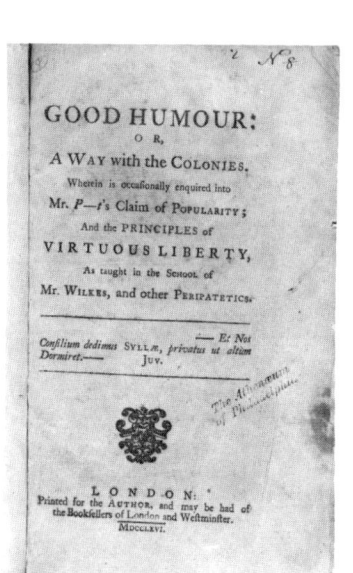

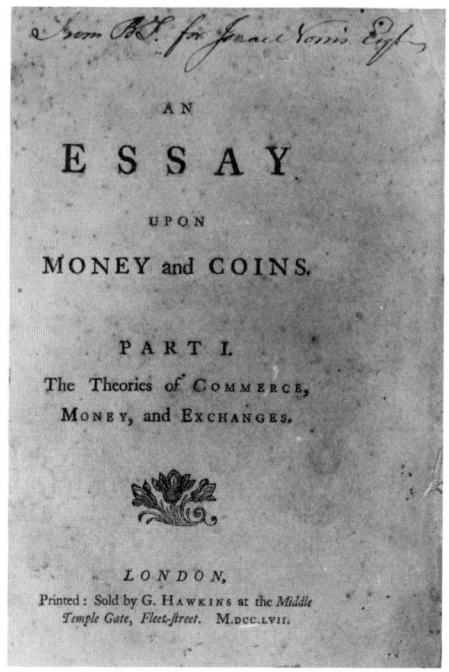

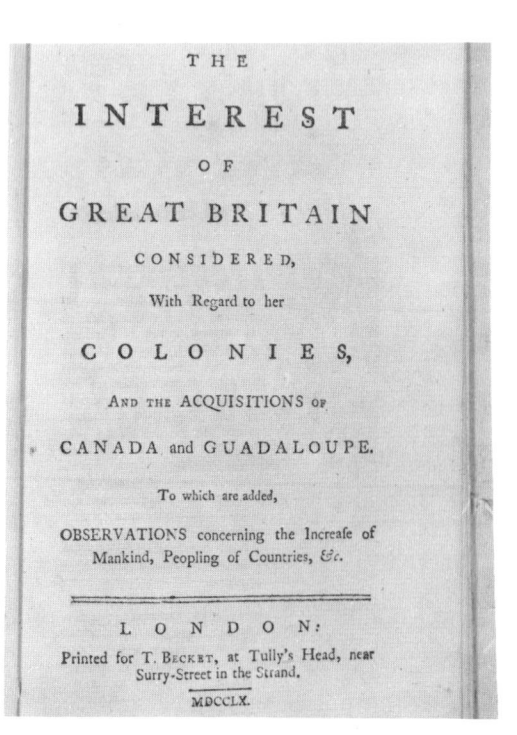

LONDON IMPRINTS OWNED OR WRITTEN BY FRANKLIN

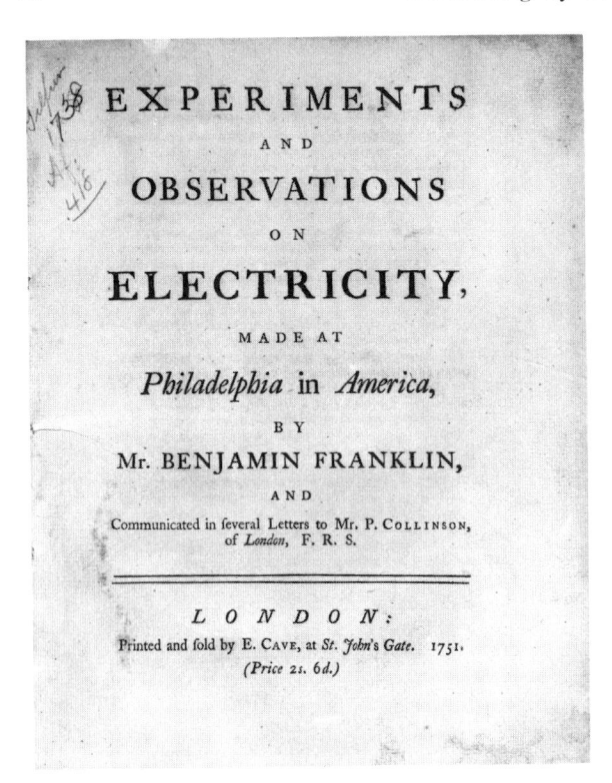

REPORT ON FRANKLIN'S EXPERIMENTS

PART OF A LETTER IN CODE TO FRANKLIN

Duane, Franklin's grandson, 148 volumes of bound pamphlets from the philosopher's library and sixty-six volumes of newspapers, including Franklin's personal copy of the *Pennsylvania Gazette* extending to 1758. The price for the lot was $260. Over the years this collection was repeatedly raided. The *Pennsylvania Gazette* disappeared; noted collectors purchased in good faith Franklin items stolen from the Athenaeum. This situation led its directors to sell its Franklin books to the Society in 1887.

Of this acquisition, which now consists of 862 pamphlets bound in 121 volumes, the distinguished Franklin scholar George Simpson Eddy has observed: "I consider this collection to be one of the great treasures of the Historical Society." Many of the pamphlets were presentation copies and some contain notes in Franklin's hand, such as *Good Humor, or a Way with the Colonies* (London, 1766), which is copiously annotated. The pamphlets deal with politics, science, medicine, and American affairs; more than two hundred are in French. Included in that category are two pamphlets from Franklin's private press at Passy.

Complementing Franklin's books is a substantial holding of manuscripts—about a hundred letters by him, five hundred received by him, and a thousand other documents in the form of notes, drafts, and official papers. The corpus of this collection had belonged to William Temple Franklin and was given in 1876 by Miss Mary Fox of Champlost. It is contained in fourteen volumes and three boxes, but, aside from these, Franklin material is scattered through many of the Society's manuscript collections.

Among the more important Franklin papers are his autograph notes of his examination before Parliament about the Stamp Act, his rules for the Junto and for the attendance of the

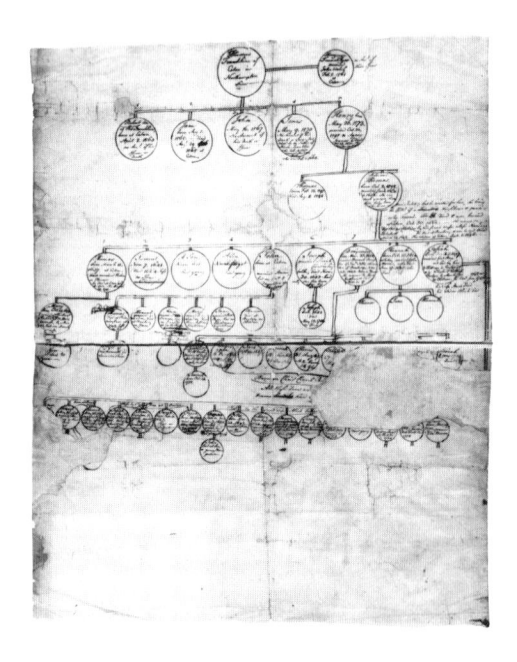

FRANKLIN'S GENEALOGICAL CHART

directors of the Library Company, the accounts of Franklin and Hall, 1747-1766, his receipt book with Samuel Rhoads for building his house in Franklin Court, and eight volumes of correspondence with Congress while minister to France. Considering the amount of genealogical research that takes place at the Society, Franklin's delvings into his family's background find an appropriate home. While in England in 1758 he conducted an extensive search, and the Society possesses two volumes of his papers on that subject—church records, births, marriages, deaths, and correspondence with distant relatives. The culmination of his work, "Memo of the Family," is his genealogical chart covering six generations of Franklins.

As for the rest of his papers at the Society, his correspondence in France with Robert Morris is of importance. One pleasant reminder of his career there is seen in the resolves of Congress of September 11 and 14, 1778, unanimously appointing him minister plenipotentiary, forwarded by Charles Thomson, Secretary of Congress. Another is a handsome passport form, printed by Franklin on his press at Passy in 1782, which begins "Nous Benjamin Franklin, Ecuyer, Ministre Plénipotentiare des Etats-Unis de l'Amerique, près Sa Majesté Très-Chrêtienne. . . ." Signed by Franklin and, as secretary, by his grandson William Temple Franklin, it was made out for young William Rawle who was later to enjoy a distinguished career as a lawyer and to serve as the Historical Society's first president.

SILHOUETTE OF FRANKLIN

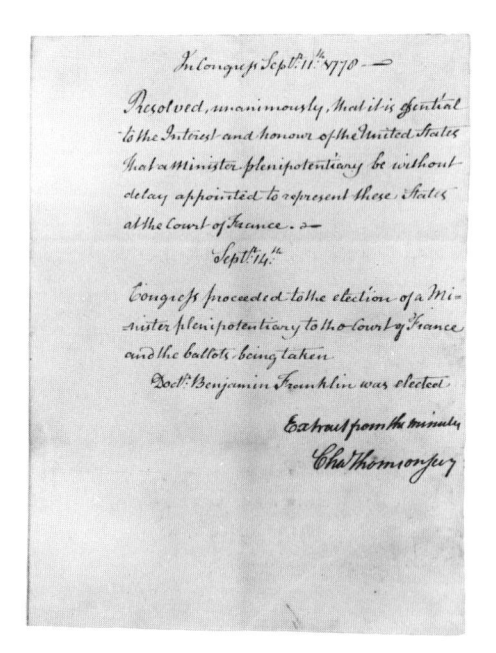

FRANKLIN'S APPOINTMENT TO FRANCE

FRANKLIN'S MUSIC STAND

In addition to books and manuscripts, the Society has a number of Franklin's possessions. They include a four-sided music stand designed so that four players could share a single support for their sheet music; his composing stick, reminiscent of his printing days; a porcelain punch keg made in Paris around 1780, the gift of the Count D'Artois; and his burning glass and thermometer. Two pieces of silver are also in the collection. One of these, a spirit lamp on which traditionally Franklin warmed his evening toddy, came from France. The other, an impressive tankard decorated with the arms of Alexander, Fifth Earl of Antrim, Franklin brought home from England in 1775. He bequeathed it to his daughter Sarah Bache, and it remained in the possession of descendants until presented to the Society in 1958.

NINI MEDALLION OF FRANKLIN

Aside from the multitude of engravings of Franklin, which the Society would be expected to have, several likenesses deserve particular mention. Among these is a marble bust by Guiseppe Caracchi. Of the sage's French ministry, the Society owns a medallion in terra cotta by Jean Baptiste Nini, who, about 1760, entered the service of the Duc de Chaumont at his ancient Chateau de Chaumont on the Loire, near Blois. Dr. I. T. Sharpless, who gave Nini's medallion to the Society in 1860 had this to say about it: "This medallion, with about 100 others of Doct. F. was found by the Duc de Chaumont in 1849 in the attic of an old chateau belonging to the estate of his father who had been a great friend of Dr. F. . . . Gotten in Paris by Donor 1850." Nini's bust-length bas-relief, showing Franklin in profile, wearing a fur hat, is inscribed "Nini F 1777."

Something of a curiosity is Joseph Sansom's silhouette. Sansom, who gave the Society its first gift and whose name is memorialized by a street in Philadelphia, stated that his collections of silhouettes, now at the Society, were "drawn from life," but later added that they were "drawn from memory." However that may be, his small painting in black ink with delicate shading in a grey wash of an aged Franklin is a plausible likeness.

The prize of the Franklin likenesses is unquestionably Charles Willson Peale's half-length portrait of Franklin wearing a blue dressing gown. This painting was given to the Society in 1852. Peale's biographer has termed it a "solid, splendidly factual portrait." Through a window lightning flashes across the sky, Franklin holds a small lightning rod in his hand and another rod lies on the table before him, upon which the artist has copied in long hand a passage from the *Experiments and Observations on Electricity* of 1769. Franklin was painfully ill in 1789 when this portrait was commissioned. "On my waiting on the Doctor I found him confined to his bed," wrote Peale, who persuaded Franklin to sit for him, "but the pain was so great that he could only sit ¼ hour, and was ill from the pressure of the stone, for 24 hours after." Peale completed the portrait on the basis of the one he had painted from life in 1785, and, while it is essentially a copy of that painting, it is, nevertheless, the last portrait for which Benjamin Franklin sat. While Franklin the genius is forever enshrined in history, in this canvas we have our last glimpse of Franklin the man.

FRANKLIN BY CHARLES WILLSON PEALE

KNIFE & FORK USED BY WASHINGTON IN CAMP

Washingtoniana

"First in war, first in peace, and first in the hearts of his countrymen," Washington has long been a foremost collector's choice. To a degree, the strength of Americana collections of broad early national interest is reflected in their holdings of our first President. There is no doubt but that those who helped build up the Historical Society's collection paid particular regard to his importance.

The reverence with which collectors approached Washington is attested to by a curious selection of artifacts now in storage at the Society. Examples are locks of the great man's hair (it was said that much of his hair was denuded from his head shortly before his burial), bricks from places he had been, slivers of wood from his original coffin, and a hatchet made from the wood of a wild cherry tree found at Washington's birthplace. Fortunately, the Society was the recipient of objects of greater merit than these.

The Papers of George Washington project credits the Society with owning the third largest

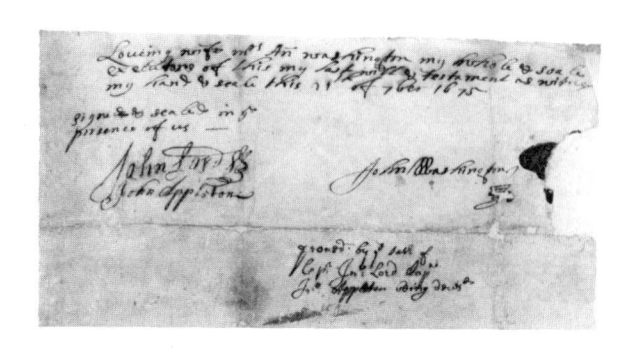

JOHN WASHINGTON'S WILL

accumulation of Washington manuscripts. This collection starts with the original will of Washington's immigrant great-grandfather, John Washington, dated September 11, 1675, and includes examples of Washington's writing at the age of twelve. In addition to early surveys, financial accounts, business papers, and signed documents, the Society owns 422 letters written by him, and 399 letters he received. Retained copies of many more letters addressed to Washington are to be found in the Society's General

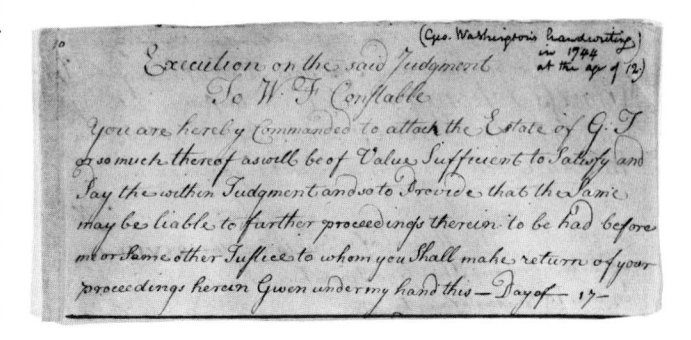

WASHINGTON'S HAND AT TWELVE

Anthony Wayne and General William Irvine papers. To cite a few will illustrate their richness and scope.

In 1754 Washington was sent with a small force to occupy the forks of the Ohio, but before he arrived the French seized the place and named it Fort Duquesne. Halting forty miles away at the Great Meadows, Washington built a fortified camp, Fort Necessity. In a lengthy letter addressed to Governor Dinwiddie of Virginia, "From our Camp, June 3, 1754," he outlined the French and Indian situation, and staunchly added: "We have just finish'd a small palisado'd Fort in which with my small numbers I shall not fear the attack of 500 men." But

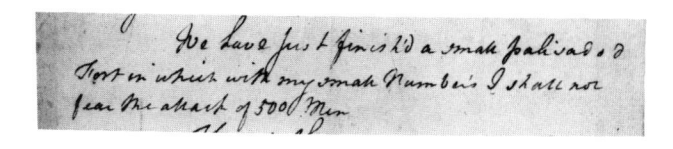

PART OF FORT NECESSITY LETTER

25

when a larger force than that besieged him exactly one month later and supplies and ammunition ran out, he was obliged to capitulate.

Another epic moment in Washington's life was his assuming command of the Continental Army at Cambridge in July, 1775. The Society has his letter written that month to his brother Samuel, describing the condition of his forces, the losses suffered by both armies at Bunker Hill, and the assault he expected the enemy to launch against him.

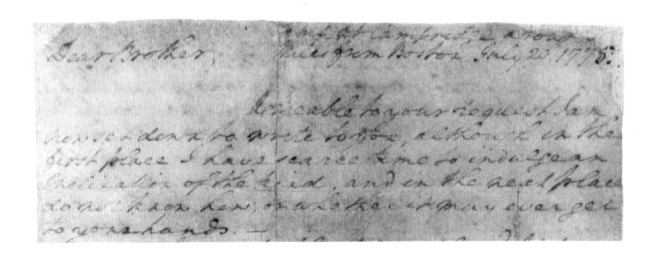

TO WASHINGTON'S BROTHER

Of greater local and dramatic interest is the commander's correspondence with General John Cadwalader in December, 1776. With New Jersey overrun by the enemy and with Philadelphia in peril, the low point in the Revolution had been reached, but Washington was about to instill new faith in the cause by brilliant victories at Trenton and Princeton. The die cast, at 6 P.M. on Christmas Day he issued orders to the Philadelphia general, writing to him from McKonkey's Ferry: "Notwithstanding the discouraging accounts I have received from Col. Reed of what might be expected from the operations below, I am determined, as the night is favourable to cross the River and make the attack upon Trenton in the morning. If you can do nothing real, at least create as great a diversion as possible."

In another letter, written during yet another gloomy period of the war, one epitomized by Valley Forge, Washington expressed his semi-humorous, semi-indignant feelings about the enemy. To Henry Laurens, President of Congress, he noted on April 18, 1778, that the British were forging his letters and publishing them in newspapers. But virtue was to have its just reward. One of the Society's most remarkable letters is that of Thomas Jefferson, writing from Monticello to congratulate Washington on the victory at Yorktown. Military cares a thing of the past, Washington and his principal officers dined in Philadelphia on New Year's Day, 1782, as guests of the Society of the Friendly Sons of St. Patrick, whose minute book in the Historical Society's collection recalls the event. A gold medal worn by Wash-

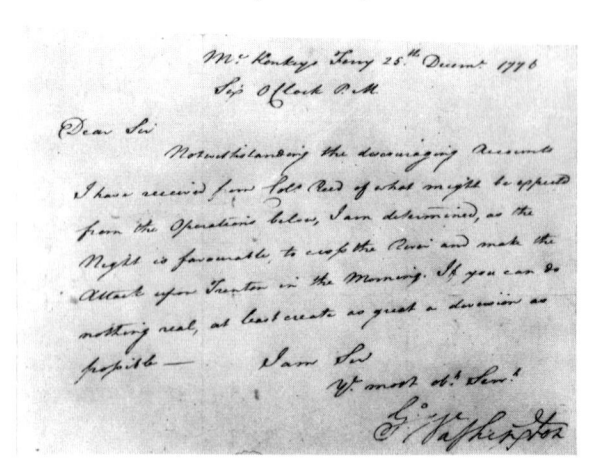

LETTER TO CADWALADER

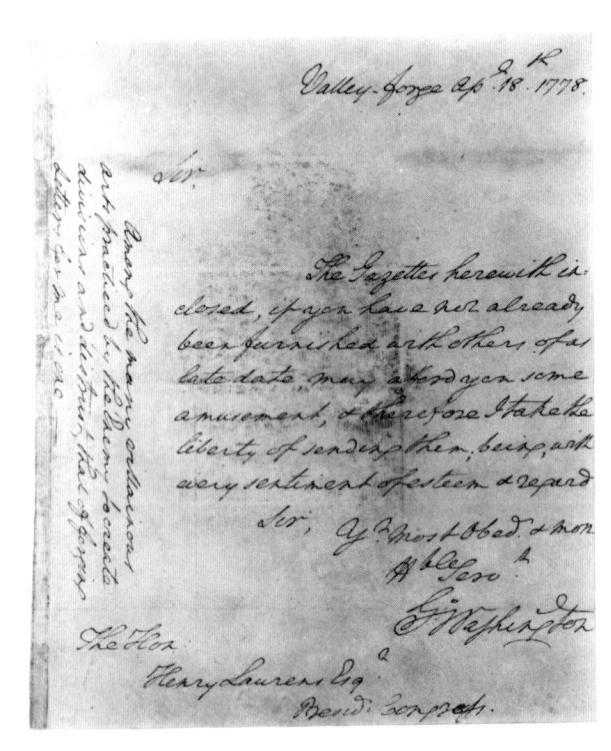

TO LAURENS FROM VALLEY FORGE

ington on the occasion, a gift of the Sons of St. Patrick who elected him a member, is also preserved at the Society.

A number of the Society's manuscripts relate to Washington's residency in Philadelphia as President. These include his diary for January

SONS OF SAINT PATRICK MEDAL

1 - June 21, 1796, and his household account book from 1793 until his return to Mount Vernon in 1797. All sorts of expenditures are recorded in the latter: castor oil for his servants, for he had at least ten domestics; three dollars to a man "who had a very sagacious dog," which performed for the family; charity to poor old soldiers; and the purchase of large landscapes by William Winstanley, which were intended for Mount Vernon. Martha Washington's cookbook, purchased long ago by the Society, was probably with the presidential couple during their Philadelphia sojourn. The appearance of the President's consort at that time may be seen in the Society's portrait of her by Rembrandt Peale.

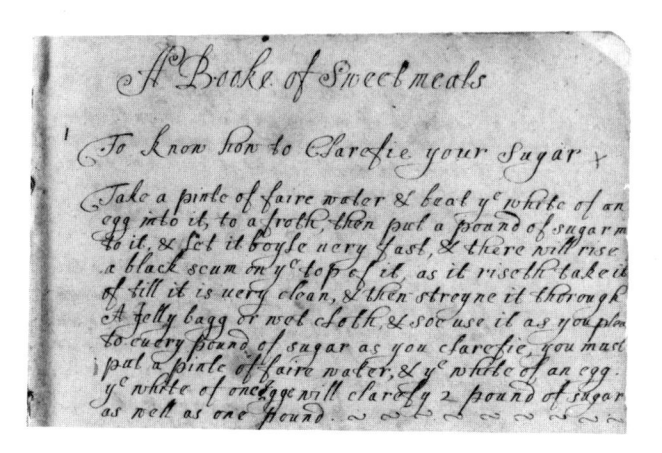

On December 13, 1799, Washington wrote to James Anderson of Norfolk on the subject of farming. This was his last letter, for he died the

MARTHA WASHINGTON BY REMBRANDT PEALE

following day. In the spring of 1800, Anderson gave the letter to a Swedish sea captain who took it home. It remained in Sweden until returned to the United States to be sold at auction in Philadelphia in March, 1893. Ferdinand J. Dreer, an Honorary Vice-President of the Historical Society purchased this prize item for $850, and gave it to the Society as part of the great Dreer autograph collection.

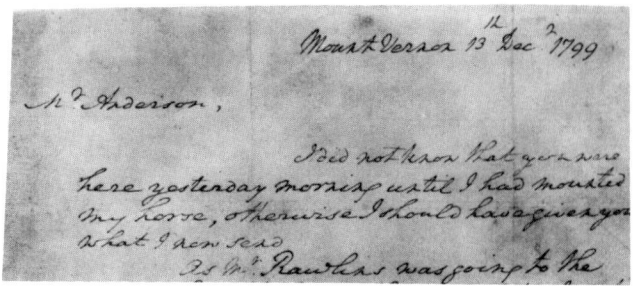

FROM MARTHA WASHINGTON'S COOKBOOK

FROM WASHINGTON'S LAST LETTER

One final Washington-related manuscript requires mention. Tobias Lear, the President's secretary, was with him when he died and kept a full account of the unfolding of the final events in his employer's life. Lear's narrative at the Society serves as the basis for subsequent descriptions of Washington's death. When all was over, Lear recorded: "Sunday Dec. 15th 1799. Fair Weather. Mrs. Washington sent for me in the morng. and desired I would send up to Al[e]x[andri]a and have a coffin made. Which I did. Doctor Dick measured the body, the dimensions of which were as follows: In length 6 feet 3½ inches exact."

Reminders of Washington's career take many forms at the Society—the knife and fork he used in camp, his tea caddy, his death mask, and relics from Robert Morris' house, 190 Market Street, which he occupied as President. Before the house was pulled down in 1830, its massive

WASHINGTON'S CHAIRS

front door lock and key were salvaged, as was a splendidly carved wooden mantel. Rescued by the Burt family, these saw service for more than a century in several of their houses before being given or bequeathed to the Society.

Nearby the mantel in the Society's museum are various contents from 190 Market Street. A set of eight handsome Hepplewhite chairs, believed to have served the President as dining room chairs, are representative of furniture auctioned at the time of his return to Virginia. Before coming to Philadelphia, Washington had occupied the departing French Minister's house in New York and purchased much of his furniture, which he subsequently sent by

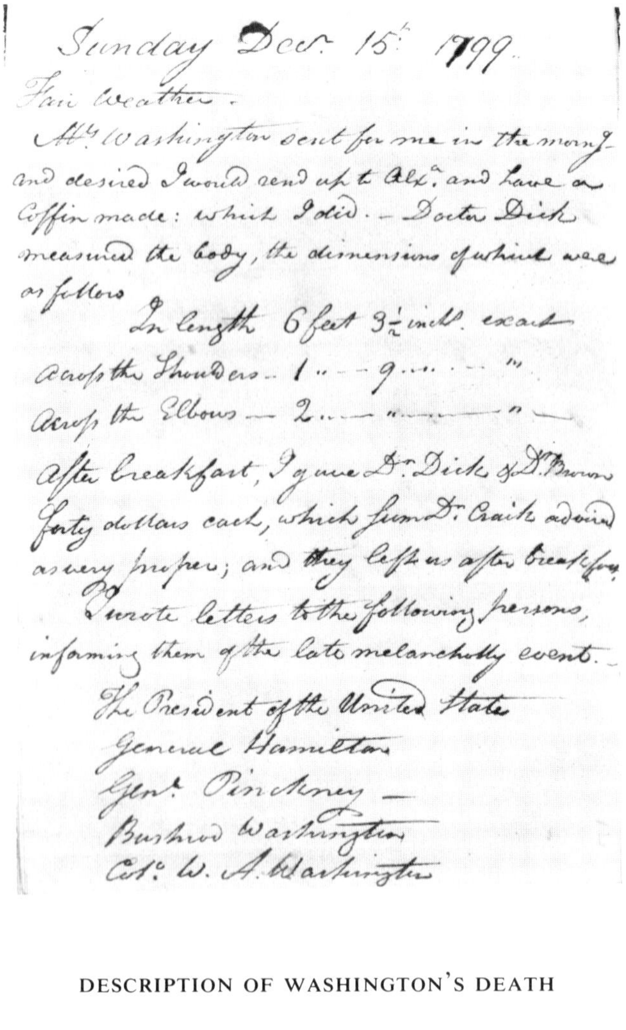

DESCRIPTION OF WASHINGTON'S DEATH

WASHINGTON'S DESK

schooner to Philadelphia. Included was a massive French desk, a ponderous object which had cost Washington £98 in New York currency and which served him throughout his presidency as his personal desk. On leaving Philadelphia in 1797, he sold it for $245, his secretary writing the purchaser: "Mr. Lear presents his respectful Compliments to Mrs. Powell and agreeably to General Washington's commands, has the honor to send her the writing desk which she bought of the General." Mrs. Powel returned a packet of letters the President had written to Martha and had inadvertently left in the desk, with the assurance that she had not read them. Subsequently, she gave the desk to her nephew, whose grandson presented it to the Society in 1867.

A description of the Society's Washingtoniana would be incomplete without mention of books from his library. Useful for his correspondence with his French allies was a 1778 printing of Chambaud's *Nouveau Dictionnaire*

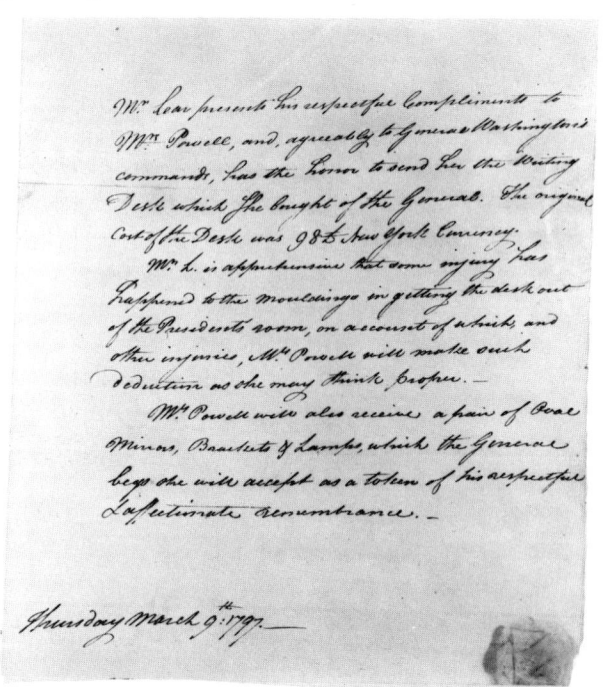

LEAR LETTER TO MRS. POWEL

Francois-Anglais, & Anglais-Francois. It bears the General's handsome bookplate. Of later interest is James Wilson's *Introductory Lecture to a Course of Law Lectures* (Philadelphia, 1791). Wilson, a signer of the Declaration of Independence, draughtsman and signer

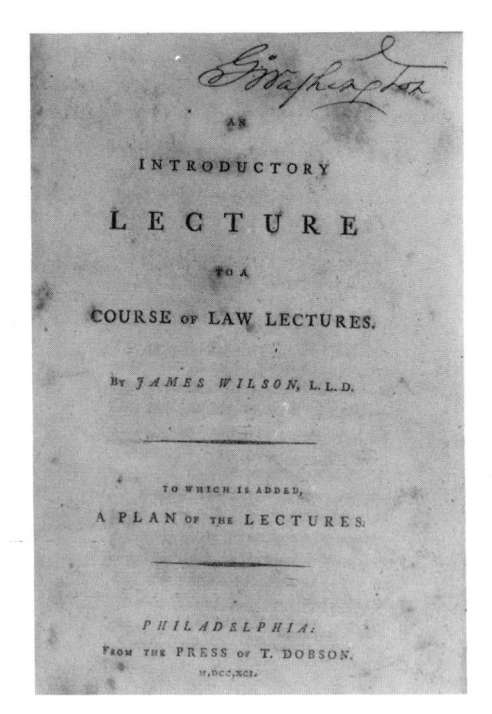

WILSON'S GIFT TO WASHINGTON

of the Federal Constitution at the convention presided over by Washington, was also the mentor of the General's favorite nephew, Bushrod Washington, in the commencement of Bushrod's eminent career in the law. Wilson gave Washington a copy of his book, inscribing on its flyleaf an elaborate presentation of respect. To this Washington added, on the title page, his signature, all in all a mouth-watering collector's item. Another volume of comparable interest is Robert Fulton's *Treatise on the Improvements of Canal Navigation* (London, 1796), a matter of great interest to the President. Fulton's presentation inscription, in which he hopes Washington will promote canals, was seemingly endorsed by the President's signature on the title page. Most impressive, however, of the Society's Washington-owned books is his two-volume set of the *Laws of the State of New York*, published in 1789. Each of these large volumes is signed by Washington, each is embellished with his bookplate, and both are distinguished by their magnificent New York bindings, an excellency for which alone they have been exhibited.

One of the Society's outstanding possessions is Washington's best watch (the Society owns two of his watches). In 1788, he commissioned

Gouverneur Morris, who was going to Paris, to procure him a carefully described gold watch. Morris obtained it from the famous Lépine, clockmaker to Louis XVI, and gave it to Jefferson to bring home. To the ribbon connecting the watch with its key, Washington added his seal, and it was this seal that he subsequently used when signing his will. On Washington's death the watch and seal became the property

WASHINGTON'S WATCH AND SEAL

of Bushrod Washington, who inherited Mount Vernon. As an Associate Justice of the Supreme Court, Bushrod spent much time in Philadelphia, and it was there that he died in 1829, leaving the watch and its seal to a Philadelphia friend, Robert Adams, "knowing that he will appreciate the gift, not for the intrinsic value of the article, but because it was worn by the Father of our Country, and afterward by his friend." Watch and seal were bequeathed to the Society in 1935 by Robert Adams' granddaughter.

Collectors of Washingtoniana have been many, but was there ever one the equal of William Spohn Baker? The foremost authority on Washington of his day, Baker was the author of numerous books on his favorite subject, among which were two catalogues, *The Engraved Portraits of Washington* and *Medallic Portraits of Washington*. In addition to collecting engravings, medals, and coins representing Washington, he specialized on books about his hero and accumulated the editions of Parson Weems's biography which came out annually for many years. Finally, having served the Historical Society as a Vice-President, he bequeathed his collection to it on his death in 1897. The Baker Collection contains 430 handsomely bound volumes relating to Washington, 1,092 engraved portraits, and 1,146 medals and coins. As far back as 1877, long before Baker had completed his collecting, an authority had "no hesitation in saying that it would be utterly impossible to duplicate, or to approach the duplication, of the many rarities contained therein."

The graphic nature of so much of Baker's collection leads to a consideration of the Society's other likenesses of the President. These are numerous and are present in media of all types, including a silhouette cut from life by Joseph Sansom. Most impressive are the paintings, twenty-five of which are described in the Society's catalogue of paintings. Among those of greatest interest is Joseph Wright's portrait from life taken at Rocky Hill, New Jersey, in the autumn of 1783. From this, one of the earliest portraits of Washington, Wright made his celebrated replica, the much larger portrait completed in Philadelphia in May, 1784, for Mrs. Samuel Powel (who was later to buy the desk). Here, in one of his most important and vital portrayals, we see a majestic, martial Washington. It was owned by the Powel family until about 1940, and then, after one more ownership, was presented to the Society in 1972 in memory of Marion Eppley.

Another impressive likeness is the portrait from life painted by the youthful Rembrandt Peale showing a much aged but still forceful face. More familiar to many is the Society's Gilbert Stuart, a replica of the Athenaeum type of highest quality. Less familiar is the rather engaging 1794-period portrait by Adolf U.

Washingtoniana

WASHINGTON BY JOSEPH WRIGHT

WASHINGTON BY CHARLES WILLSON PEALE

WASHINGTON BY REMBRANDT PEALE

WASHINGTON BY CHARLES PEALE POLK

Wertmüller. Among the remaining portraits, one of interesting background is Charles Willson Peale's small painting of Washington as a Virginia colonel. Taken from an earlier portrait, Peale painted it to hang in his museum. From the brush of Peale's nephew, Charles Peale Polk, a victorious Washington is revealed, Nassau Hall in the background.

Remaining for final mention is a pamphlet, *The Journal of Major George Washington, Sent by the Hon. Robert Dinwiddie, Esq.; His Majesty's Lieutenant Governor, and Commander in Chief of Virginia, To the Commandant of the French Forces on Ohio*. This was published in Williamsburg in 1754, its author being just twenty-two years of age. One of its copies survived in perfect condition, still in its original blue paper covers, and was presented to the Society by Charles R. Hildeburn in 1887.

This account of Washington's visit to the French forces on the headwaters of the Ohio late in 1753 is a narrative of profound significance to early American history, an initial step in the development of the French and Indian

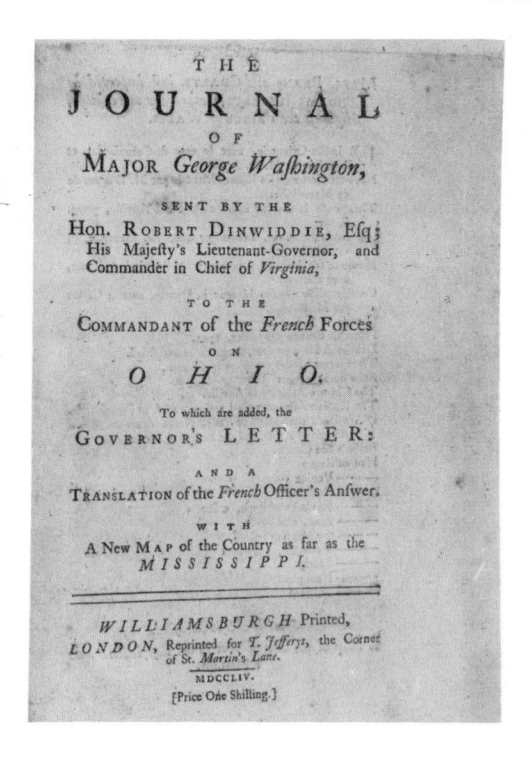

WASHINGTON JOURNAL OF 1754

WASHINGTON BY ADOLPH WERTMÜLLER

War. Rarer than the *Bay Psalm Book*, only eight copies of it are known, the auction record of those copies lists a sale in America in 1880, another in Europe in 1907, and a third, again in America, in 1955, when Mrs. John D. Rockefeller, Jr. purchased the last-known copy for Williamsburg at a price of $25,000. Somehow it seems more appropriate to close this description of the Society's Washingtoniana with mention of the *Journal*, rather than conclude with Tobias Lear's account of the great man's death. A living presence seems to emanate from this slim printing of Washington's heroic early adventures, when, young and vigorous, he took his first step toward a career in public service unmatched in American history.

WASHINGTON BY GILBERT STUART

LAWS

OF THE *G. Washington*

STATE of NEW-YORK,

COMPRISING

THE CONSTITUTION,

AND

The ACTS of the LEGISLATURE since the Revolution,

FROM

The First to the Twelfth Session, inclusive.

PUBLISHED ACCORDING TO AN ACT OF THE LEGISLATURE, PASSED THE 15th APRIL, 1786.

IN TWO VOLUMES.

VOL. I.

Quum Leges aliæ super alias accumulatæ, eas de integro retractare, et in Corpus sanum et habile redigere, ex Usu sit. BACON.

Misera Servitus est ubi Jus est vagum aut incognitum. 4 Inst. 246.

NEW-YORK:

Printed by *Hugh Gaine*, at his Printing-Office and Book-Store, at the Bible, in Hanover-Square.
M,DCC,LXXXIX.

FROM THE CHARLEMAGNE TOWER COLLECTION

Munificent Collectors

The Society's collections have been immeasurably enriched through the generosity of collectors who either gave, bequeathed, or made possible the acquiral of their libraries and manuscripts. The earliest of these benefactors was George W. Fahnstock, a man very much in the mold of William Spohn Baker, whose gift of Washingtoniana has been mentioned.

Fahnstock was born in Chambersburg in 1813. Inheriting large wealth, he devoted himself to antiquarian studies and became an ardent collector of pamphlets relating to American history. His private secretary and librarian attended sales and bought without stint. Meanwhile, Fahnstock moved to Philadelphia in 1849. Upon his tragic death in a steamboat disaster on the Ohio River twenty years later, the Society learned that he had left it his matchless collection of pamphlets, estimated at seventy thousand, the largest private pamphlet collection in America, far more extensive than the Society's own library. The arrival of this mass of material necessitated a search for larger quarters.

Unfortunately, no catalogue was ever compiled of the Fahnstock library. Early resolves to keep it intact proved impractical, and, in the next sixty years, all his pamphlets were blended into the general collection and lost their separate identity.

The Society had barely begun to digest the Fahnstock material when, ten years later, it learned of the Brinley bequest. George Brinley of Hartford was one of the first, one of the most discriminating, and the most successful collector of early Americana. Following his death, his family, acceding to his wishes that his books be sold at auction and that certain institutions be given credit so that they could purchase free of cost, set aside $25,000 for the latter purpose. Of this, the Society's share was $2,000.

It took from 1879 to 1893 to dispose of the 9,501 lots from the Brinley library. Remarkable for rarity, value, and interest, this was the greatest number of books ever offered at an Americana auction. Total sales realized $127,138 at prices which today appear unbelievably low. The Society's principal purchases were made at the second sale in 1880, which contained the Pennsylvania materials. Among the imprints secured were twenty-five books printed by William Bradford, the first printer in the Middle Colonies, four by Renier Janson, Philadelphia's second printer, and three by Samuel Keimer, Franklin's employer.

Among other titles bought in were Gabriel Thomas' *An Historical and Geographical Account of the Province and Country of Pensilvania* (London 1698), with its map of Pennsylvania and West Jersey (a copy superseded in 1938 by the acquisition of a better copy). Reaching into New England, the Society secured John Eliot's *Indian Bible*, the second edition,

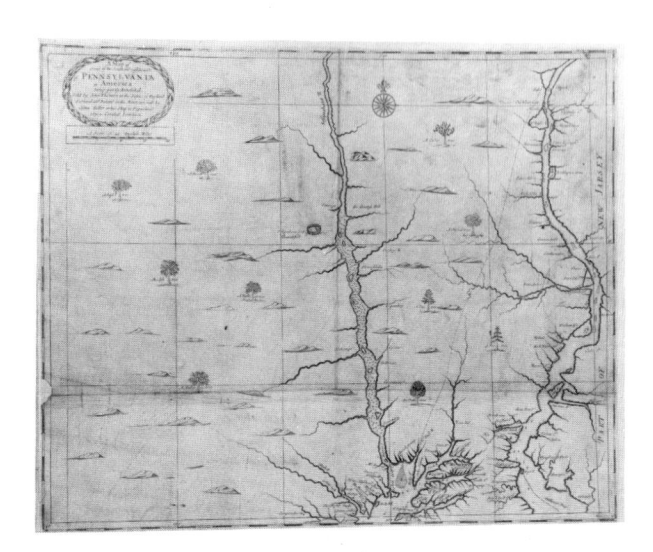

MAP FROM THOMAS BOOK OF 1698

printed at Cambridge in 1685 by Samuel Green. For fifteen dollars George Keith's *The Christian Quaker: Or George Keith's Eyes opened. Good News from Pensilvania* (London, 1693) was added to the shelves. Appropriate as the many purchases were, the great accession was the first two volumes of the *Pennsylvania Gazette* in superb condition, knocked down at $560. These contained Samuel Keimer's advertisement of his intention to issue a newspaper, dated October 1, 1728, followed by numbers 1-39 of the *Gazette* (December 24, 1728—September 25, 1729, lacking issues 4 and 5), and numbers 40-111 complete, printed by Franklin (October 2, 1729—December 22, 1730).

At the 1883 sale the Society acquired an attractive reminder of versatile, young Francis

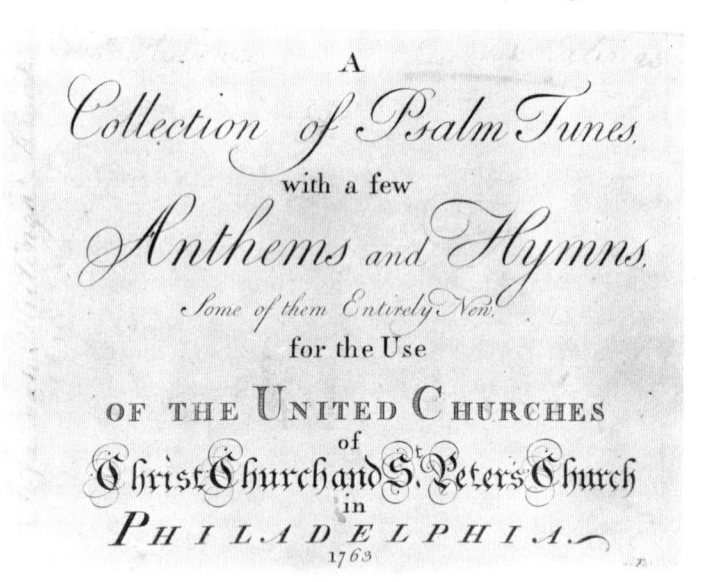

KEITH'S CHRISTIAN QUAKER AND HOPKINSON'S COLLECTION OF PSALM TUNES

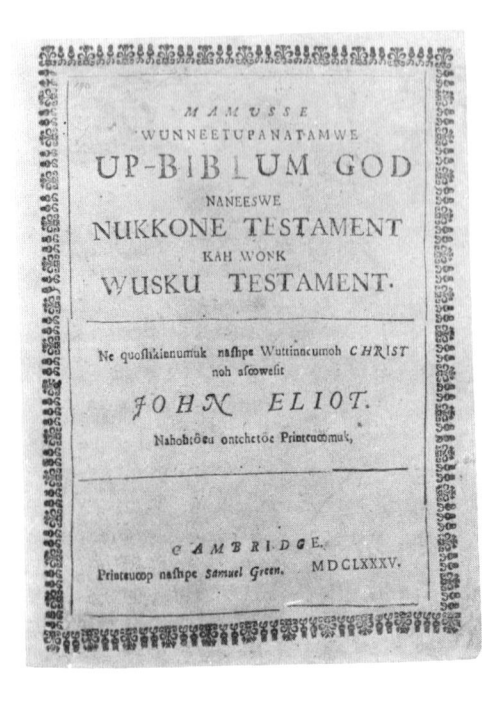

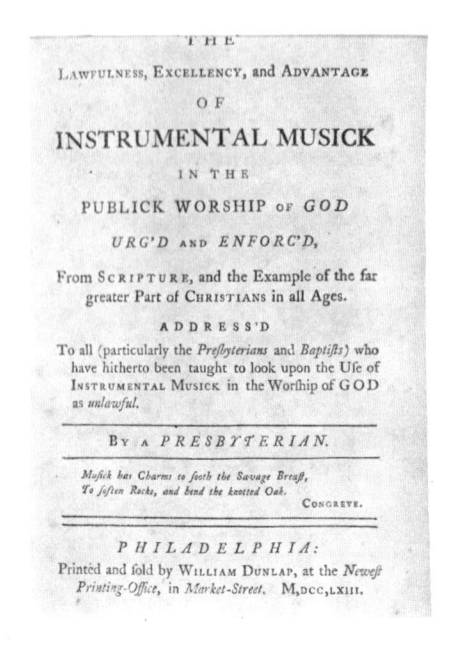

ELIOT'S INDIAN BIBLE AND HOPKINSON'S DEFENSE OF INSTRUMENTAL MUSIC

Hopkinson's interest in music, *A Collection of Psalm Tunes with a few Anthems and Hymns, Some of them Entirely New, for the Use of the United Churches of Christ Church and St. Peter's Church in Philadelphia,* 1763. This complemented a title from another source of the same year, Dunlap's fine printing of Hopkinson's *The Lawfulness, Excellency, and Advantage of Instrumental Musick in the Publick Worship of God.*

A few more books from the Brinley library were acquired later. Of these, the outstanding purchase was the only known copy of the anonymous [Thomas Story] *Tribute to Caesar,* which justified to Quakers the payment of a wartime tax. Presumably printed by Andrew Bradford in Philadelphia in 1715, it was acquired at the Leiter sale in 1933 at what, even

FRAMPTON'S JOYFULL NEWES

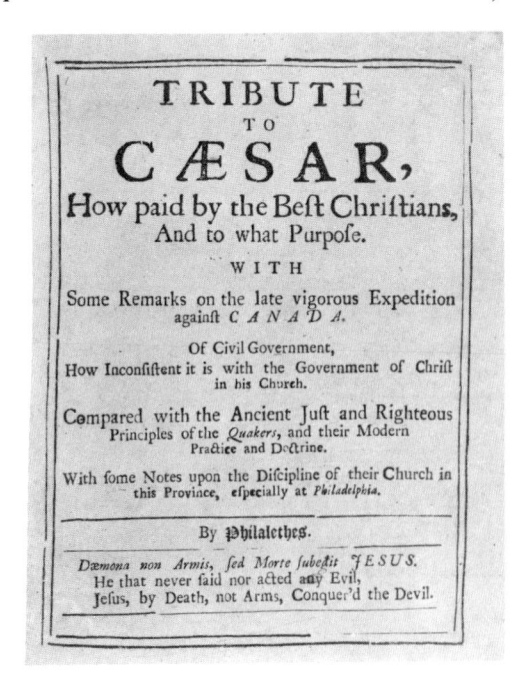

STORY'S TRIBUTE TO CAESAR

considering its previous Brinley sale at $45, was considered a third of its value—$1,000.

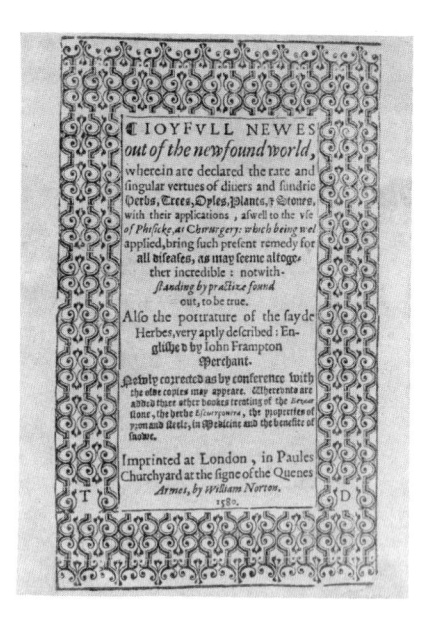

The Society's purchases at the Brinley auctions were guided by Charles R. Hildeburn, the noted bibliographer and compiler of the *Issues of the Press in Pennsylvania.* Munificent in his own right, Hildeburn bestowed many rarities upon the Society, including his splendid copy of Washington's Williamsburg *Journal.* It

VAN LINSCHOTEN'S VOYAGES

was Hildeburn, the widely recognized authority, who advised Charlemagne Tower in his collecting.

Born in 1809, Tower achieved a lucrative legal practice, specializing in cases involving the Pennsylvania coal fields, before his retirement to Philadelphia in 1875. In a subsequent career, he helped develop the iron resources of Minnesota, the Vermilion Range, and was tremendously successful. After his death in 1889, his widow gave his collection of colonial laws to the Society. One of the most important ever formed in Philadelphia, and, in its special field, unequalled in the world, it represented nearly forty years of collecting. Of the laws there were 942 titles, and in rare Americana of general interest 87 more. The laws include those of the British and Danish West Indies, Barbados, Bermuda, Jamaica, Nova Scotia, Quebec, and other jurisdictions. The set of Pennsylvania laws is unrivalled. In pristine condition, wonderously bound, some of the Tower laws are unique. George Washington's matchless set of the laws of New York is one of the Tower gems.

The miscellaneous Tower Americana consists of the earliest general histories of the colonies and many volumes printed in the sixteenth and seventeenth centuries, such as: *Joyfull Newes out of the newfound World Englished by John Frampton* (London, 1580); Linschoten's *Voyages* in English (London, 1598), a very fine copy complete with twelve maps; Smith's *Virginia* (London, 1627); and the first of the series of reports from New England relative to the conversion of the aborigines, known as the Eliot *Indian Tracts* (London, 1643).

Tower's emphasis on condition was one with which Frederic R. Kirkland wholeheartedly agreed. Long-time Treasurer of the Society, Kirkland was influenced by his partner Morris Parrish, whose collection of Victorian novelists is at Princeton. "Parrish condition" became an expression recognized as meaning virtually mint condition. It did not mean putting magnificent bindings on old books, which was Tower's fancy. In line with this advance in conserving rarities, Kirkland had boxes or slip covers made for his special prizes, all of which are in outstanding condition.

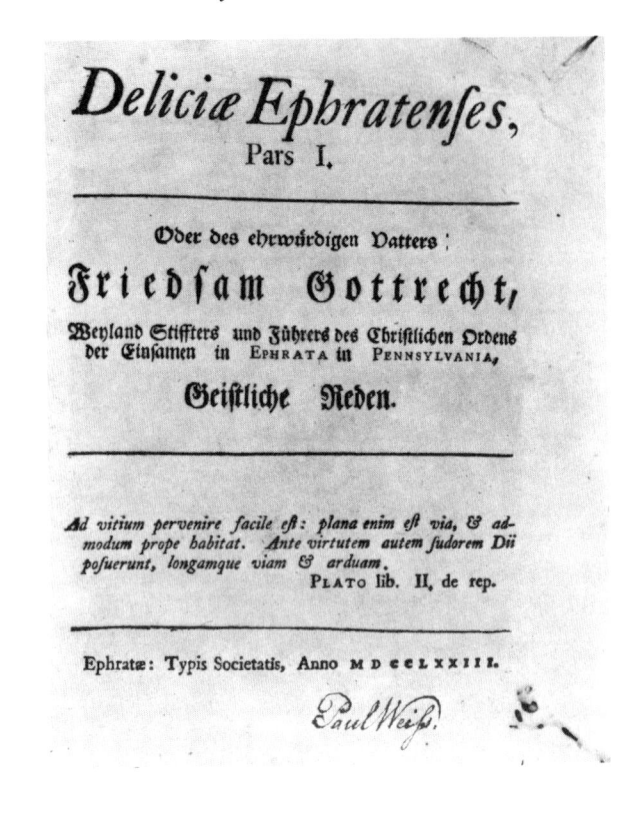

EPHRATA GERMAN IMPRINT

The focus of Kirkland's large collection was on the Revolution, with sections for each state, as well as for biographies, other studies, and a strong bibliographical section. With the gift of his library in the 1940s and 1950s, the Society gained depth in its Revolutionary holdings for areas other than Pennsylvania.

Like Tower, Kirkland also had an interest in general Americana. He, too, had a Smith *Virginia* (1632). To mention several other titles of interest, he owned the extremely rare Bartolomi de las Casas, *The Tears of the Indians* (London, 1656), the best known of the two English translations of Las Casas' tracts relating to the cruelty of the Spaniards, a perfect copy, dedicated to Oliver Cromwell. Of antiquarian interest is a *Tacitus*, printed in Basel in 1544. It is inscribed by Franklin's grandson: "The Gift of Citizen Fouchet, Minister of the French Republic to B. F. Bache 1795," and one of Kirkland's finest books is the first edition of Hakluyt's *Voyages* (London, 1589).

Midway between book collectors and manuscript collectors stand the extra-illustrators of books. Dr. Thomas Addis Emmet, the eminent New York collector, strayed into this field, and the Society owns his four-volume set of *Hugh Wynne*.

Presumably, the outstanding extra-illustrator was David McN. K. Stauffer, Philadelphia railroad and consulting engineer, a collector of engravings and autographs. He used these to enhance books by the expansion of their volume through the insertion of prints and documents pertinent to their contents. The pre-eminent authority in his field, his great work was *American Engravers Upon Copper and Steel*, published in 1907 in two volumes.

Many of the works he extra-illustrated are in the Society's collection, among them Simpson's *Lives of Eminent Philadelphians* (four volumes), *Diary of Christopher Marshall* (three volumes), Graydon's *Memoirs* (three volumes), the *Shippen Papers* (five volumes), and, a precious volume, *A List of the Proprietaries and Governors of Pennsylvania*. Extremely deep in manuscripts of interest, it took Stauffer seventeen years to complete this latter work. It is definitive to 1890, when his interest flagged.

Stauffer's most ambitious undertaking was the extra-illustrating of "Westcott's History of Philadelphia," a newspaper serial. Devoting many years of his life to that project, he barely completed it by his death in 1913. His widow saw to it that the collection was handsomely bound in thirty-two folio volumes for presentation to the Society. The more than 12,000 inserts represent a wealth of illustrative and documentary value and has been a boon to researchers. Stauffer's accomplishments as a collector rank him high on the list of the Society's patrons.

While many book collectors acquired some manuscripts, collectors were basically either seekers of books or seekers of documents. The book collectors had only peripheral interest in manuscripts, and the collectors of manuscripts seem to have had little time to pursue printed rarities. Prior to 1850, there were only four notable collectors of autographs in the United States—Lewis J. Cist, Israel K. Tefft, Robert Gilmor and the Rev. William B. Sprague. Sprague enjoyed unrivaled opportunities as a collector. On his death in 1876 his collection of

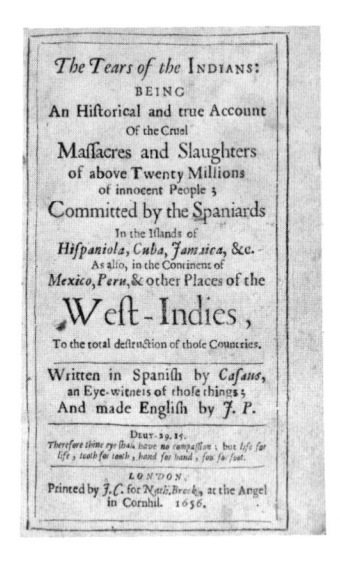

DE LAS CASAS ON INDIANS

TACITUS PRINTED IN BASEL

90,000 items was deemed the largest in the country. As we shall see, both the Gilmor and Sprague collections were to come to the Society.

By the middle of the nineteenth century a number of Philadelphians, including George M. Conarroe, became collectors. Conarroe's interest was in assembling letters of individuals prominent in American history. On his death, his collection, mounted in thirteen volumes, was given to the Society. Other early Philadelphia collectors were Ferdinand J. Dreer, who started in 1848, Frank M. Etting, who took it up about 1852, and Simon Gratz, who entered the field in 1856. All three were to give their collections to the Society.

Colonel Etting, born in Philadelphia in 1833, was a Civil War veteran whose historical bent led him to writing books on the Liberty Bell and Independence Hall, and to his recognition as historian for the Centennial. Above all, he was a collector of manuscripts. A descendant of colonial families, he inherited papers relating to the Indian trade, the Ohio Company, and the old frontier. Adding to these, he also built up an assembly of letters of distinguished Americans and Europeans in groups such as generals of the Revolution, members of presidential cabinets, officers of the colonial wars, British literary lights and a wide variety of other subjects. Shortly after his death in 1890, his collection of some 20,000 items was delivered to the Society; it remains its third most important autograph collection, one which has attracted many scholars.

At nearly the same time that the Etting manuscripts were received, Ferdinand J. Dreer donated his collection which was twice as large as the Etting and of extraordinarily high quality. It covered the entire range of American history and was rich in European manuscripts, letters and documents of such figures as Galileo, Ben Jonson, John Locke, Lorenzo De'Medici, surnamed Il Magnifico (a long letter begging an indulgence from the Pope so that he could eat meat in Lent), Martin Luther, Macciavelli, Milton, Horatio Nelson to Lady Hamilton, and royalty (James VI, King of Scotland, later to be James I of England, a letter of September 3, 1597, to Henry IV, King of France, on the relations between the crowns of France and Scotland). Jefferson, Robert Morris, and Lafayette are represented by volumes of letters, as are William Penn and Washington.

Dreer had the good fortune to purchase the Gilmor collection in 1851. Retiring from business in 1863, he devoted his entire energies to his hobby. Such were his circumstances that prices were a secondary consideration. After 1870 he began extensive purchasing through dealers in London, Paris, and Berlin.

Fortunately for posterity, he resolved that his collection would never be sold, but would be kept intact and devoted to the public benefit. "With this object in view," wrote Dreer, "I

GRATZ COLLECTION IN VAULT

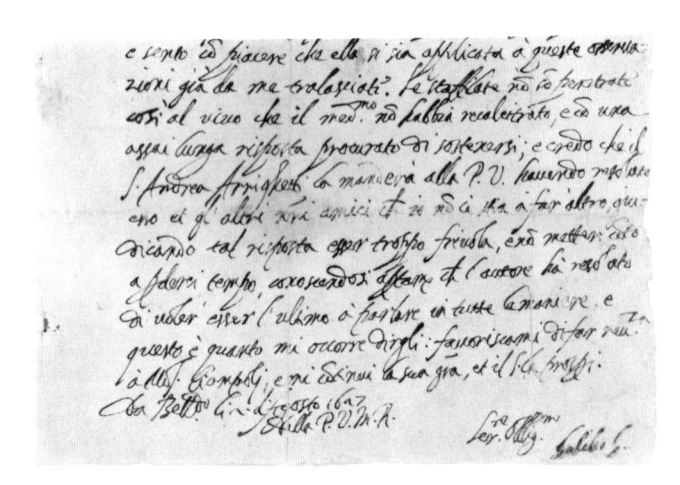

END OF A GALILEO LETTER

chose the Historical Society of Pennsylvania, one of the useful and flourishing institutions of my native city, Philadelphia, as a perpetual custodian."

And what treasures he bestowed upon the Society! Highlights concerned with the Civil War take their start with the John Brown papers. These Dreer secured in two lots, one of which he purchased from Brown's son. It includes extensive correspondence on the organizing of the raid on Harper's Ferry. This is followed by Brown's subsequent letters to his family from jail, his touching last letter condemning slavery, his will dated December 1, 1859, and a document of December 2, the day of his execution, instructing his wife on the inscription for his tombstone. The second lot comprises the correspondence of Governor Henry A. Wise of Virginia relating to the raid.

Dreer was also happy in acquiring the Buckner-Grant letters of 1862. In these, the besieged Confederate commander of Fort Donelson offers to surrender his force of 14,000 and asks Grant's terms of capitulation, to which Grant made his historic reply: "No terms except an unconditional and immediate surrender can be accepted." Unconditional surrender—U. S. Grant. Finally, in this category there is Dreer's magnificent Lincoln letter to Grant in 1863, relating to Grant's victorious strategy at Vicksburg, and ending: "I now wish to make the personal acknowledgment that you were right and I was wrong."

It seems ungenerous to add that Dreer's is not the Society's greatest autograph collection, but it has to bow to that of Simon Gratz, the largest, most comprehensive, and richest of all American collections. Born in Philadelphia in 1838, Gratz was a member of one of the city's old families. He was prominently identified

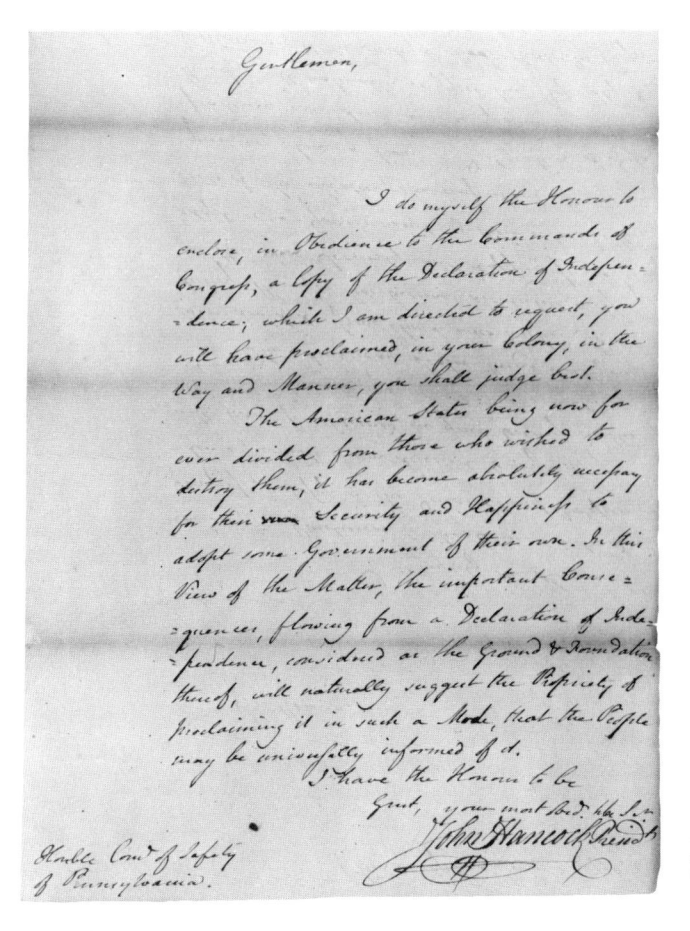

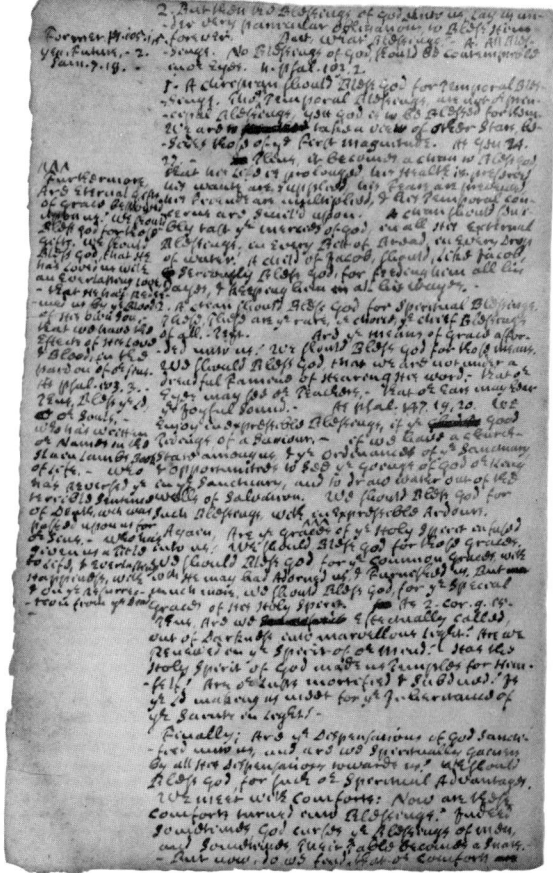

LETTER FROM HANCOCK TO PENNSYLVANIA

LEAF OF COTTON MATHER SERMON

with public education and served on many cultural boards, including that of the Society. An autograph collector from his youth, he purchased the Sprague collection in 1881. Unlike other collectors, he did not mount his manuscripts in volumes, but kept them in folders. He was insistent on fine condition and endeavored to preserve his documents in the appearance they had when they came from the hands of their authors.

In 1917 he resolved to give his collection to the Society. Before the transfer was made, he wrote: "The manuscript department of the Historical Society of Pennsylvania exceeds, in size and importance, that of any other Historical Society in the United States." That was in 1920. Since then the collection has increased five-fold.

It was in 1922 that Gratz began sending in the main parts of his collection, series by series, which the bachelor donor called his children. Miss Catharine Miller was added to the staff and for the next fifteen years devoted her time to cataloguing the Gratz. The collection remains in the same order in which Gratz arranged it in two large rooms on the second floor of his Spruce Street residence. Numbering more than 200,000 documents, it fills more than 1,000 boxes. Like Dreer before him, Gratz set up a trust fund for the increase of his collection. In addition to that, his bequest to the Society's endowment in 1925 was the second largest it has received. By all odds, Simon Gratz was the Society's most munificent benefactor.

As for his manuscripts, space permits only a general statement that they cover much of the history of the western world. Virtually all significant historical figures are represented from the time autographed documents became available down to modern times. So many superlative specimens are included that it is difficult to select one to serve as an example. While of no overweening historical importance, there is reason, however, to believe that Gratz's sentimental favorite was John Keats's love letter to his fiancée, Fanny Brawne. Written on July 8, 1819, it is probable that Keats knew his future was hopeless. Poverty and ill-health, which brought on the poet's death nineteen months later, prevented the match.

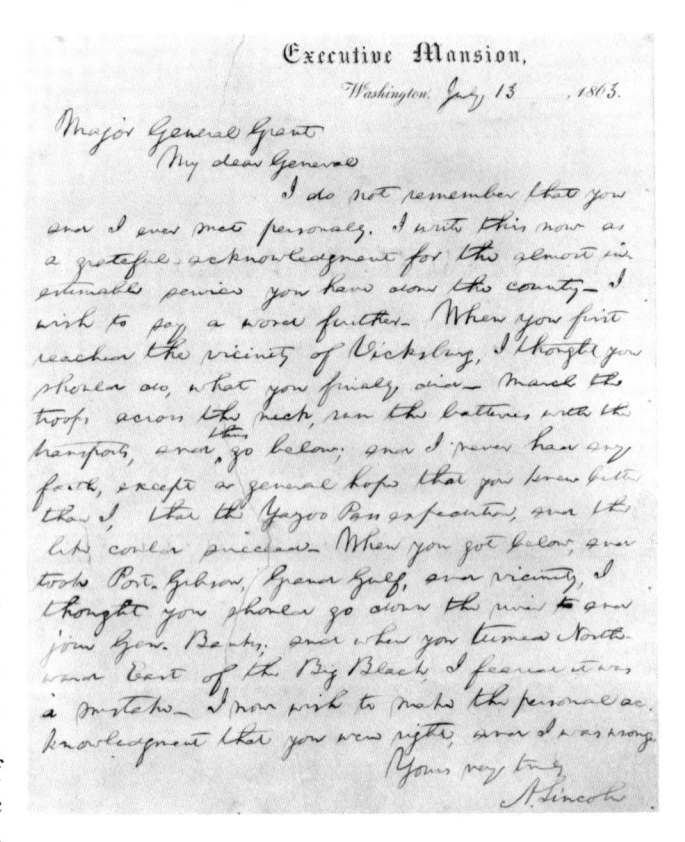

LINCOLN LETTER TO GRANT

Like most major collectors, Gratz collected in series, filling them in much as a stamp collector strives to obtain every stamp in a set. Among the most popular series were the Albany Convention of 1754, the first coming together of representatives of as many as seven of the colonies; delegates to the Stamp Act Congress, held at New York in 1765 to register the first deep rumble of colonial discontent; First Continental Congress, 1774; officers of the Continental Army; Presidents of the United States. However, none of these equalled in prestige the fifty-six Signers of the Declaration of Independence, complete sets of which were limited by the scarcity of the signatures of Button Gwinett, who died early, and Thomas Lynch, Jr., for whom collectors had to depend on signatures cut from books in his library.

By 1889 there were twenty-one complete sets of Signers in the United States and one in England. Although forty-five other sets were in process of forming, only six more are known to have achieved completeness by 1925.

Etting's set continued to lack the two notable rarities, while another set at the Society wanted but one. Of the sets completed by 1925, four were at the New York Public Library, three were at the Historical Society of Pennsylvania, two were at the Morgan Library and the rest were scattered among other institutions and collectors. Beyond question, the two best sets were those of Thomas Addis Emmet, at the New York Public, and Simon Gratz. Emmet's set was outstanding in that it contained the only known letter of Thomas Lynch, Jr., but, in the round, Gratz's set was the most perfect for its depth. It boasted more autographed letters dated in 1776—thirty-three—than any other collection, and was wonderfully rich in duplicates. Of its fifty-six components, fifty-three were full autograph letters. Its Gwinett item is a document signed, signed in fact by all three Georgia delegates. While the Lynch is the usual cut signature, nine of the rest are dated in July, 1776. James Wilson's is July 5, as is John Hancock's on a document transmitting a copy of the Declaration to the Council of Safety of Pennsylvania. For the number of items in the Gratz set of Signers, their perfect condition and the historic value of their contents, it has no equal. The Historical Society's other sets were those formed by Dreer and the one Thomas Addis Emmet gave to Sprague, which was purchased by the Society in 1881 for $2,000, at the time Gratz bought in the rest of the huge Sprague collection. For prestigious documents, the Society bows to none.

OPENING AND CLOSING PAGES OF LETTER FROM KEATS TO HIS FIANCÉE

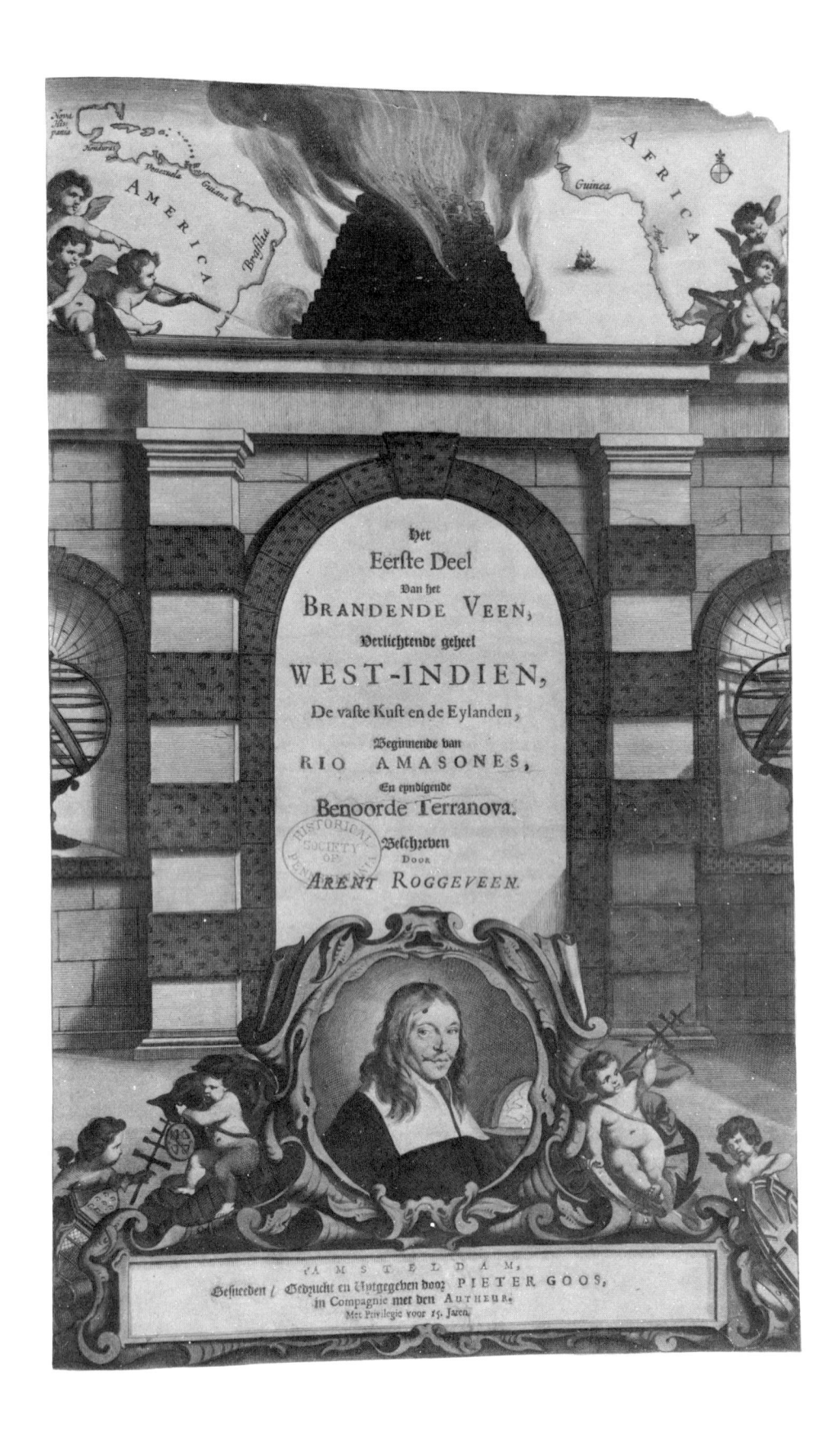

ROGGEVEEN'S ATLAS OF THE WEST INDIES

Colonial Days

In early times Pennsylvania's prosperity depended on the port of Philadelphia. The export of furs and deerskins, lumber, and flour to other colonies, the West Indies, and Europe brought in the manufactured objects which could not yet be made at home, and such necessities and luxuries as sugar, tea, wine, and clothing. For the safe conduct of this waterborne traffic, charts were a requirement.

Several of the Society's atlases represent Dutch contributions to navigation. Arent Roggeveen's of the West Indies (Amsterdam, 1675) has handsome decorations in color but cannot compare with Arnold Colom's *Zee-Atlas Ofte Water-Wereldt* (Amsterdam, *c*. 1700). The Society's copy is a large folio in magnificent condition with gloriously colored cartouches, fantastically designed. No detail for Pennsylvania is given, although Delaware Bay and River are fairly well represented.

The standard work on American coastal charts from 1689 through the eighteenth century was *The English Pilot. The Fourth Book*. The Society has various editions of this atlas, notably the 1698 one which contains the desirable chart of Boston Harbor as well as "A New Description of . . . Dellewar Bay . . . By the Information of divers Navigators of our own and other Nations."

Primitive as were the navigational aids available to Penn, the virtual absence of a map delineating his new province was even more distressing. Several to which he had access are in the map collection. The most current one for Penn's use, printed in 1680, was *A Mapp of Virginia, Mary-Land, New-Jarsey, New-York & New England*. On it are located New Castle, Upland (Chester), and Philadelphia's future site Wicoco (Wicacoa). An edition of this map published the following year replaces the designation Hore Kill with Skoole Kill, but Wicoco remains unchanged.

Nor was it displaced on John Thornton's 1681 *A Map of Some of the South and East Bounds of Pennsylvania in America*. This, the first distinct map of the colony, actually offers nothing new and was used merely to advertise the venture. Penn referred to it in his 1681 *A Brief Account of the Province of Pennsylvania*. Attached to the Society's copy, which came from the library of the Marquess of Lansdowne, a descendant of William Penn's friend Sir William Petty, is a printed description of the colony. There is only one other like it in Ameri-

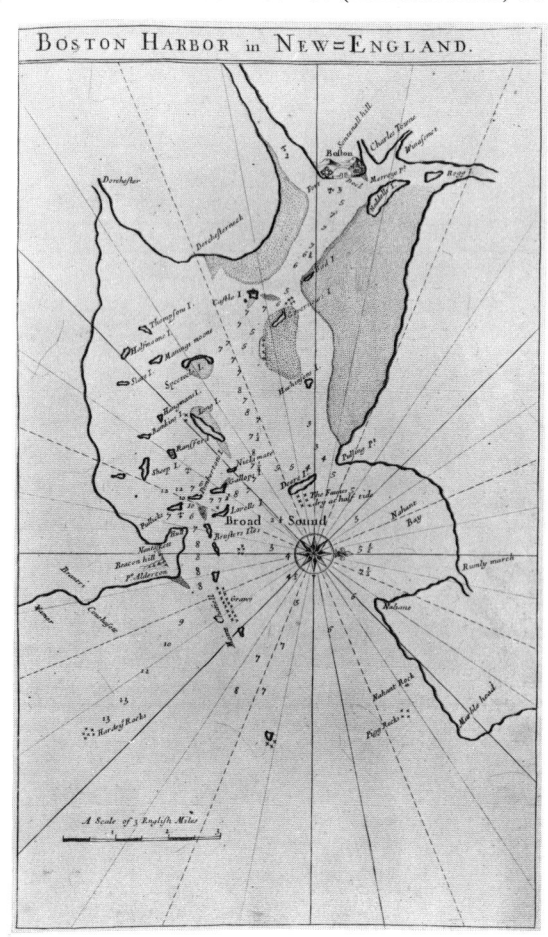

ENGLISH PILOT MAP OF BOSTON

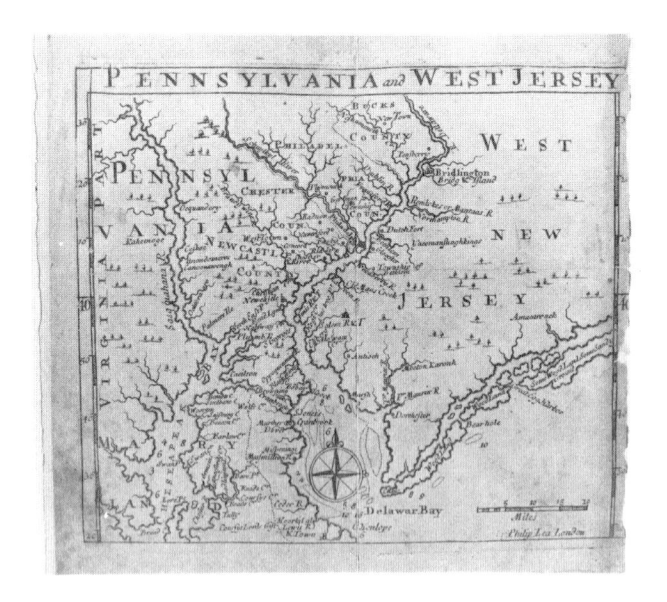

EARLY MAP OF AREA

HOLMES MAP OF PHILADELPHIA

ca. The British Museum holds the other known copy.

Maps of greater precision and usefulness were urgently needed for the attraction of settlers. The first of these was Surveyor General Thomas Holme's 1683 *A Portraiture of the City of Philadelphia in the Province of Pennsylvania in America*. This plan showing city lots served as the basis for their allotment and was bound into Penn's *Letter to the Free Society of Traders*. It was also published separately and the Society has a variety of copies of it in different states.

After repeated urgings by Penn, Holme completed in 1687 a far more ambitious project, his large *Map of the Improved Part of the Province of Pennsylvania* on which are inscribed the names of the owners of each plot of land. The Society owns the finest copy of this, for it is in its original condition in six uncut plates.

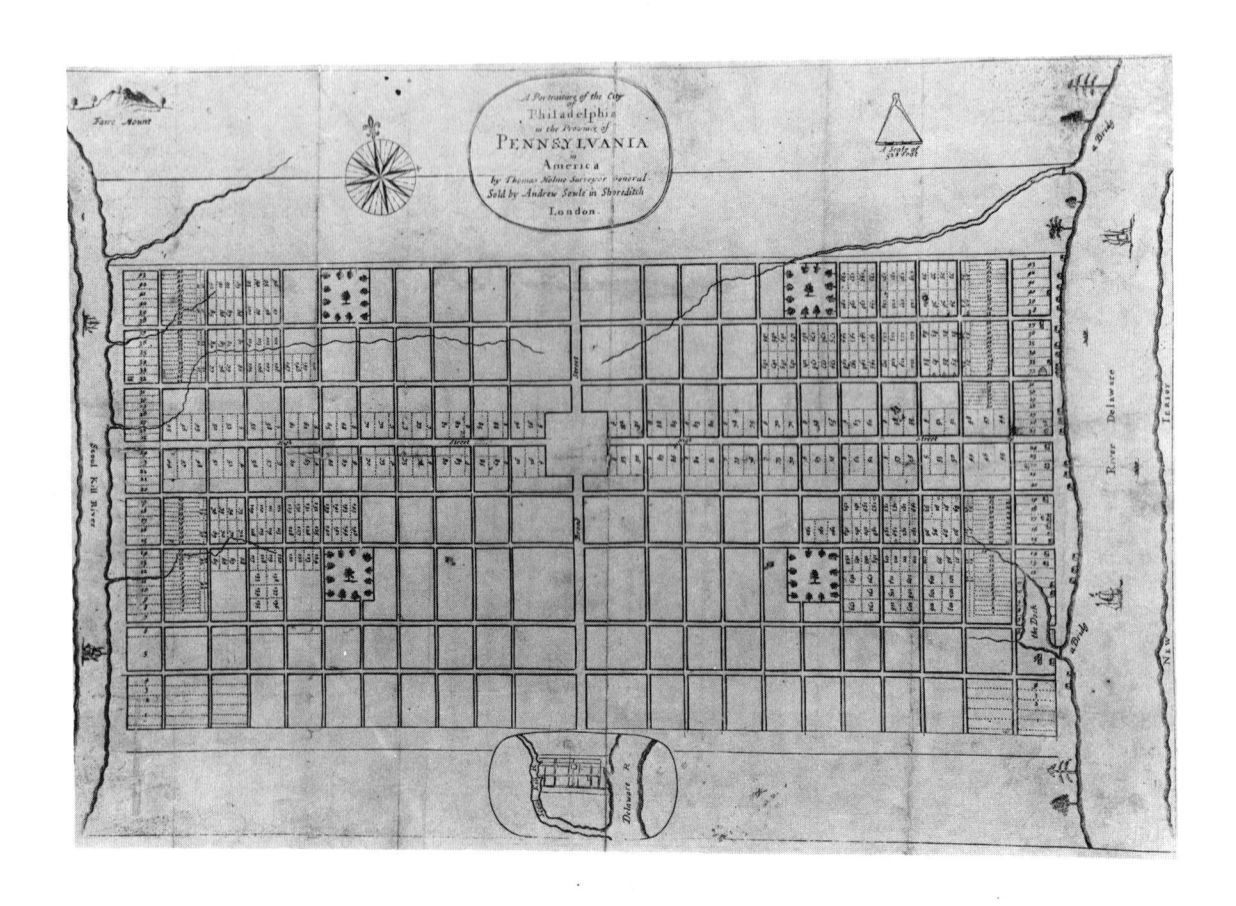

Not long after Penn's death in 1718 maps became relatively numerous and their contents often controversial. The Society has a number relating to the Maryland boundary argument as well as probably all the pamphlets and printings on that well-nigh endless subject. One of these, *Articles of Agreement . . . Touching the Limits and Bounderies of the Two Provinces*, printed by Franklin in 1733, is illustrated with a woodcut map, the first map printed in the English colonies south of New York.

The most ambitious cartographic undertaking of colonial times was Nicholas Scull's monumental *Map of the Improved Part of the Province of Pennsylvania*, engraved and printed in Philadelphia in 1759. Of seven known copies, the Society's is outstanding because, in immaculate condition, its plates were never cut to be joined together, but remain entirely untrimmed. After Scull's death his daughter Mary Biddle and Matthew Clarkson published the surveyor's map of Philadelphia in 1762, which illustrates the city's tremendous growth. Of three known copies, the Society owns two. Scull's grandson was also a cartographer. In 1770 he published a condensed and revised version of the large 1759 map of the colony. Engraved in Philadelphia by Henry Dawkins, it shows the entire line run by Mason and Dixon, and has survived in but seven copies, one of them at the Society.

To enable pilots to bring ships safely up to the city, Joshua Fisher of Philadelphia in 1756 provided the first comprehensive and accurate survey of Delaware River and Bay. However, the British were engaged in a war with the French and Fisher's large-scale chart was instantly suppressed. The Society does not own one of the two surviving copies. Fortunately, Fisher was not to be denied his labors. He had the chart re-engraved on a smaller plate, but one encompassing a larger geographic scope. Printed in Philadelphia, Fisher's *Chart of Delaware Bay and River . . . from the Capes to Philadelphia* was extensively copied in Europe and proved to be of unusual influence, for it retained its usefulness for nearly a hundred years. The original survives in three copies, of which the Society has one. It also has two manuscript versions, one of them evidently Fisher's own draft for the earlier publication of 1756, and the other more closely related to the second edition, possibly the engraver's rendering for use in preparing the plate. One of these two manuscripts was presented by Joseph Wharton, who wrote in 1856: "I send herewith for preservation among the archives of the Society the original draft of a survey of Delaware Bay by my greatgrandfather Joshua Fisher."

Four years after Wharton's gift the Society received some books printed before 1500, incunabula presented for reasons now unknown by the Royal Library of Munich. Interesting as curiosities, they have nothing to do with America. The Society's earliest Americana is Richard Eden's translation from the Latin of the pertinent part of Sebastian Münster's *Cosmographia Universalis*, which Eden published in London, 1553, *A treatyse of the newe India, with other new founde landes. . . .* Acquired by Frederick D. Stone, Librarian

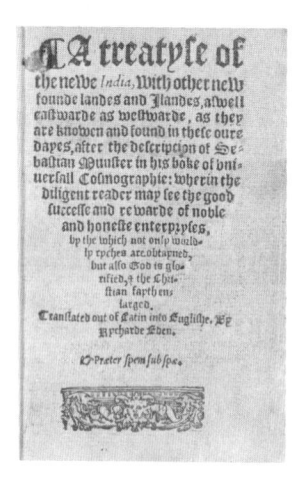

FIRST BOOK ABOUT AMERICA IN ENGLISH

from 1877 to 1897, for five guineas, one of six known copies, this volume is in excellent condition. As the first book printed in England about America, it is of great geographical importance. With mention of the names and deeds of Columbus, Vespucci, Magellan, Albuquerque and Vasco da Gama, Eden's translation is the foundation stone of English geographical literature.

In the Society's library are a large number of titles of pre-Pennsylvania Americana, among them another work by Eden, *The History of*

Trauayle [sic] *in the West and East Indies... With a Discourse on the Northwest Passage* (London, 1577). Closer to home is *The Relation of the Right Honourable the Lord De-La-Warre, Lord Gouernour* [sic] *and Captaine General of the Colonie, Planted in Virginia* (London, 1611); Marc Lescarbot's *Histoire de la Nouvelle-France* (Paris, 1611); works by William Usselinx who gave the first impetus to Swedish colonization by persuading Gustavus Adolphus in 1626 to found the South Sea Company whose activities were to embrace America; publications of the Dutch West India Company; and early publications of New England. Also of note is George Alsop's *A Character of the Province of Maryland* (London, 1666), containing the rare map of both Delaware and Chesapeake Bays.

While such books furnish background history, the Society's chief collecting interest has been in books printed in Pennsylvania. It boasts an unexcelled collection of seventeenth- and eighteenth-century Pennsylvania imprints. When such material was reasonably accessible, the Society was the only institution in the state vigorously collecting it. Fortunate in the advice of the two men most knowledgeable in the field, the bibliographer Charles H. Hildeburn and Librarian Stone, it benefited also from many generous benefactors. From time to time, windfalls added greatly. In 1882 Dr. John Dickinson Logan presented a large number of books from the libraries of his distinguished ancestors, Isaac Norris II and John Dickinson. It was also in 1882 that the Society purchased some thousand titles from the Pennsylvania-German collection of Abraham H. Cassel. Cassel was a descendant of Christopher Sauer, who with his sons were Germantown printers from 1739 to 1778.

The Society's imprint collection had its advent with the establishment in Philadelphia of William Bradford's press, the first in the Middle Colonies. In December, 1685, Bradford published its initial issue, an almanac compiled by Samuel Atkins—*Kalendarium Pennsilvaniense, or America's Messinger. Being an Almanack For the Year of Grace, 1686*. One of its pages was largely made up of a chronology of so many years since a given event. Thus,

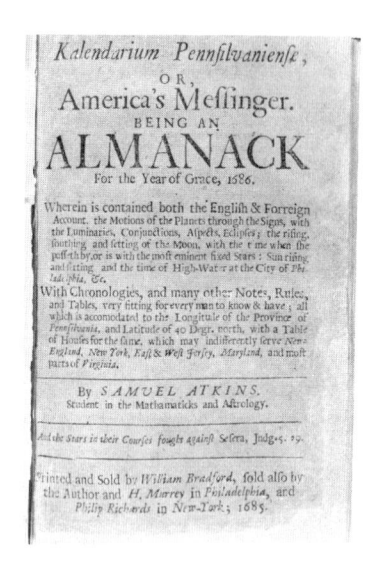

FIRST PENNSYLVANIA IMPRINT

3,979 years had passed since "The Flood of Noah." An event but five years back was recorded as "The beginning of Government here by Lord Penn." Shocked by the terminology, the authorities ordered the words "Lord Penn" blotted out, and so they are in the two surviving copies, one of which, a symbol of the beginning of printing in Pennsylvania, is at the Society.

Of the early issues of the press, the Society has the major collection of the works produced by successive generations of the Bradfords. In part, the primacy of its Bradford holdings rests on an extraordinary gift by the printers' descendant William Bradford in 1883. He had assembled through inheritance and collecting a large number of Bradford imprints, including a bound volume of *The American Weekly Mercury*, 1737-1739, and seven volumes of the *Pennsylvania Journal* starting in 1742.

Pennsylvania's second printer, Reynier Jansen, worked in Philadelphia from 1699 until his death in 1706. Only thirty-three of his titles are known, of which the Society, owning sixteen, three of them unique, is by far the major holder. And so it is of printings by Samuel Keimer, who operated his press in Philadelphia from 1723 to 1729. Also the major holder of Christopher Sauer imprints, the Society has the

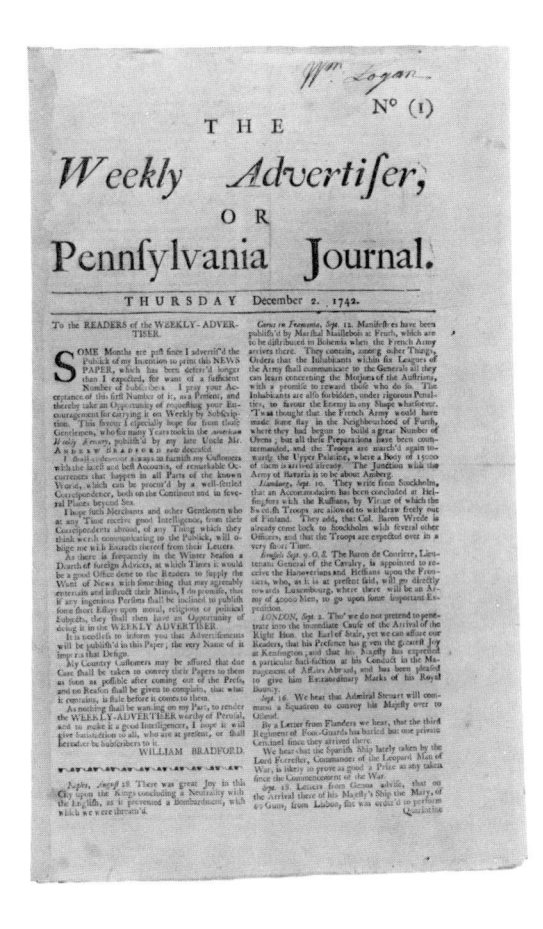

FIRST NUMBER OF THE JOURNAL

SAUER'S GREAT BIBLE

first issues from his press beginning in 1739, and a splendid copy of his great Bible of 1743, the first Bible printed in a European language in America. Of the German press at Ephrata, it owns not only its first title (a Mennonite prayer book prepared by Conrad Beissel and printed in 1745) but the press as well. A bequest of 1872, this printing press has been on loan since 1949 to the Pennsylvania Historical and Museum Commission for exhibition at Ephrata Cloisters.

The old books at the Society are interesting for their provenances, the signatures on their title pages, the armorial bookplates of former owners. A *Hudibras* (London, 1761) has inscribed on its title page "Anty Wayne Anthony Wayne Anthony Wayne his book God give him grace thereon to Look and may he evermore incline to read all books that are sublime." *The Manners of the Times; A Satire. By Philadelphiensis* (1762), aimed at local fashionables, bears Quaker Phineas Pemberton's approving signature. Dr. William Smith's influential *A General Idea of the College of Mirania* (New York, 1753), which led to his being called to preside over the College of Philadelphia, is inscribed to one of its trustees, "For Isaac Norris, Esq." Printed in 1756, the Society's copy of Nicholas Scull's *Kawanio Che Keeteru: A True Relation of a Bloody Battle Fought Between George and Lewis in the Year 1755* bears that humorous versifier's notation, "By Nicholas Scull." Yet another volume of historical background is Harrington's *Oceana*, for it contains the bookplate of William Byrd of Westover and the signature of a subsequent owner, James Madison.

Of other forms of printing, the Society's outstanding run of Franklin's *Gazette* has been noticed. Earlier than the *Gazette* was Andrew

Bradford's *Mercury*, 1719-1746, of which the Society owns only the third best run. But of William Bradford's *Pennsylvania Journal*, 1742-1793, it can again claim first place.

The newspapers chronicled much of the colony's Indian relations, which are amplified by the Society's manuscripts, perhaps most notably in the papers of James Logan. For many years Logan was not only the principal merchant in the fur and deerskin trade but also the Proprietors' chief negotiator with the natives. Included in his manuscripts is a handsome map of the Walking Purchase, drawn for him by Lewis Evans in 1738, "A Map of that Part of Bucks County released by the Indians to the Proprietaries of Pennsylvania in September 1737." Nicely designed, it is decorated with the figure of an Indian striding purposely along, followed by his dog.

When Logan retired from the Indian trade about 1730, Edward Shippen became its largest operator, and most of his papers are at the Society, as are those of George Croghan, "King of the Traders" and later Pennsylvania's most prominent land speculator and Indian agent, deputy to Sir William Johnson. The colony's effort to regulate the Indian trade is represented by much correspondence, many

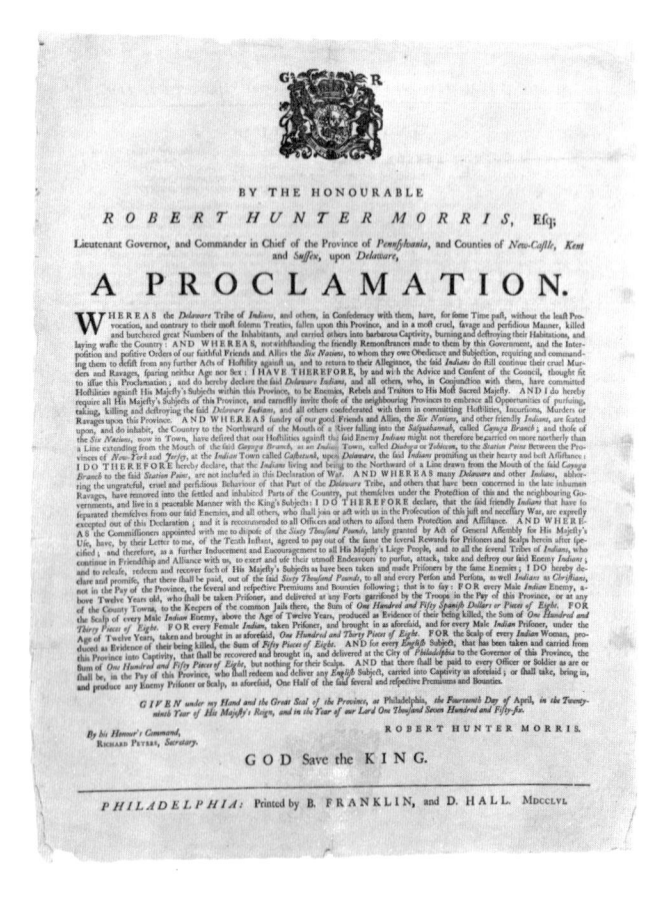

DECLARATION OF WAR ON INDIANS

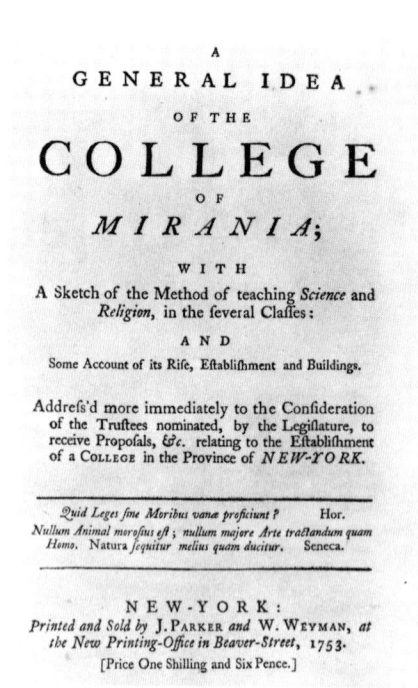

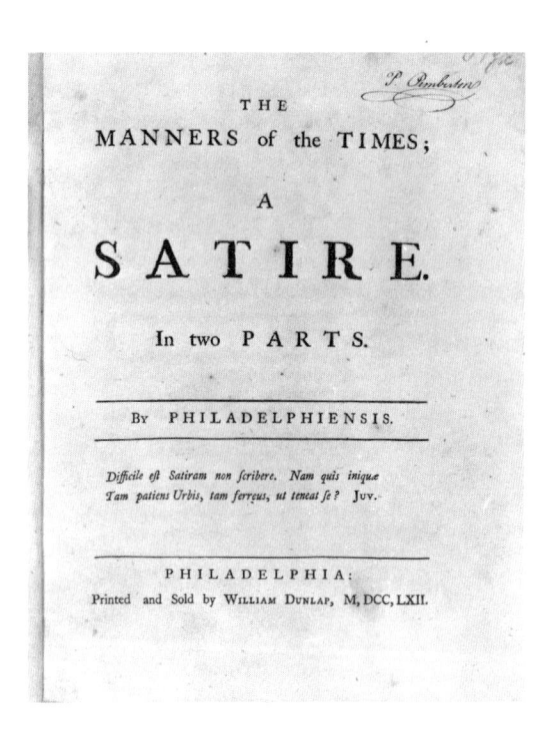

TWO ASSOCIATION BOOKS

journals, and the diaries of its agent James Kenny.

Following Braddock's disaster, the Indians descended on the frontier, massacring the pioneers. Franklin and Hall printed Governor Robert Hunter Morris' proclamation formally declaring war on the Delawares and offering bounties for scalps, 138 pieces of eight for the scalps of males above the age of twelve. This gory memento among the Society's broadsides is complemented by another relic of the colony's retaliation, a silver medal made by Joseph Richardson. Gift of the Corporation of the City of Philadelphia, it commemorated Colonel John Armstrong's destruction of the hostile Indian village of Kittanning in western Pennsylvania on September 8, 1756. Each of Armstrong's commissioned officers received one of these and they are believed to be the first medals struck from dies in the colonies. The Society's was a gift in 1880 from Dr. William A. Irvine whose grandfather commanded at Fort Pitt during the Revolution.

The Quakers, deploring military operations, founded the Friendly Association for Regaining

KITTANNING MEDAL

and Preserving Peace with the Indians. Their minutes at the Society record that in March, 1757, the Association ordered "a parcel of silver medals suitable to be presented" to the Indians. Once again silversmith Richardson, a trustee of the Association, went to work. The medal he designed has a portrait of George II on one side and on the other an Indian and a Quaker exchanging the peace pipe while the sun beams approval. John Richardson, grandson of Joseph, gave the Society one of these in 1827. Joseph Richardson also made gorgets for Indian presents, engraved with the same peace scene as the medal. The Society's Richardson gorget is evidently the only surviving example.

The skill of the colonial silversmith was one of that period's greatest glories. Of historical

HAMILTON'S FREEDOM BOX

interest is the gold Freedom Box presented in 1735 by the Common Council of the City of New York to Andrew Hamilton, who had come on from Philadelphia to attain the first major victory for the freedom of the press in America. Made by Charles Le Roux, the box is engraved with the seal of the City of New York and is accompanied by a parchment expressing the appreciation of the Mayor and other officials for Hamilton's remarkable services in his "learned and generous [*he did not accept a fee*] Defense of the Rights of Mankind and the Liberty of the Press in the Case of John Peter Zenger lately tryed," for which Hamilton was presented with "the freedom of this Corporation." The Freedom Box and the certificate were the gift of a descendant of Hamilton more than two centuries after the event.

The collection contains some English silver of association interest. Particularly curious are two large plates retrieved after the earthquake which destroyed Port Royal, Jamaica, in 1692. They were found in a cradle with a Negro child, floating on the water. Formerly owned by Thomas Norris, who had perished in the calamity, the silver was sent to his son Isaac in Philadelphia and was presented to the Society by Dr. Charles C. Norris in 1948.

The importance of the Society's silver rests, however, not on association pieces made elsewhere, but on its substantial collection of locally made silver, mention of a few pieces of which will indicate its attraction. Johannis Nys (1671-1734) is represented by two wedding items—a porringer engraved with the initials of Francis Knowles and Sarah Lee, who were

FOOTED TRAY BY SYNG

married on March 10, 1714/15 (the mate of the porringer is at the Philadelphia Museum of Art), and a splendid tankard initialed for George Emlen and Mary Heath, married on April 24, 1717. A footed tray, wonderously worked, part of the wedding silver of Sarah Shoemaker who married Edward Penington on

SAUCEBOAT BY JOSEPH RICHARDSON

November 26, 1754, reflects much credit on its maker, Philip Syng, Jr.

Along with examples of other Philadelphia silversmiths, the collection is strongest in the work of all three generations of the Richardsons, particularly of Joseph Richardson (active 1736-1771). A noted tea set is a good specimen of his skill, as are a pair of sauce boats of about 1760, engraved with the arms of the Pembertons, and an impressive stuffing spoon of the same period for the same family. That he enjoyed a carriage trade is seen in the porringer he made for Caspar Wistar, a tray for the Logan family, and a pair of cans purchased from him in 1737 by Hugh Roberts.

Much of the Society's silver is on display in its museum together with a wide variety of other objects, the oldest of which is an intriguing reminder of Swedish settlements along the Delaware decades before William Penn's arrival. Long ago a grave was uncovered at the site of a fortified Indian town in Lancaster County. In the grave, on the skull of its occupant, was an iron helmet. Of the type introduced by Gustavus Adolphus and made between 1620 and 1640, it was worn by pikemen and musketeers and is the only specimen of

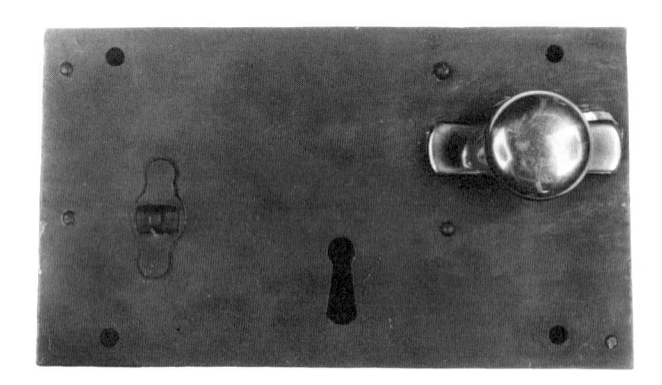

LOCK OF DOOR OF SLATE-ROOF HOUSE

Swedish armor used in America in existence. It was sent to the Society as a Centennial contribution in 1876.

Among other antique objects is the initialed and 1687-dated lintel from Phineas Pemberton's house, the lock and key of the Slate Roof House where William Penn lived during his second visit, and a large, black-framed mirror, a 1711 wedding gift imported on the *Greyhound* by Samuel Preston for Hannah Preston and Samuel Carpenter II, as the bill of lading still attests. Improved craftsmanship soon made possible the purchase of locally made objects of fine quality. A masterpiece of this description is the Society's tall-case clock, the work of Peter Stretch, who came to Philadelphia in 1702. Made prior to 1720, it has a restrained, flat-topped mahogany case and a single pointer for its brass dial. For the thoughts they evoke, a variety of other objects are of interest: James Logan's massive watch; Governor James Hamilton's strong box; Henry W. (Baron) Stiegel of Manheim's spinnet, imported from Germany in 1760; and a boundary stone from the Mason-Dixon Line with the Penn arms on one side and Baltimore's on the other, presented in 1903 when the line was resurveyed.

The colony's early iron industry is represented by ornamental fire backs and plates from iron stoves. The Society has three plates

FIRE BACKS FROM THE COLLECTION

with the "War and Peace" design featuring two tall grenadiers personifying War and two short, bearded men with long hair and broad brimmed hats, emblematic of Peace. A plate from another stove is of "The Family Quarrel." Husband and wife, urged on by their children, flail at each other. A side plate from a six-plate stove is dated 1764. Made by Robert Thornbury and Francis Sanderson, ironmasters at Carlisle Furnace, this is the earliest plate known to have been cast so far west.

Among the Society's fire backs is one dated 1728 on a raised cartouche between two floral

STRETCH TALL-CASE CLOCK

festoons, the same pattern as fire backs at Graeme Park and Stenton. Inscribed in German with the words "The Life of Jesus Was a Light" is yet another made by John Potts in 1751, probably at Warwick Furnace. One of several massive fire backs boldly decorated with the British coat of arms reveals itself as cast in 1754 at Oxford Furnace.

Only a portion of the Society's collection of some 800 oil paintings and miniatures can be exhibited together with its museum objects.

WITT'S WATER COLOR OF KELPIUS

Those which date back to early colonial times are numerous enough. The Society's earliest portrait is not an oil but a water color by Dr. Christopher Witt of the mystic Johannes Kelpius who died near Philadelphia in 1708. Painted about 1705, it is believed to be the oldest portrait of a Pennsylvanian. Perhaps nearly as old are the coat of arms of Queen Anne. Dating from sometime in her reign of 1702 to 1714, these arms are on a heavy sign board which was affixed to the Courthouse completed in 1708 at Second and Market. Unlike the work of Dr. Witt, a fairly skilled amateur, the arms illustrate the crude artistry of a primitive sign painter.

Among the Society's likenesses of early governors is an India ink drawing on parchment of Sir William Keith, governor of Pennsylvania and Delaware from 1717 to 1726. It was drawn during that period by John Watson. An attractive pastel, English, about 1735, presents the appearance of George Thomas. Ablest of the governors, he held the office from 1738 to 1747.

GOVERNOR KEITH BY WATSON

Throughout most of the administration of these officers, Gustavus Hesselius was active in Philadelphia. A Swede who settled in the city in 1712, he was the founder of painting in the Middle Colonies. The Society is fortunate in the ownership of his self-portrait of about 1740 and its companion painting of Mrs. Hesselius. His Indian chiefs and Governor Patrick Gordon have been mentioned. There remains one more, his important canvas of James Logan, acting governor in 1736-1738. There is reason to believe that this likeness may have

Jane Galloway by Benjamin West

been taken in 1716.

Of talented young John Meng, who was born in Germantown in 1734 and who died about 1754, the Society owns all three of his known works, one of them a pleasing self-portrait. While not holding a monopoly on the American works of Benjamin West (1738-1820), the Society has more of them than any other owner. West was about seventeen years of age when he painted the portraits of the Lancaster gunsmith William Henry and his wife. Crude yet forceful, they illustrate how greatly the artist's skill had developed two or three years later when he painted young Thomas Mifflin and Jane Galloway. These four portraits rank among the Society's most important. Further evidence of West's Philadelphia years is seen in his sketch book of some seventy pictures of men, women, and children. They include pencil portraits of West's father and of Francis Hopkinson, a dilettante in the arts.

Among others of the Society's paintings of this period are Copley's miniature of Sir John St. Clair, Braddock's quartermaster general; Robert Feke's Mrs. William Peters; John Wollaston's portrait of Mrs. Peters' husband,

JOHN MENG'S SELF-PORTRAIT

an important official; Wollaston's likeness of Colonel Henry Bouquet, the premier soldier on the Pennsylvania frontier during the French and Indian wars, and the same artist's large, impressive portrait of Mayor William Plumstead. From the brush of Matthew Pratt have come miniatures of Mr. and Mrs. Thomas Hopkinson; James Claypoole, Jr. is represented by a portrait of a young girl; the collection contains four portraits of Moravians by John Valentine Haidt of Bethlehem.

The lives of early Pennsylvanians, whose portraits and other possessions are displayed at the Society, are fleshed out by their papers, the letters they received and those they wrote, many thousands of which are represented by retained copies entered in their letter books. Diaries also furnish a valuable source of information about their times. Fortunately, our ancestors were apt to save their papers and in many cases they have survived reasonably intact. The backbone of the Society's colonial manuscripts, other than collections mentioned in previous chapters, are to be found in its

THOMAS MIFFLIN BY WEST

56   Collecting by The Historical Society

archives of the Bartram, Bradford, Cadwalader, Clifford, Drinker, Gilpin, Hollingsworth, Hopkinson, Logan, Meredith, Norris, Pemberton, Peters, Powel, Rawle, Shippen, Wharton, Wistar, and Willing families.

Most of these family collections are large, some cover many generations. The Cadwalader papers cover a time span of 1680 to 1900 and number some 65,000 documents. Larger yet are the Hollingsworth manuscripts, which, spanning a period from 1748 to 1887, amount to 165,000 papers dealing with the political and economic interests of a flour manufacturing family.

The papers of James Logan and of Isaac Norris I and II are extremely rich. Their letter books, which are virtually complete, are the authority for much that has been written about the early decades of Pennsylvania's eighteenth-century history.

PAGE FROM THE LOGAN PAPERS

Among earliest records are those relating to the Dutch and the Swedes. In 1867 the Society purchased at auction in Amsterdam a collection of Dutch West India Company papers bearing on Delaware. From the Penn family came a 1683 file of affidavits executed

PENN PATENT TO SAMUEL CARPENTER

by "ancient" Swedes describing their original settlements. A prime Philadelphia source is James Claypoole's letter book of 1681-1683. Interesting exhibition pieces are two deeds executed by Penn: a 1682 sale of 1,500 acres to Robert Greeneway "Marrinor," captain of the *Welcome* on which Penn sailed to his colony; and a 1684 patent to Samuel Carpenter for the large city lot on which he built the celebrated Slate Roof House. In this category belongs a confirming patent to John Key, reciting Penn's gift of a lot on Sassafras Street in 1683 to Key "then an Infant being the first born in the said city of Philadelphia."

Other manuscripts of interest include Jonathan Dickinson's description of his shipwreck while on a journey from Jamaica to Philadelphia in 1696, published as *God's Protecting Providence, Man's Surest Help and Defense*; the letter book and other records of Germantown's founder, Francis Daniel Pastorius; a vast collection of account books of forges and furnaces; Baron Stiegel's glass works records; original minute books of early Quaker meetings; 146 volumes of transcripts of Journals of the Lords of Trade, 1675-1782; Germantown court records, 1691-1707; ledgers and letter books of the silversmith Joseph Richardson. Some forty-one manuscript volumes preserve the hymns of German settlers; sixteen of them come from the Ephrata Cloisters. Many of these choral books are most beautifully illuminated.

The scope of the collection covers every aspect of early colonial life in Pennsylvania—religious, political, social and economic—and dramatically illustrates the colony's growth. Perhaps if a person living in the period under discussion were asked what object in Philadelphia filled him with the greatest sense of satisfaction, he might point to the State House, erected in the 1730s. Preserved on parchment at the Society are its earliest designs (1732), its elevation and floor plans. Found in the papers of John Dickinson about 1890, these have been attributed to Andrew Hamilton, defender of John Peter Zenger and superintendent for the construction of the State House. The Society also has the bill for its floor plans and elevation drawings of 1735-1736, submitted by Edmund Woolley. Woolley, a master carpenter, was probably the building's actual architect, possibly guided by Hamilton.

We cannot leave this period and Pennsylvania's most famous building without mention of the role of Isaac Norris II, Speaker of the Assembly and one of the Superintendents of the State House. His letter book at the Society contains all the correspondence relative to the ordering of a bell in 1751 to be hung in the tower. According to his instructions, the bell was to carry the legend "Proclaim Liberty thro' all the Land to all the Inhabitants thereof."

EARLIEST PLAN OF THE STATE HOUSE ATTRIBUTED TO ANDREW HAMILTON

I have numbered the Questions for the sake of making References to them.—

Qu. 1. is a Question of Form; ask'd of every one that is examin'd.—

Qu. 2. 3. 4. 5. 6. 7. were ask'd by Mr Hewit, Member for Coventry, a Friend of ours, and were design'd to draw out the Answers that follow, being the Substance of what I had before said to him on the Subject, to remove a common Prejudice, that the Colonies paid no Taxes, & that their Governments were supported by burthening the People here.— Qu. 7. was particularly intended to shew by the Answer, that Parliament could not properly & equitably lay Taxes in America; as they could not by reason of their distance be acquainted with such Circumstances as might make it necessary to spare particular Parts.

Qu. 8. to 13. ask'd by Mr Huske, another Friend, to shew the Impracticability of distributing the Stamps in America.

Qu. 14. 15. & 16. by one of the late Administration, an Adversary.

Qu. 17 to 26. by Mr Huske again.— His Questions about the Germans and about the Number of People were intended to make the Opposition to the Stamp Act in America appear more formidable.— He ask'd some others here that the Clerk has omitted; particularly one I remember.— There had been a considerable Party in the House for saving the Honour & Right of Parliament by retaining the Act, and yet making it tolerable to America, by reducing it to a Stamp on Commissions for Profitable Offices & on Cards and Dice. I had in conversation with many of them objected to this, as it would require an Establishment for the Distributors, which would be a great Expence for that the Stamps would not be sufficient to pay them, & so the Odium & Contention would be kept up for nothing.— The Notion of Amending however still continued, & one of the most active of the Members for promoting it, told me he was sure, I should if I would assist them to amend the Act in such a manner as that America should have little or no Objection to it.— I must confess, says I, I have thought of one Amendment, that if you will make it, the Act may remain & yet the Americans will be quieted. 'Tis a very small Amendment, too, 'tis only a Change of a single Word. Ay! says he what is that? It is, says I, in

FRANKLIN'S NOTES OF HIS QUESTIONING BY PARLIAMENT

Dawn of a New Nation

When Isaac Norris in 1751 selected the line from *Leviticus*, "Proclaim Liberty thro' all the Land," to be inscribed on the State House bell, he was not motivated by antagonism toward his mother country. On the contrary, the expression conveyed the exultation Pennsylvanians felt over the liberties they had long enjoyed. Following the costly French and Indian War, however, England sought to raise revenues from the colonies, and some Americans became fearful. It was about 1763, the First Continental Congress was later to agree, that the British Ministry adopted a form of administration calculated to enslave the colonies. Taxation without representation was tyranny. One step after another led inexorably to the drama of July 4, 1776. Of this long series of events the Society holds significant records.

Parliament's first most aggressive action was the passing of the Stamp Act in 1765 to help meet the expense of administering the colonies. Benjamin Franklin, Pennsylvania's agent in England, was not aroused by the Act. He saw to it that his Philadelphia friend John Hughes was appointed distributor of stamps. Among Hughes' papers at the Society is a pamphlet, *Instructions To be observed by each Distributer of Stamped Parchment and Paper*, and the manifest of the ship *Royal Charlotte* covering three cases and seven packages of stamps for America.

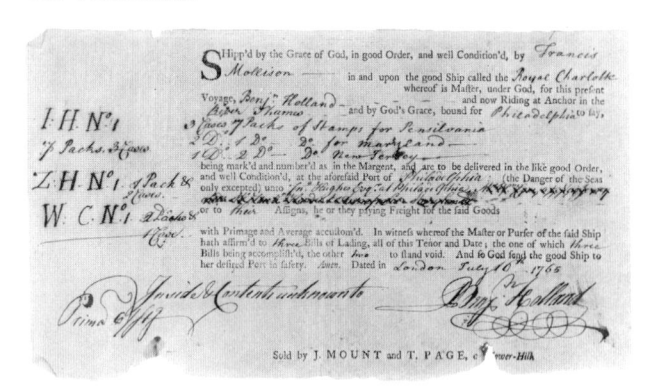

MANIFEST FOR STAMPS

Franklin and Hughes had misjudged their colleagues; the merchants and leading men were outraged. They passed nonimportation agreements to bring pressure on Parliament to repeal the Stamp Act. In Philadelphia, the printer William Bradford played a major role. He sent his son Thomas from house to house to obtain signatures to a document headed by the following: "That none of the Subscribers hereto shall or will vend any Goods or Merchandize whatsoever that shall be ship'd them on Commission from Great Britain after the first Day of January next unless the *Stamp Act be repeal'd*." Of the 374 names of the principal residents of Philadelphia whose signatures are on the protest, most were obtained by Thomas Bradford. Others were added at his father's office in the London Coffee House at the south-

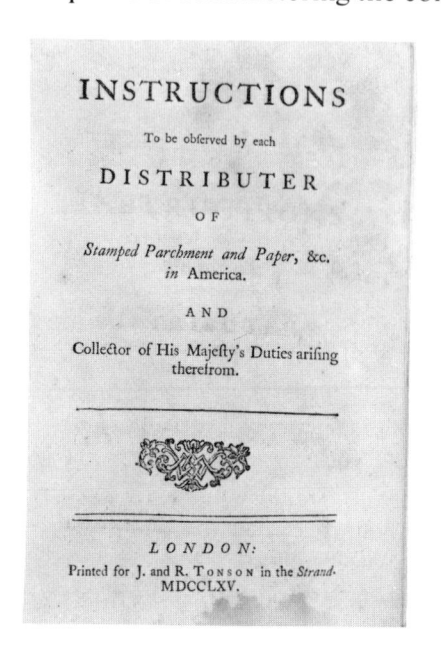

STAMP ACT INSTRUCTIONS

west corner of Front and Market Streets, where the document was displayed for public view. The Americans won this round, for the Stamp Act was repealed. Toward the end of his long life Thomas Bradford gave the Philadelphia nonimportation agreement to his grandson, who, in turn, presented it to the Society in 1854.

hold on the American tea trade. In the recently acquired papers of Thomas Wharton, an eminent Quaker merchant of Philadelphia, is a broadside dated October 13, 1773, which conveys the urgency of local reaction: "A Very dangerous Attempt to render ineffectual your virtuous Exertions, against the Inroads of Op-

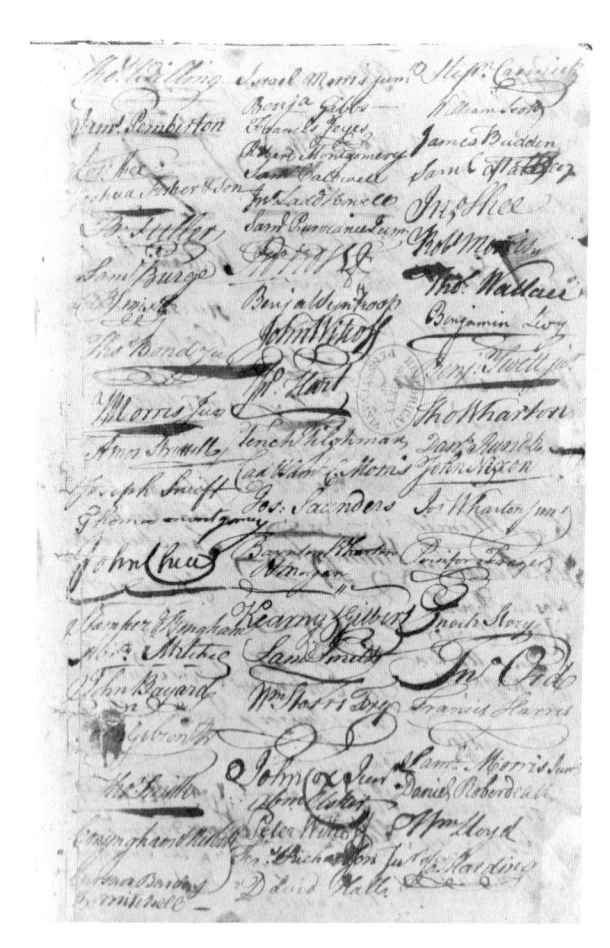

NONIMPORTATION AGREEMENT, FIRST PAGE OF TEXT AND OF NAMES

The next most severe shock occurred in Boston and had Philadelphians reading such pamphlets as the following in the Society's collection: *A Short Narrative of the horrid Massacre in Boston, Perpetrated In the Evening of the Fifth Day of March, 1770;* and *The Trial* [of soldiers of the 29th Regiment of Foot] *For the Murder of Crispus Attucks, Samuel Gray, Samuel Maverick, James Caldwell, and Patrick Carr.* The kettle was beginning to steam.

Then came the Tea Act, which, if effective, would give the East India Company a strangle-

pression and Slavery, being now meditated by the East-India Company, under the Direction of a corrupt and designing Ministry; you are most earnestly requested to meet at the State-House, on Saturday next at two o'Clock in the Afternoon; to consider what Measures will be necessary to prevent the Landing of a large Quantity of TEA which is hourly expected; and which, if allowed a footing in the Land of Liberty, will speedily and effectively change your present invaluable Title of American Freemen to that of Slaves." Strong sentiments these! In the face of them the captain of the Philadelphia tea ship returned to England without landing his cargo.

In Boston it was a different story. Three hundred and forty-two chests of tea were thrown into the harbor and this brought on the Boston Port Bill, closing the port of Boston on June 1, 1774, until the tea was paid for. This "massacre of American liberty" resulted in the calling of the First Continental Congress, which met in

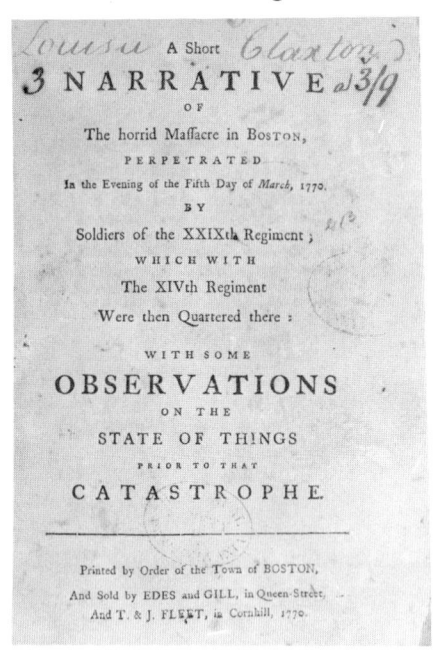

REPORT OF BOSTON MASSACRE

Philadelphia that September to discuss colonial grievances. The upshot of congressional deliberations was another nonimportation agreement. Dated "In Congress, Philadelphia, October 20, 1774," these resolves were published in a pamphlet which concluded: "The foregoing Association being determined upon by the Congress, was ordered to be subscribed by the several Members thereof; and thereupon we have hereunto set our respective names accordingly." Two of these pamphlets actually signed by the delegates have survived. The Society's copy bears forty-two signatures, including those of both Adamses for Massachusetts Bay, Washington for Virginia, and Edward Biddle, Joseph Galloway, Thomas Mifflin and Charles Humphreys for Pennsylvania.

In accordance with the nonimportation resolve, the Philadelphia Committee of Observation appointed a Committee of Inspection, which met at the Bradfords' Coffee House to pass on the sale of cargoes. The original minutes of their meetings are at the Society. Among the committeemen were Thomas Mifflin whose portrait and that of his wife, painted by John Singleton Copley in Boston in 1773, is one of the Society's chief adornments, and Joseph Dean, whose likeness taken by Charles Willson Peale about 1785 also hangs on the Society's walls.

The rising Revolutionary tempo was sparked in Philadelphia by the arrival at the City Tavern of an express rider at 5 P.M. on April 24, 1775. He carried news from Watertown, Massachusetts, which was certified from town to town until it reached Trenton: "To all friends of American Liberty be it known that this Morning before break of day a Brigade consisting of about 1,000, or 1,200 men landed at Phips farm at Cambridge and Marched to Lexington where they found a company of our Colony Militia in Arms upon whom they fired without any provocation and killed six men. . . ." The Bradfords immediately printed the dispatch. Ninety-eight years later, in 1873, the original manuscript was purchased by the Society. It bears an endorsement of about 1790 by that historical editor and antiquarian Ebenezer Hazard: "Acco of the Battle of Lexington sent by Express from Town to Town. This is the paper sent to Phila. & delivered to me by one of the Comm. Eben Hazard."

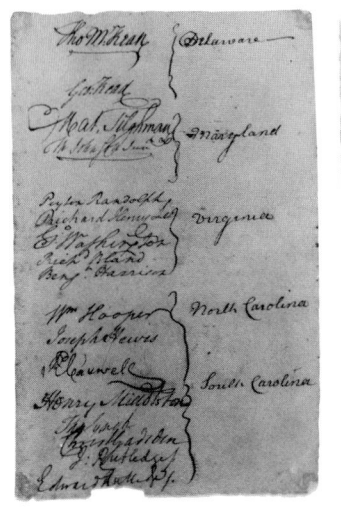

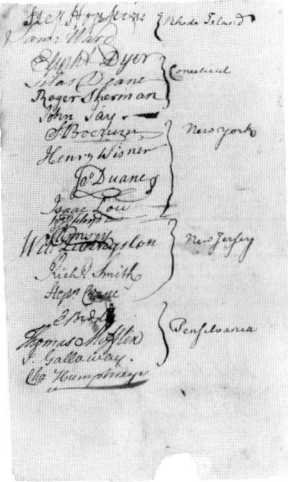

ASSOCIATION SIGNATURES

Lexington was followed in 1775 by Bunker Hill, but still the Continental Congress hoped for a peaceful union with Great Britain. It decided to send a message to George III setting forth the case for the colonies. The Society has a draft of this Olive Branch Petition as drawn up by John Dickinson. The copy sent to London was rejected by the King.

And so events moved on to the publication early in 1776 of Thomas Paine's *Common Sense*, which called for an immediate declaration of independence. The Society's copy is autographed by that sturdy patriot Timothy Matlack and is a second issue of the first edition. Six months later Paine had his wish and John Dunlap the satisfaction of being the first to print the Declaration. Perhaps eighteen copies of that broadside have survived. The Society's copy is only the top half, but it is unique, being evidently a proof before corrections. The differences between it and all other known copies lie in punctuation. A copy of Dunlap's broadside was sent to the Governor of Rhode Island, and from it on July 13, 1776, Solomon Southwick printed the first Newport edition, of which the Society has one of six original copies. Other mementos of the Declaration are a marble mantel from the Graff House in which Jefferson wrote the document, and the well-known Pine-

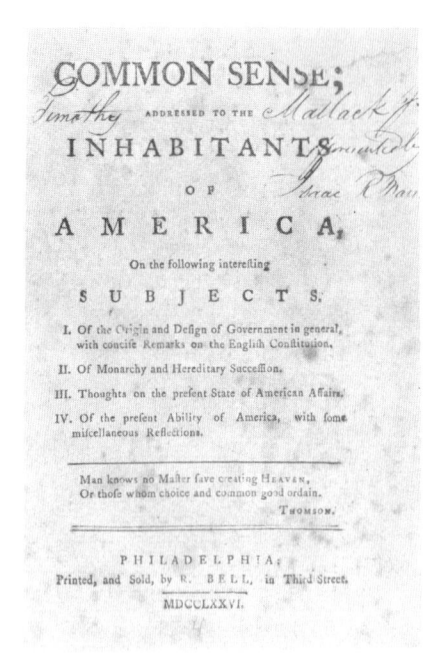

PAINE'S COMMON SENSE

Savage painting of the signing of the Declaration which was used as a basis for the restoration of Independence Hall's Assembly Room.

The time had now come to write new constitutions. On July 12, 1776, John Dickinson, author of the influential *Farmer's Letters*, reported to Congress a set of articles of confederation. In his papers at the Society is his much

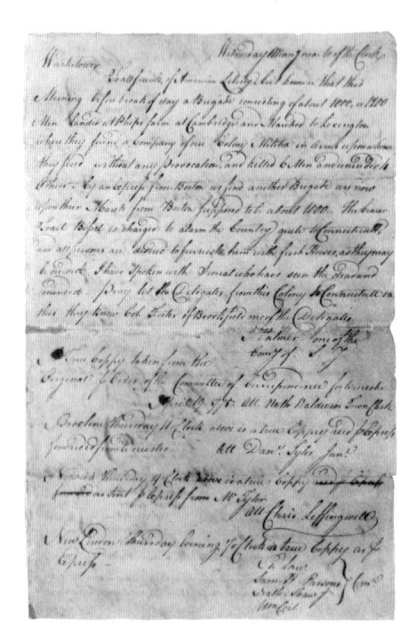

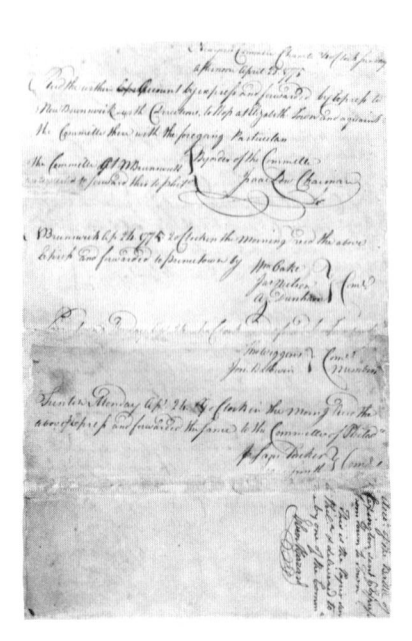

MANUSCRIPT AND PRINTED REPORT OF BATTLE OF LEXINGTON

corrected draft of "Articles of Confederation and perpetual union between the Colonies of New Hampshire etc [in General Congress met] at Philadelphia the [blank] Day of [blank] 1776. Art. the name of the Confederacy shall be 'The United States of America.' " The sovereign state of Pennsylvania went through similar proceedings, first by a *Provincial Conference of Committees . . . Held at the Carpenter's Hall, June 18-25, 1776.* The Society's copy of this pamphlet belonged to John Dickinson, but it also bears the signature of Thomas McKean who was president of the conference. From this initial step came the printing by John Dunlap in the following September of *The Constitution of the Common-Wealth of Pennsylvania*. This was a highly controversial, very radical instrument and greatly distressed Dickinson. He virtually rewrote his copy, now at the Society, but to no avail; the constitution-makers were not interested in his ideas.

Among the Society's most important Revolutionary manuscripts are the papers of Generals Anthony Wayne, William Irvine, Edward Hand, Thomas Hutchins and John Cadwalader. It owns nine volumes of Secretary to Congress Charles Thomson's papers, a major portion of John Dickinson's papers, Chaloner and White's accounts of provisioning the army, the Bradfords' records of British prisoners of war, muster rolls and lists of citizens able to bear arms in 1775 gathered by George Clymer, the Thomas McKean papers, and those of Thomas Willing, including Willing's statement of the part he played in transmitting General Howe's peace offer to Congress in 1778 (an episode his biographer chose to overlook). A number of journals are devoted to the Quebec expedition of 1775-1776 and there is intensive coverage of the Virginia Exiles, those Philadelphians suspected of Loyalism and banished to Winchester in 1777. Diaries further illumi-

CONGRESS VOTING INDEPENDENCE BY PINE & SAVAGE

nate the period, particularly those of Sarah Logan Fisher, Elizabeth Drinker, Christopher Marshall and Grace Growdon Galloway, and the autobiography of Charles Biddle is another notable primary source for the times. Much of these writings have been published.

Also in the collection are eight maps believed to have been used by General Knox in the early stage of the conflict. They show roads around Philadelphia, the course of the Delaware River, plans of roads from Trenton to Princeton, January, 1777, and the Whitemarsh area. These are complemented by several French maps of the defenses of Forts Mifflin and Mercer. It was at Fort Mercer that the Hessian Colonel Count Donop was killed. His watch was subsequently auctioned in Philadelphia and has found its way to the Society.

Another of its Revolutionary maps is a large one drawn by Jacob Broom, Surveyor of New Castle County, of the Brandywine area in August, 1777, two weeks before the Battle of Brandywine. This was used by Washington in that disappointing encounter which failed to stop the British from taking Philadelphia. Of the Battle of Germantown, which shortly followed, the Society displays the red ensign which belonged to the British General Agnew who was killed in the fight. One of the Society's most charming diaries is that of Sally Wister. On December 12, 1777, she relates how the six-foot figure of a British Grenadier, painted on wood, was used to frighten an American officer. Sally Wister's journal was presented to the Society by Owen Wister, the novelist, in 1931 at the same time that Dr. James W. Wister presented the Grenadier.

Comfortably ensconced in Philadelphia, the British issued the *Royal Pennsylvania Gazette*, of which the Society has one of three complete runs, and published such various pieces to be found in the Society's collection as *A List of the General and Staff Officers . . . Under the Command of His Excellency General Sir William Howe*. One of the Society's prizes is a unique recruiting broadside for the First Battalion of Pennsylvania Loyalists. Volunteers were exhorted to fight against "the arbitrary Usurpations of a tyrannical Congress. . . . Such spirited Fellows, who are willing to engage, will be rewarded at the End of the War, besides their Laurels, with Fifty Acres of Land in any County they shall chuse, where every gallant Hero may retire, and enjoy his Bottle and Lass."

Meanwhile, Washington at Valley Forge wanted supplies. On December 20, 1777, John Dunlap, who had taken refuge at Lancaster, issued the General's proclamation requiring all persons within seventy miles of Headquarters to thresh their grain by March 1, or else it would be purchased as straw. This relic of the Valley Forge winter at the Society is joined by many maps of the British defenses at Philadelphia and American troop locations at Valley Forge, some of them drawn by French engineers and one of them owned by General Duportail. The

BRITISH GRENADIER

> TEUCRO DUCE NIL DESPERANDUM.
>
> First Battalion of Pennsylvania Loyalists, commanded by His Excellency Sir WILLIAM HOWE, K. B.
>
> ALL intrepid, able-bodied HEROES, who are willing to serve His Majesty King GEORGE the Third, in Defence of their Country, Laws, and Constitution, against the arbitrary Usurpations of a tyrannical Congress, have now not only an Opportunity of manifesting their Spirit, by assisting in reducing their too-long deluded Countrymen, but also of acquiring the polite Accomplishments of a Soldier, by serving only two Years, or during the present Rebellion in America.
>
> Such spirited Fellows, who are willing to engage, will be rewarded at the End of the War, besides their Laurels, with Fifty Acres of Land in any County they shall chuse, where every gallant Hero may retire, and enjoy his Bottle and Lass.
>
> Each Volunteer will receive, as a Bounty, FIVE DOLLARS, besides Arms, Cloathing and Accoutrements, and every other Requisite proper to accommodate a Gentleman Soldier, by applying to Lieutenant-Colonel ALLEN, or at Captain STEVENS's Rendezvous, in Front-street.
>
> PRINTED by JAMES HUMPHREYS, JUNR. in Market-street, between Front and Second-streets.

LOYALIST RECRUITING POSTER

collection is also rich in muster rolls and orderly books. It contains Colonel William Bradford's muster roll of the Army at Valley Forge and an orderly book which describes in detail the celebration there of the French entry into the war: "Upon a signal given the whole army will Huzza long live the king of France. The Artillery then begin again and fire 13 rounds. This will be succeeded by a 2nd Genl Discharge of the Musquetry. . . ."

The evacuation of Philadelphia by the British in June, 1778, was followed by an effort to obtain oaths of allegiance renouncing George III from all those who had not already subscribed in pursuance of an act of 1777. Plunket Fleeson was in charge of this task and collected more than a thousand signatures. They included those of most of the state officials, notably Joseph Reed, President of the Supreme Executive Council, whose portraits by Charles Willson Peale, in oil and in pencil, are at the Society. On July 15, 1778, the old Indian agent George Croghan signed. The certificate he was given as proof of his oath came to the Society with his papers. As for Fleeson's two volumes of signatures, they were acquired from his heirs in 1793 by someone unknown and were given to the Society in 1893 by its President, Brinton Coxe.

Among the Society's John Paul Jones letters is one to Robert Morris of October 13, 1779, which has been described as "without doubt the most interesting letter extant in reference to the Naval History of the American Revolution." This gives a detailed account of the fight between the *Bon Homme Richard* and the British *Serapis*, a bloody victory gained by Jones.

Victory was in the air, and at last it came at Yorktown on October 19, 1781. The Society's military journal of Lt. William Feltman of the First Pennsylvania Regiment gives a full account of how Major Alexander Hamilton took possession of the British batteries and hoisted the American flag. And then "The British Army march'd out & Grounded their arms in front of our Line. Our Whole Army drew up for them to march through. The French Army on their right & the American Army on their left. The British Prisoners all appeared to be much in Liquor." Daniel Miller, a Pennsylvania soldier, was mustered out at Yorktown after the surrender. His complete mustering out pay is on exhibit at the Society, a fat wad of Continental notes still in their original parchment wrapper. Inflation was so severe that Miller never bothered to redeem his pay.

Among the Society's paintings, there are some that recall the stirring days of the Revolu-

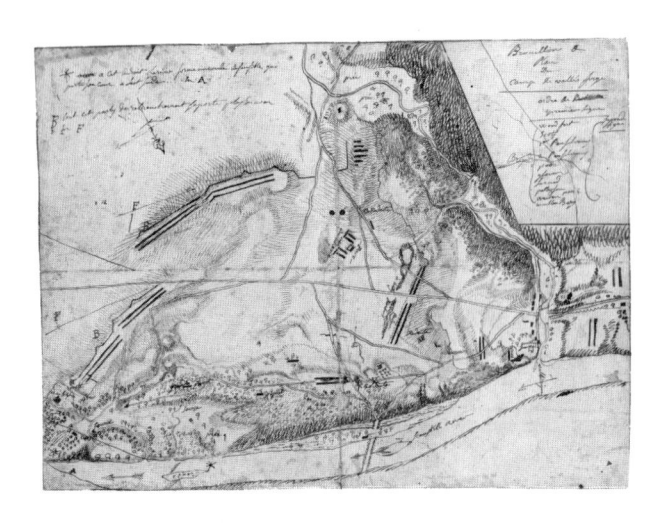

MAP OF VALLEY FORGE

tion. William Mercer, a deaf mute artist, painted the Battle of Princeton which depicts his father, General Hugh Mercer, dead or dying on the field. From the brush of an unknown painter was created a dramatic portrayal of the blowing up of the British man-of-war *Augusta* on October 23, 1777, during the invaders' opening up of the Delaware River. Of persons prominent in those years, the Society is fortunate in its ownership of Charles Willson Peale's fine 1770 portrait of John Dickinson and that of Mrs. Dickinson. Robert Edge Pine is represented in his well-posed portrayal of the Signer Francis Hopkinson, and Edward Savage through his likeness of Signer Robert Morris. Lawrence Sully's miniature of Cyrus Griffin recalls the last President of the Continental Congress, whose tall-case clock is also at the Society. Another miniature, this one by Walter Robertson, gives us the face of one of Philadelphia's most fiery characters, Blair McClenachan, privateersman and politician. Arthur Lee of Virginia is present in William Birch's miniature. Lee was one of the commissioners who negotiated the French alliance. David Rittenhouse, astronomer and Patriot, can be seen in John Trumbull's small painting. Rittenhouse was versatile. The Society owns one of his impressive clocks. Yet another personage of eminence was Dr. John Morgan, who served for a time as physician-in-chief of the American Army. His portrait is by Thomas Spence Duché.

Then there were those thrust by fate into the other camp, notably the Rev. Jacob Duché. The first Chaplain of Congress, Duché later became a defeatist and was exiled. The portrait of this unfortunate man was taken by his son, Thomas Spence Duché. A more romantic note is struck by Peggy Shippen, who in 1779 married the then hero General Benedict Arnold. Her portrait, painted by Daniel Gardner in London in the 1780s, was a gift she sent to her mother. Deserving mention of those on the "other side" are Benjamin West's small portraits of George III and Queen Charlotte.

The return of peace unleashed creative energies. A Philadelphia printer, Robert Aitken, published the first complete English Bible printed in America, popularly called the Congress Bible. A copy of the Bible and Aitken's portrait by Peale are at the Society. Joseph Richardson's sons, Nathaniel and Joseph, Jr., followed their father's trade in creating beautiful silver, many pieces of which are owned by

FATHER AND SON DUCHÉ

MRS. BENEDICT ARNOLD AND CHILD

the Society as well as their receipt book for 1780-1800. Outstanding in the collection is their coffee pot with the Pemberton arms. The art of the cabinetmaker is also evident in Chippendale chairs owned by John Dickinson and furniture from Stenton, the Logan countryseat. To the curious, cabinetmaking tools used by William Savery will be of interest.

Philadelphia had long been fortunate in the skill of its clockmakers. Benjamin Rittenhouse, like his brother David, was skilled in this craft as may be seen in his tall-case clock which has inscribed on its dial "Made by Benjamin Rittenhouse for Jonathan D. Sergeant Esq. Anno 1788." Sergeant had just married the clockmaker's niece, Elizabeth Rittenhouse. A few years ago this clock was bequeathed to the Society by a descendant.

The Society owns a large number of historical "grandfather clocks" as well as many watches. Early watches had an inner and outer case. Before the middle of the eighteenth century it became the custom to place a small circular piece of paper between these cases to keep out dust and to advertise the name and location of the watchmaker's shop. The Society's collection of watchpapers has been acclaimed as "rare and valuable," bits of paper, like lottery tickets, of interest to antiquarians.

No longer a part of the British Empire, denied traditional trade in the West Indies, Americans looked elsewhere with Robert Morris leading the way. In partnership with another man he dispatched the *Empress of China* from New York in 1784, the first American venture in the China trade. The ship's commander, Captain John Green, brought a fan home from Canton, the gift of Chinese officials. Painted by a Chinese artist, it shows his ship at the Whampoa anchorage. Many years later this souvenir of the birth of a great trade was presented to the Society by Mary M. Green. Only a month after the *Empress* sailed from New York, the *United States* left Philadelphia for the Orient. Her journal is also at the Society.

A nation that yearned for wealth and power required a stronger form of government than that supplied by the Articles of Confederation. In 1787 the Constitutional Convention convened at Philadelphia for this purpose. In the Society's James Wilson papers are two drafts of the Constitution in Wilson's hand, with marginal notations on one of them by John Rutledge, chairman of the committee on detail. These represent Wilson's labors as a member of that committee in collating and reducing to form the materials submitted. To promote the passage of the Constitution, *The Federalist* was

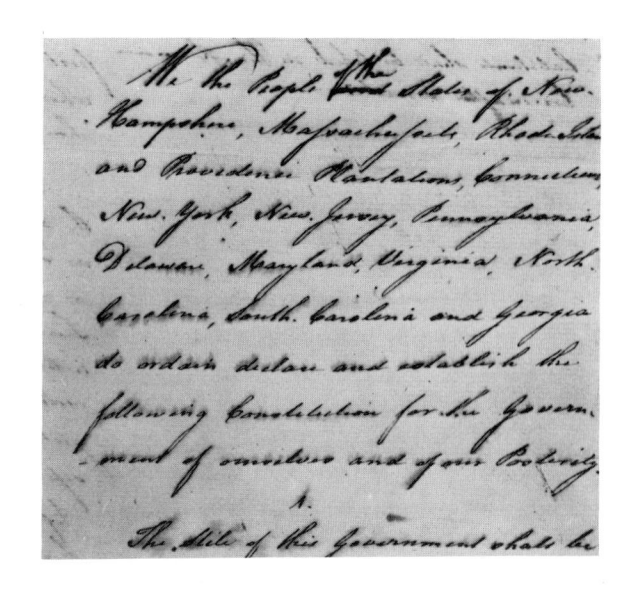

PART OF WILSON'S DRAFT

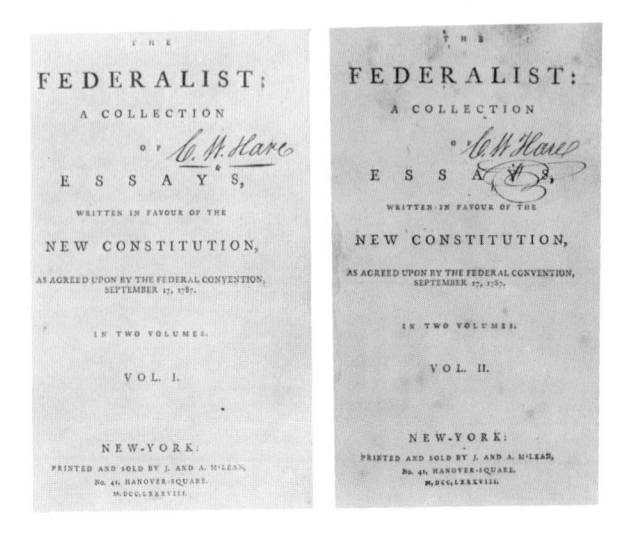

TWO-VOLUME FEDERALIST

written by a few supporters including Alexander Hamilton; his gift copy to William Bingham is in the Society's library. The passage of the famous document was celebrated in Philadelphia on July 4, 1788, by the greatest parade ever. One of the flags carried on the occasion was given to the Society in 1869. It represents the interior of a brass foundry, with the motto: "In vain the earth her treasure hides."

Long the chief publishing center of the country, Philadelphia was fortunate in the arrival in 1784 of Mathew Carey, after Franklin the city's outstanding publisher. The Society holds his voluminous correspondence from 1785 to 1822. For the Revolutionary years and the Federal Era, the Society has outstanding coverage in its nearly complete runs of the most important local newspapers: the *Pennsylvania Journal*, *Pennsylvania Gazette*, *Pennsylvania Chronicle*, *United States Gazette*, *Aurora*, and the *Pennsylvania Packet*. Started in 1771, John Dunlap's *Packet* became America's first successful daily in 1784. The *Packet* was the first newspaper to print the Declaration of Independence, the Constitution of the United States, and, under a different name and ownership, Washington's Farewell Address.

The country was by now mature enough to be able to take a backward glance and to support historians. To be sure, as far back as 1760 Samuel Smith had composed a two-volume history of Pennsylvania, but it was never published and reposes today in one of the Society's vaults. Ebenezer Hazard was more successful. In 1792-1794 he published his two volumes of *Historical Collections*. The Society owns his broadside *Proposals For Printing by Subscription a Collection of State Papers*, to which is attached a sheet on which subscribers entered their names. Washington's signature heads the list followed by John Adams. Other signers include Jefferson, Monroe, Charles Carroll, Robert Morris, and Richard Henry Lee.

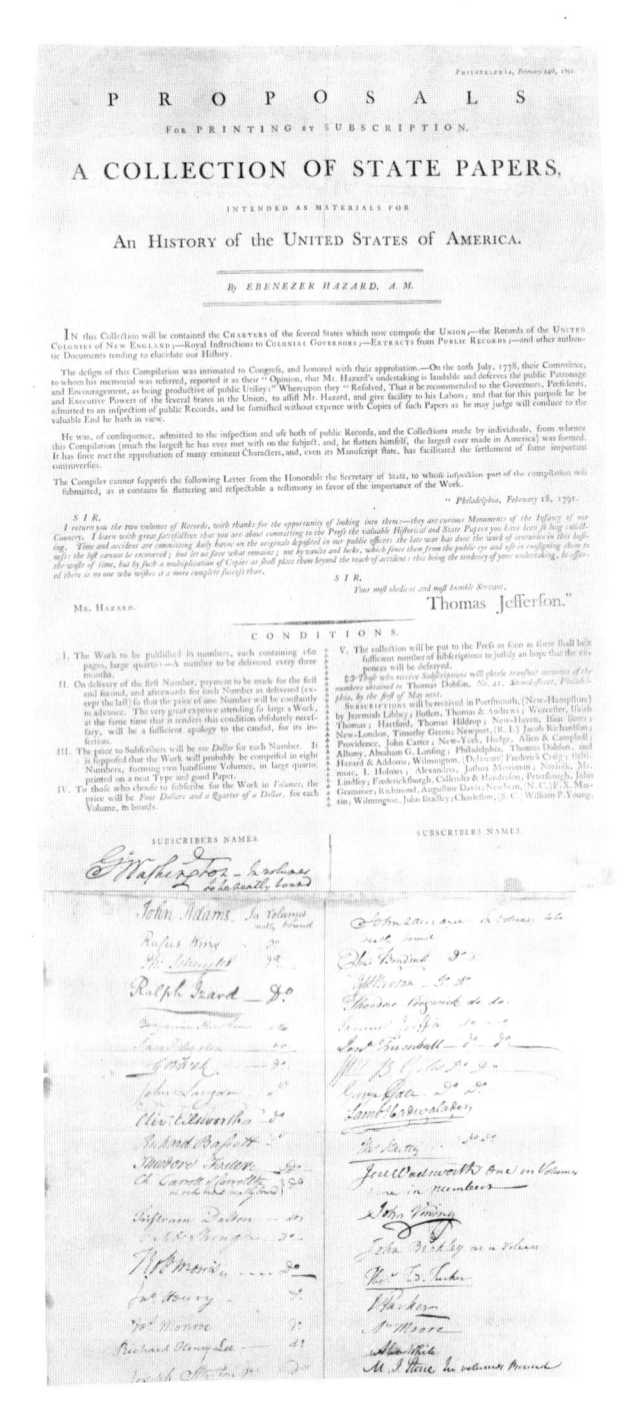

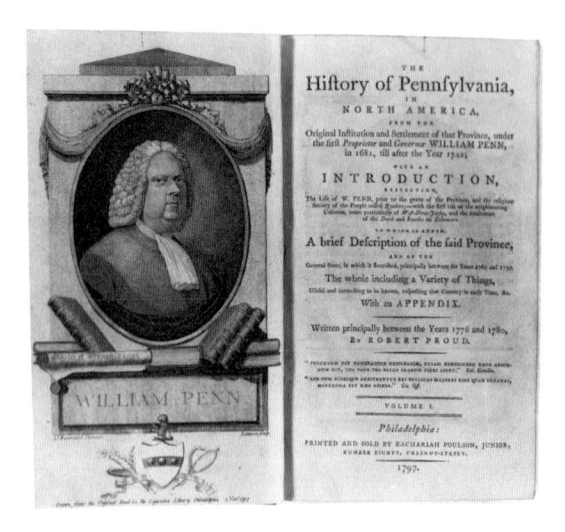

PROUD'S HISTORY OF PENNSYLVANIA

PROPOSAL FOR HAZARD'S WORK

Pennsylvania's first published history was produced by a Quaker schoolteacher, Robert Proud. His *History of Pennsylvania in North America* appeared in two volumes in 1797-1798. When the Robert Proud papers came up at auction in 1903, the Society purchased the lot, forty-three volumes and four boxes containing the manuscripts of all his writings. Half a century earlier, in 1852, William Cogswell had presented the Society with a portrait he had painted of Proud after a pencil sketch. It shows Proud in profile holding a cane with a silver knob and with a distinctive chair in the background. Proud's chair and cane were among the Society's earliest gifts, having been received in 1826.

ROBERT PROUD BY COGSWELL

In 1798, the year William Birch began to issue his fine set of engraved Philadelphia views, of which the Society has a splendid copy, Joseph Hopkinson wrote "Hail Columbia." This remained our national hymn until superseded by Francis Scott Key's "Star Spangled Banner." The Society owns copies in their authors' hands of both these patriotic pieces, and it is worth mentioning that it has a copy of "Home Sweet Home" in the autograph of John Howard Payne, and "Listen to the Mocking Bird" in that of Septimus Winner.

After the nation achieved its independence corporate records become more numerous. Of such for this period at the Society are those of the Bank of North America, chartered in 1781, the country's first government incorporated bank. This collection of minute books, letter books, and ledgers numbers 620 volumes. The records of the Society for the Relief of Poor and Distressed Masters of Ships, starting in 1765, fill fifty-four volumes and those of the Pennsylvania Prison Society are also numerous.

The early minutes of the Pennsylvania Abolition Society, founded in 1775, are part of the Society's large collection of Afro-American history. Slavery in Pennsylvania was doomed in 1780 when the legislature passed a bill calling for gradual abolition. Later in the decade 1,475 people signed a petition to the legislature, which is one of the Society's outstanding antislavery pieces. The petition called for a halt to be put to the slave trade, since vessels were still being equipped at Philadelphia for the African adventure, and this should be pre-

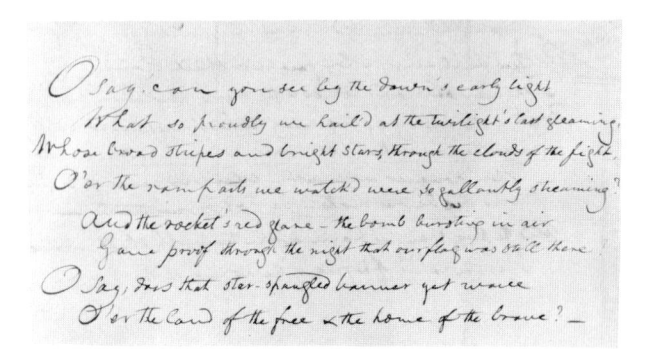

KEY'S STAR SPANGLED BANNER

vented as well as to "answer other purposes of benevolence and justice to an oppressed part of the human species."

Those looking for data at the Society on the formative years of the nation, those years brought to a close with Washington's death in December, 1799, will find much of value that can barely be suggested here. And the collection continues to grow. After years of cataloguing, the Society opened the papers of Tench Coxe (1756-1824) to the public in 1973. Of the voluminous manuscripts of this political economist, a scholar has observed that they will necessitate the rewriting of much of the history of the young republic. Virtually all of the leaders of the day were numbered among Coxe's correspondents.

FRANCIS HOPKINSON BY ROBERT EDGE PINE

Nineteenth Century from 1800 to 1860

Washington's death inspired Chief Justice John Marshall to write a five-volume biography of the national hero. Proposals for publishing it by subscription were circulated in 1802 and 1803 when its publisher traveled about the country obtaining thousands of signatures of subscribers. At a later date this enormous autograph collection was bound in book form. Although many of the names in it were of people who had yet to make their mark—among New Haven signatures is that of Yale student John C. Calhoun—it is fair to say that the volume contains the names of the most prominent citizens of their day. Included are the signatures of ten Signers of the Declaration, among them Presidents Adams and Jefferson. Secretary of State James Madison was another subscriber as were others in Jefferson's cabinet, and the Philadelphia subscribers represent a who's who of the town. The precious volume which contains this unique collection of autographs is one of the Society's most interesting early nineteenth-century possessions. It is complemented by the bulky manuscript volumes four and five of Marshall's biography. The manuscripts of the first three volumes were accidentally destroyed by fire after their printing in 1804-1807.

While Marshall was formulating his biographical plans, inventive genius strove to bring the nation into a semblance of modern times. In Philadelphia, this took the form of a public water supply introduced in 1800. At Center Square, where City Hall now stands, an engine house was built, a round marble edifice which pumped Schuylkill water into a tank overhead for distribution through hollow log pipes throughout the city. The Society holds the list of subscribers to this system. Among the portraits at the Society is one of Frederick Graff, painted in 1804 by James Peale. Graff was superintendent of the works and is pictured against a background of the pump house from which smoke industriously rises. Graff's work was so outstanding that when the initial system was replaced by the Fairmount Water Works he continued in charge and was twice honored by presentation pieces made by Philadelphia

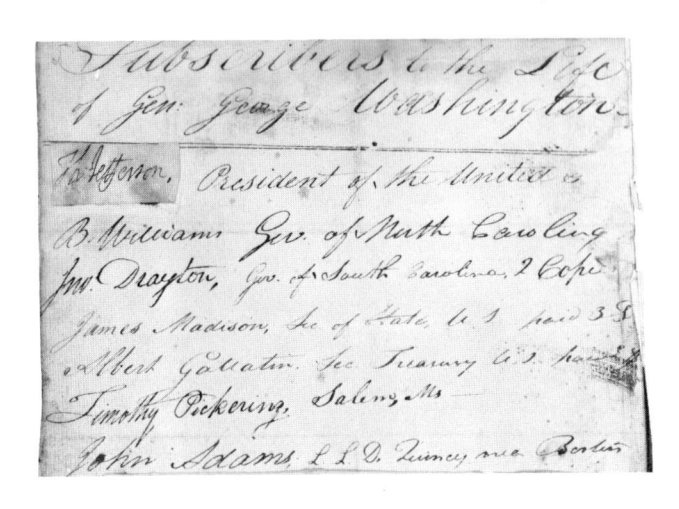

SOME SUBSCRIBERS TO MARSHALL'S BOOK

MARKET STREET BRIDGE BY BARRALET

silversmiths and now in the Society's collection. In 1822 he was given a vase with splendidly engraved views, made by Harvey Lewis, "for prosecuting to a conclusion the public works at Fairmount"; and in 1826 he received from the Watering Committee a pitcher, the work of Edward Lownes.

The city's next triumphant improvement was its first "permanent" bridge over the Schuylkill, the Market Street bridge, opened in 1805. In the Society's collection is a volume of autographs, 1800-1809, of the stockholders in the bridge company as well as a splendid large painting of the bridge by John J. Barralet, taken when the bridge was new. As fate would have it, the structure proved only semipermanent, since it was destroyed by fire in 1875.

The years leading up to the Civil War were relatively placid but there were two wars which did much to awaken native patriotism. An event preliminary to the War of 1812 was the capture of the frigate *Chesapeake* by the British *Leopard* in 1807. Of this humiliating event, the Society has Stephen Decatur's report on the condition of the injured vessel. When the war came on, however, the Americans gained their share of victories at sea. Two of these occurred in 1812, the first when Captain Isaac Hull captured the *Guerrière*. Before he sank the ship, Hull removed from the captain's cabin an ornamental panel showing water and a volcano. In 1909 one of his descendants gave this souvenir to the Society. The other 1812 victory was that of Decatur and his *United States* when he captured the British *Macedonian*, which was subsequently to see so many years of service in the American Navy. Paintings of both these naval battles by Thomas Birch are in the Society's collection, as is a handsome silver wine cooler made by Whartenby and Bunn of Philadelphia

BIRCH'S PAINTING OF THE CONSTITUTION AND THE GUERRIÈRE

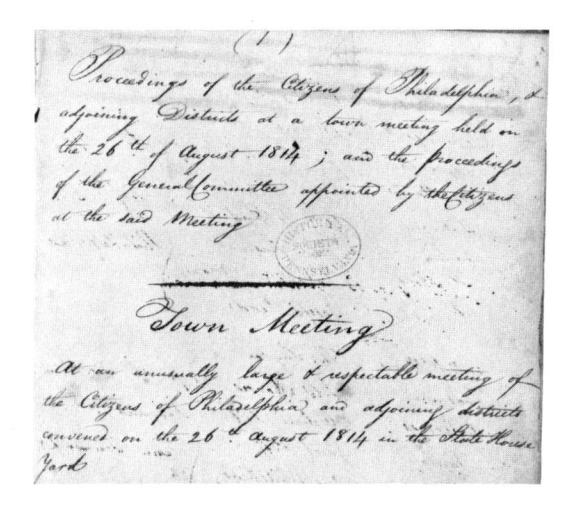

CITY DEFENSE COMMITTEE MINUTES

in 1818 and presented to Decatur by citizens of Philadelphia in recognition of his valor.

Oliver Hazard Perry's victory on Lake Erie in 1813 is recalled at the Society by a gold medal, one of those presented by the Commonwealth of Pennsylvania to Perry and his officers. And further by Louise Steinmetz Birch's little replica of the large, well-known Thomas Birch scene of Perry's victory: "We have met the enemy and they are ours."

With the British threatening the Chesapeake and Delaware areas, having burned Washington on August 24, 1814, a town meeting was called at Independence Hall on August 26. There a committee was appointed to organize the defense of the city, with Charles Biddle named chairman. The committee's work is recorded in three volumes of minutes kept by its secretary, who presented them to the Society in 1845.

Not long after the Committee of Defense was formed, the authorities dispatched a brigade under General Thomas Cadwalader to protect the powder mills on the Brandywine. Camp du Pont was established on grounds now part of Winterthur. Cadwalader's papers, part of the Society's vast Cadwalader family archive, cover the bloodless campaign in much vivid detail.

Other aspects of the war are recorded in the Society's voluminous official War Department correspondence of Daniel Parker, Adjutant General and Inspector General, 1810-1845, which contains many presidential letters on the conflict. An odd victim of the war was a tall-case clock ordered by Thomas Jefferson in 1811 and made by Thomas Voigt of Philadelphia. After many delays the clockmaker was at last ready to see it loaded on a ship scheduled to sail for Richmond, when the British bottled up the Delaware. It was not until November, 1815, that the clock at last left on its journey to Monticello. There it was placed in Jefferson's bedroom, where, in 1826, it ticked out its owner's final moments. Given by the family to Dr. Robley Dunglison, who had attended the President in his last illness, the clock was subsequently presented to the Society by the doctor's son.

The conclusion of the war was marked by efforts to re-establish the nation's economic life. In 1816 the Second Bank of the United States was chartered by the federal government and scores of new banks were incorporated by the Commonwealth. Of the great bank, the Society has many records, including papers of its first president, William Jones, who proved more successful as a War of 1812 Secretary of the Navy than as a banker. The Society also holds a significant amount of the papers of Nicholas Biddle, the man most intimately associated with the Bank's history, and much on the liquidation of the Bank after 1840. As for the state chartered banks, the Society owns the minute books of quite a few, a collection bolstered in 1967 when the Philadelphia National gave the Society 170 volumes of its own minutes and those of banks it had taken over.

Records of other enterprises operating prior to the Civil War abound at the Society. Some 475 volumes of shipping records attest to the pre-eminence of Thomas P. Cope's trans-Atlantic packet line and allied interests. Other large manuscript collections of the period are those of David S. Brown & Company, Philadelphia commission merchants and manufacturers; the Lewis-Neilson papers, which cover trade with Russia and Philadelphia banking; 702 volumes of Lippincott Company papers deal with international trade in sugar and other commodities; 20,000 papers of a Philadelphia chemist, 1815-1853, are contained in the Rosengarten Collection; while heavy industry is represented in 70,000 manuscripts of the Bush & Lobdell Carwheel Company of Wilmington, which specialized in railroad equipment, and in 175 volumes of letter books and correspondence of Matthias W. Baldwin and others, being the archives of the Baldwin Locomotive Works from 1834 to 1868.

Yet another notable business venture, which blossomed in the 1820s, was the Schuylkill Navigation Company which carried, first, the produce of the interior, and then coal to the city's Schuylkill wharves. Its early prosperity may be viewed in an elegant silver vase made by Thomas Fletcher and presented in 1833 to the Company's former president, Cadwalader Evans. It is splendidly engraved with Schuylkill River scenes near the city. Alas, ere long the Schuylkill Navigation Company was engaged in ruinous competition with the Reading Railroad, a large collection of whose records are also owned by the Society.

NEAGLE'S STUDY OF PAT LYON

Fortunately, the area's overall economic health was good and this made it a center for the arts. Of portrait painters, Thomas Sully was the most popular. He settled in Philadelphia in 1808, and continued painting there until his death at the age of eighty-nine in 1872. His original manuscript Register records 2,631 of his works, forty-three of which are at the Society, including two self-portraits, and the Register as well.

Perhaps next in popularity to Sully was Rembrandt Peale. Among the eight paintings from his studio owned by the Society is the artist's sensitive portrait of his father, Charles Willson Peale. John Neagle was another who ranked high. Two studies for his famous "Pat Lyon at the Forge" are among the baker's dozen of his paintings at the Society, as well as his portrait of Gilbert Stuart. The Society also owns his commonplace book of 1839, in which the artist describes his techniques of mixing colors, use of oils, canvases and varnishes. Neagle had studied under Bass Otis who is represented in the collection by nine portraits, of which those of the Patriot Thomas Leiper and his wife are perhaps the most important. Yet another portraitist who spent many years painting in Philadelphia before his death in 1841 was Jacob Eichholtz of Lancaster. Rebecca J. Beal's catalogue of his works, published in 1969 by the Society, describes 924 of them, and, of these, ten, two of

JOHN A. SHULZE BY EICHHOLTZ

Mr. and Mrs. Thomas Mifflin by John Singleton Copley

Nineteenth Century from 1800 to 1860

JANE PENN-GASKELL BY THOMAS SULLY

ISAAC PENN-GASKELL BY THOMAS SULLY

MRS. PETER PENN-GASKELL BY THOMAS SULLY

MRS. WILLIAM HALL BY THOMAS SULLY

them of Governor John A. Shulze, are owned by the Society.

Chronologically interspersed with the Society's portraits are numerous landscapes, some appealing genre subjects, and Raphaelle Peale's popular still life of 1815, a smoked herring and various objects. The tradition of ornamental sign painting, which stemmed from earliest times, was nobly carried on by John A. Woodside, who was also celebrated for his decorating of fire engines. His documentary painting of the Lemon Hill estate above Fairmount in 1807 is one of the Society's gems. Four years later, William Strickland, not yet established as the city's outstanding architect, painted his large, important canvas of Christ Church, which was presented to the Society in 1891 by the children of Strickland Kneass.

Meanwhile, John Lewis Krimmel was at work laying the foundations of his short-lived career as the American Hogarth. The Society is fortunate in two of his lively water colors, marvelous historical documents—"Election Day at the State House, 1816," and "Fourth of July Celebration at Centre Square, 1819." Another local genre painter, William E. Winner, began to make his mark about fifteen years after Krimmel's untimely death in 1821. Among the Society's best-liked paintings are Winner's "Crazy Nora" and "The Pie Man." Two more Winners of this sort have recently been added to the collection.

Of all Pennsylvania's landscape painters active before 1850, none was as prolific as Thomas Birch. The earliest of the thirteen examples of his work at the Society is the large painting of the Treaty Tree at Kensington, which blew down in 1810. Two of Birch's Philadelphia Harbor scenes show the river front respectively from upstream and from downstream. One of the artist's most impressive views is of the Upper Ferry Bridge at Fairmount. Believed to be the longest single-span bridge in the world, it was completed in 1813 and was destroyed by fire in 1838. The bridge company's minute books from 1811 to 1834 are in the Society's archives.

Bits and pieces of the lives and accomplishments of Philadelphia artists are to be found in many of the Society's manuscript collections. Its Peale Papers relate mainly to Peale's Museum and include Charles Willson Peale's "A walk through the Philadelphia Museum," minute books of the Museum, and various other of its records from 1794 to 1845. One of the features of the Museum was its portrait gallery of famous Americans, which, ultimately, was sold at auction in 1854. Half a dozen of those paintings are now in the Society's collection. Evidence of Charles Willson Peale's antiquarian interest is seen in an 1877 gift of letters and papers he had gathered on the background and early history of the Pennsylvania Academy of the Fine Arts, 1794-1808, and a run of the Academy's minutes beginning in 1817. The Society also has the minutes and papers of the Artist Fund Society, 1835-1858.

In addition to oil paintings, the Society has many drawings. In 1938, it purchased 125 by B. R. Evans, a delineator of Philadelphia street scenes in the mid-nineteenth century. Drawings are to be found in the John Sartain (1808-1897) Collection, which contains the correspondence, letter books, and engravings of Philadelphia's best-known engraver, as well as the manuscript of his autobiography and his set of engraving tools. Included also are 122 drawings by Thomas Birch.

Although Sartain's influence was not felt until the 1830s, the number of Philadelphia engravers had been increasing rapidly since 1800. Their work was much in demand for illustrations, advertisements, and other commercial purposes. As major art expressions, engravers had not followed in the footsteps of William Birch, author of various editions of his celebrated views of the city and his portfolio of country mansions. However, in 1830 Cephas G. Childs, "Engraver," completed his set of twenty-five *Views in Philadelphia and Its Environs from original Drawings taken in 1827-30*. Prior to its publication, the Historical Society "Resolved that the Council regard the preservation of such skillful delineations of objects illustrative of history and which are liable to decay, or to be otherwise removed, as an important auxiliary of the purposes of the Society." In gratitude, Childs printed this resolution in his book, which he dedicated to the Society "as a token of zeal for its objects, and of esteem for its valuable

JOHN QUINCY ADAMS BY CHARLES WILLSON PEALE

labours." Among its copies of this work, the Society owns a large paper one which came from Childs's estate.

The Society has two portraits of Childs, one of them by John Neagle. He was a remarkable man, artist, innovator, militia officer, journalist and art collector. Moreover, it was he who successfully established lithography in Philadelphia after several other firms had experimented with it in the late 1820s. As an enterprising engraver, Childs realized the possibilities of the less expensive art of lithography. In 1829 he entered the business. Among his staff of artists was the deaf mute Albert Newsam who was to develop into the best lithographic portraitist in the country and whose personal collection of hundreds of his own pictures is at the Society.

Since French technicians were considered unexcelled, Childs persuaded P. S. Duval to come to Philadelphia, where within a few years Duval took over the business from Childs and continued for decades as the city's most important lithographer, rivaled only by J. T. Bowen and Thomas Sinclair. From their presses, and those of their many rivals, poured a stream of inexpensive art prints, most of which are now reasonably rare, some excessively so, and a great volume of commercial work, the most attractive of which were the trade cards, large portrait views of business houses.

CEPHAS G. CHILDS BY NEAGLE

GILBERT STUART BY NEAGLE

Some of the lithographers' efforts were ambitious. In 1839-1842 Huddy and Duval published the *U. S. Military Magazine* with its brilliantly hand-colored plates depicting the elaborate uniforms of the day. Earlier, Childs had sponsored Thomas and John Doughty's *The Cabinet of Natural History and American Rural Sports*, which featured birds and animals. Childs and his partner Henry Inman, prior to the Duval take-over, had also published the Landreths' *The Floral Magazine and Botanical Register. The Orchardists' Companion* was a similar work devoted to fruit.

It was J. T. Bowen, however, who was the

most prominent in the publication of art series. It was he who completed in 1844 McKenney and Hall's *History of the Indian Tribes of North America*, a large folio, three-volume work illustrated with 120 Indian portraits. While engaged in that task between 1839 and 1844, he printed an octavo edition of Audubon's *Birds of America*, and in 1848 completed the impressive large plates for Audubon's *Quadrupeds of North America*. Bowen was, moreover, the publisher of J. C. Wilds's Philadelphia views. These sets, published in numbers for subscribers, have considerable charm, and a quality which would fast disappear after 1850 with the development of chromolithography. The Society's collection of early Philadelphia lithography is unexcelled and formed the basis for a book, *Philadelphia in the Romantic Age of Lithography*, published by the Society in 1958.

Artistic expression in these pre-war decades was not limited to the art of the painter, engraver, or lithographer. The silversmiths continued to flourish. One of the most remarkable pieces of silver at the Society was made by Thomas Fletcher about 1830 for the United Bowmen, an archery club instituted in 1828. Inside the top rim of their large bowl are inscribed the names of the members from 1828 to 1855. The winner of the annual shoot was required to provide a silver ornament to hang from the lip of the bowl, and so it is decorated. This bowl is believed to be the oldest sporting challenge cup in America.

While the Bowmen were ceremoniously conducting their matches in the 1830s, Thomas Tucker for a few brief years operated a porcelain factory nearby. Today, his colorful, attractive products are highly esteemed by collectors. The Society is fortunate in having some examples of Tucker china. One of these was presented in 1868 by Thomas Tucker himself, a fine porcelain pitcher of his own manufacture, "made now over thirty years ago."

Mechanical techniques, the steam press for speed, chromolithography for cheap, garish color, were typical of the processes that undermined the hand crafts of previous decades, and among these innovations must be numbered the daguerreotype. Information about this photographic process reached Philadelphia in the summer of 1839 and stirred the ingenuity of Joseph Saxton, an employee at the Mint. Applying Daguerre's principles, he constructed a crude camera out of a box and took the first American daguerreotype—a picture of the nearby Central High School. Shortly afterward

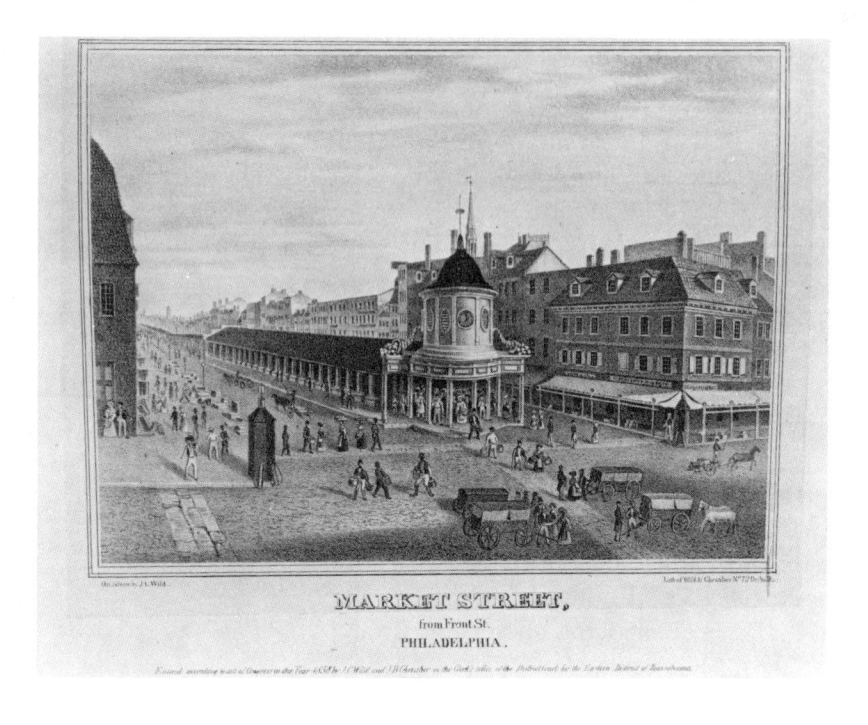

LITHOGRAPH VIEW OF MARKET STREET BY WILD & CHEVALIER

FIRST AMERICAN DAGUERREOTYPE, SAXTON'S PICTURE OF CENTRAL HIGH SCHOOL

he presented this historic triumph of American photography to the Historical Society, where it is kept concealed from light to prevent further fading.

Artistry is not limited to the graphic arts, there is also the world of literature, and Philadelphia was the publishing capital of the country in the early decades of the nineteenth century. Mathew Carey's successors, his son and succeeding partnerships, whose archives enrich the Society, published the most famous authors of the day, including James Fenimore Cooper. In 1838, Cooper chose to leave the latter part of the original manuscript of his *Home as Found* with his publisher, who presented it to the Society in 1887.

More pertinent to its collections, however, are the original manuscripts of John Fanning Watson. An amateur historian and author of the city's first history, Watson's *Annals of Philadelphia* was published in 1830. A founder of the Society, he was the first author to carry on a title page the phrase "Member of the Historical Society of Pennsylvania." On June 30, 1830, he gave the Society three folio volumes of manuscripts, including that of the *Annals*, and this collection has since grown to seventeen volumes, a tribute to the indefatigable labors of the annalist and of the Society's ability to gather in such original fruit. At the request of the Society, who selected the artist, Watson sat for A. B. Rockey in 1849. The portrait, showing Watson at the age of seventy, was the gift to the Society by the artist in 1852. That year the Society also received as an artist's gift, William E. Winner's fine painting of Samuel Hazard, distinguished historical editor and later Librarian of the Society.

Historians such as Watson are fortunate when they can locate material bearing on their subject recorded by eye witnesses, diarists. While more have since been added, the 1949

SAMUEL HAZARD BY WINNER

Guide to the Society's manuscripts listed 176 diaries for the period 1800-1860.

One of the most fascinating of these records is the seventy-volume account kept by Samuel Breck from 1800 until his death in 1862. Breck, one of Philadelphia's leading political and cultural figures, provides an invaluable glimpse of his time. Deborah Norris Logan, mentioned earlier, resided after her marriage to Dr. George Logan at Stenton, surrounded by the papers of James Logan. Perhaps it was these that gave her her interest in history. The seventeen volumes of her diary from 1815 until her death in 1839 are an eloquent witness to enlightened Quakerism and to common sense observation. Another Philadelphian who started a diary in 1831 and did not cease making entries in it until three days before his death in 1854 was Joseph Sill who filled a total of 4,838 pages. Merchant and art fancier, he captured in his diary "the delights of living in this beautiful world." No student of Philadelphia history of his era can afford to neglect Joseph Sill.

Sidney George Fisher, whose diary in sixty-five volumes covers the years 1834 to his death in 1871, represents the supreme accomplishment of a diarist. His insights, perceptions, observations and literary ability are unsurpassed. To him his diary was "a sort of father confessor to me, unluckily without the power of giving me either advice or absolution." It is a great record of his times, as well as a document of poignant human interest. In 1967 the Society published excerpts from Fisher's diary in *A Philadelphia Perspective*, a 626-page volume.

Allied to diaries are autobiographies, of which that of Horace Binney, Philadelphia's most famous nineteenth-century lawyer, in three unpublished volumes, is one of the Society's most important.

While heavy emphasis has been laid on Philadelphia manuscripts, the Society has major holdings for many other counties. These, buttressed with an astonishing depth in cultural, philanthropic, military, religious, business, and tax records, as well as large accumulations of club and fire company records, log books (such as that of Elisha Kent Kane, carried by him on his Arctic expedition of 1853-1855) add depth

PAGE FROM FISHER'S DIARY

to the sources of understanding of the pre-Civil War era and furnish a guide to the activities of the central figures of the times.

Many of these are well represented in the Society's manuscript collection. It has, for example, the largest number of manuscripts of Thomas Jefferson outside of institutions to which went parts of the corpus of the President's papers, or political units which retained them. In addition, hundreds of letters of Presidents Madison, Monroe, and John Quincy Adams are present.

Among public figures for which the Society holds a significant part of their papers are William Shaler (1778-1833), United States agent in Mexico and counsul general to the Barbary States and to Cuba. These reveal much on American diplomatic relations, particularly on foreign interference with American commerce. Others of eminence strongly represented in the collection are Josiah Stoddard Johnston (1784-1833), congressman and senator from Louisiana; Jonathan Roberts (1771-1854), Pennsylvania congressman and senator, active in the Jefferson, Madison, and Monroe administrations; and Charles Jared Ingersoll (1782-1862) who enjoyed a career as congressman, literary light, and partisan Democratic leader. Of George Wolf (1777-1840) the Society has much of his political correspondence covering his term of office as Governor of Pennsylvania,

1829-1835, and of William Bigler (1814-1880) it holds a far larger collection of his papers as Governor of Pennsylvania and senator in the 1850s.

One of the Society's collections of interest to Latin American scholars is that of Joel R. Poinsett (1779-1850). He held various diplomatic posts in South America and in 1825 was appointed minister to Mexico. From Mexico he introduced a plant to which Robert Buist, a Philadelphia florist, gave the name of poinsettia. Secretary of War for Van Buren, Poin-

PAGE FROM THE POINSETT PAPERS

sett was a great friend of Philadelphia's Henry D. Gilpin, among whose papers is another large and important segment of Poinsett's correspondence. Gilpin (1801-1860) left a large accumulation of manuscripts covering his long and varied career, informative of many aspects of national history. Attorney General in Van Buren's cabinet, brother-in-law of Josiah Stoddard Johnston, he was a patron of the arts and a Vice-President of the Historical Society.

In George Mifflin Dallas (1792-1864) Philadelphia had its most successful public figure of his day. Between 1828 and 1861 he served as its mayor, as federal district attorney, senator, attorney general of Pennsylvania, minister to Russia, Vice-President of the United States and minister to Great Britain. Most of his surviving papers are at the Society.

Dallas and James Buchanan were rivals for the presidency and hence not politically harmonious, but at least their literary remains have been brought together. In 1898 President Buchanan's nieces donated some 20,000 of their uncle's manuscripts to the Society, representing about ninety per cent of his surviving correspondence. And these the Society has published in a microfilm edition of sixty reels. Thus, it is pleasing to note that the Society holds the papers of Pennsylvania's only President and Vice-President.

Throughout the years that these public men were building their careers, all of them were

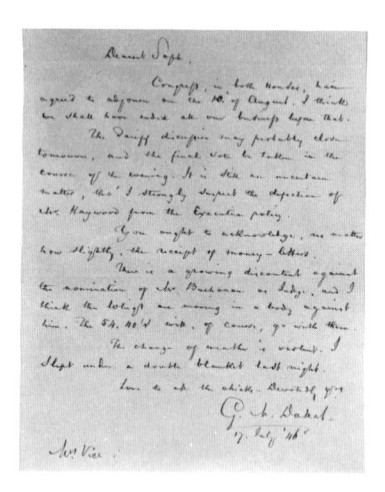

PAGE FROM THE DALLAS PAPERS

concerned at what came to be known as the impending crisis, the southern question—slavery. Antislavery agitation was anathema to the South, which underwent its most sensational slave rebellion in 1831. The Society owns one of five known copies of the first printing of that event, *The Confessions of Nat Turner, the Leader of the Late Insurrection in Southamp-*

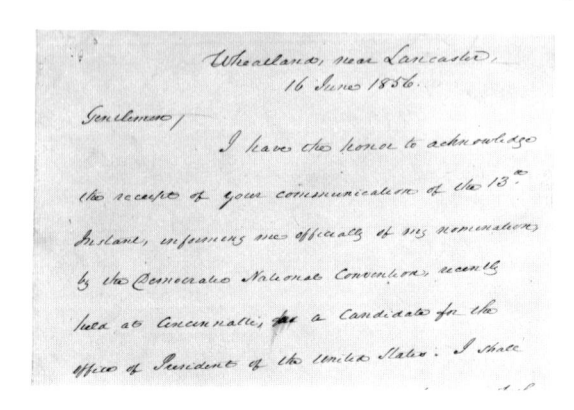

PAGE FROM THE BUCHANAN PAPERS

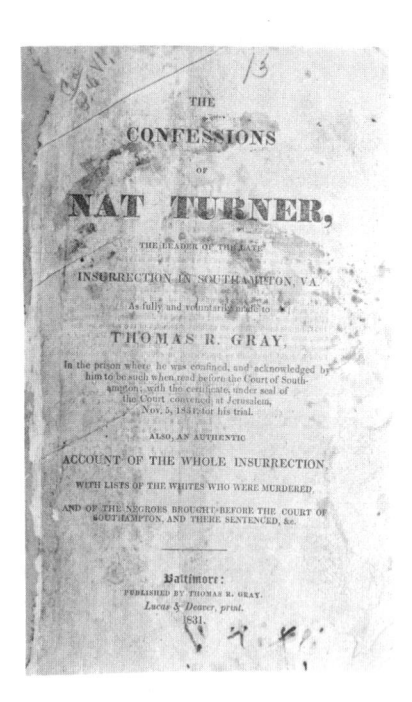

NAT TURNER'S CONFESSIONS

ton, Va. (Baltimore, 1831). A few years later the actress Fanny Kemble married Pierce Butler who, with his brother, had inherited large rice and cotton plantations in Georgia, worked by a thousand slaves. Fanny was immeasurably shocked by her plantation visit. The records of the Butler plantations are at the Society. Pierce Butler's insolvency forced the sale of his share of the slaves at auction at Savannah on February 21, 1859, when Butler gave each one of his Negroes a parting gift of a silver dollar. In the plantation records is a manuscript catalogue and prices obtained at the auction, the last important sale of slaves before the impending crisis ceased to impend and the nation found itself in flames.

The Negroes' lot in Philadelphia was not an easy one, but they had their champions. Mention has earlier been made of the extensive records of the Pennsylvania Abolition Society in the collection, and the Historical Society also has those of the Antislavery Society of Pennsylvania and of the Philadelphia Antislavery Society. Of those active in the Pennsylvania Colonization Society, including Negro leaders in the Liberian venture, forty-one portraits were painted which were ultimately presented to the Historical Society, disclosing the appearance of leaders in the fight against slavery. One who preferred to make his contribution on an individual basis was the lawyer and orator David Paul Brown. For his freely given legal services Bard & Lamont of Philadelphia made a pair of silver trays and pitchers inscribed: "Presented to David Paul Brown Esqr by the disfranchised citizens of Philadelphia, 1841." The pitchers are decorated with the figure of a kneeling, supplicant slave. One of these trays and pitchers is at the Detroit Institute of Arts, the other set was given by the Brown family to the Society in 1898 with the manuscript tribute which originally accompanied them on their presentation.

The Society's Negro history collection is extremely large, and, together with the holdings of the Library Company of Philadelphia, was

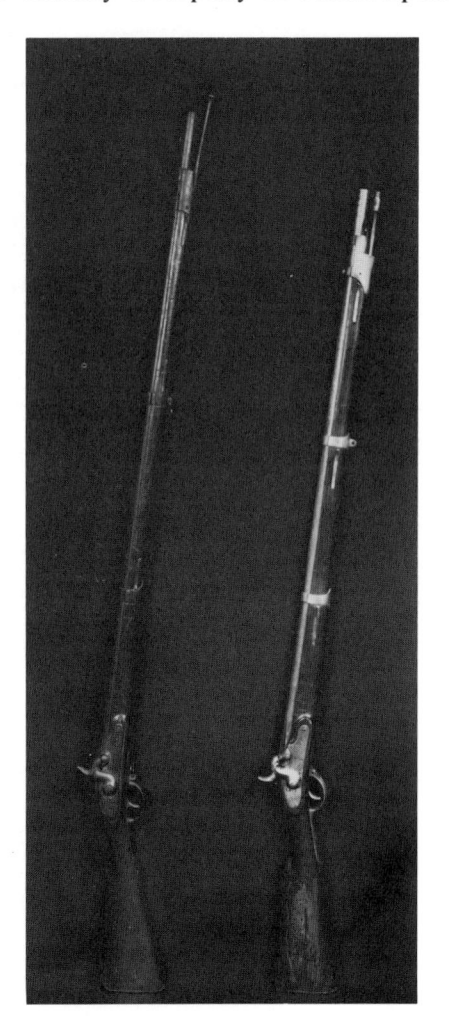

MUSKETS USED BY BROWN'S MEN

published in a 700-page catalog in 1973—*Afro-Americana, 1553-1906*. Among the Society's manuscripts recorded in that volume is the minute book and record of cases, 1839-1844, of the Negro Vigilant Committee, which aided indigent blacks on their escape to New England or Canada. A later similar record, 1852-1857, is William Still's manuscript journal of slaves who passed through Station No. 2 of the Underground Railroad.

The sectional tensions created by the fervor of the abolitionists, by the pin pricks of the Underground Railroad, by fear of that new party, the Black Republicans, were heightened by John Brown's effort to rid the South of slavery in his raid on Harper's Ferry in October, 1859. A year later Abraham Lincoln was elected President and the deep South could stand no more.

While many steps led to secession, two muskets made about 1812 and a pike in the Historical Society's modest armory are emblematic of the final phase. They were carried by John Brown's men in their abortive raid.

GIFT TO DAVID PAUL BROWN BY "THE DISFRANCHISED CITIZENS OF PHILADELPHIA, 1841."

Civil War to Twentieth Century

In February, 1861, President-elect Lincoln was in Philadelphia preparing to move on to Washington via the Philadelphia, Wilmington & Baltimore Railroad. However, the president of the Railroad, Samuel Morse Felton, and many others were convinced that if Lincoln traveled through Maryland he would be attacked. Felton, who was employing Allan Pinkerton's detectives to guard his road's bridges and tracks, changed Lincoln's advertised route to the capital for a secret passage from Harrisburg. Shortly afterward, he received a letter dated Baltimore, February 26, from J. H. Hutcheson, an alias assumed by a Pinkerton agent: "As you are aware ere this our Party arrived safely at Washington on Saturday morning. Every thing worked to a charm, every thing was right, and the President often repeated the sense of the many obligations he is under to you. There is no doubt but that he would have been assassinated had he come here." The Felton manuscripts at the Society, which include the above, contain his correspondence on the conduct of a railroad of great strategic importance on the outbreak of the war, one which rendered important services in the transporting of Union troops. Along with this collection are the papers of a later Samuel Morse Felton who was also a railroad president and who served as Director General of Military Railways in France during World War I.

Although Pennsylvania supported the Union, it contained many "Copperheads." To express their southern sympathy and extreme racist views, a newspaper was established in Philadelphia called *The Palmetto Flag*. Starting off rather grandly on March 30, 1861, it issued Volume I, Number 1. On April 6 and 13 it produced succeeding numbers, but April 13 was an epic date, the day Fort Sumter capitulated. Undaunted by the mood of the town, the editor hung out a palmetto flag which so enraged the mob that his office was sacked on April 15 and his newspaper ceased to exist. Of its three rare issues, the Society has the first and third, with the intervening number in photostatic form.

Philadelphia had now become a military city, and through it began to pour troops from the east on their way to the seat of war. They came by water, landing at the foot of Washington Avenue, on which lay the tracks of the Philadelphia, Wilmington & Baltimore. To systema-

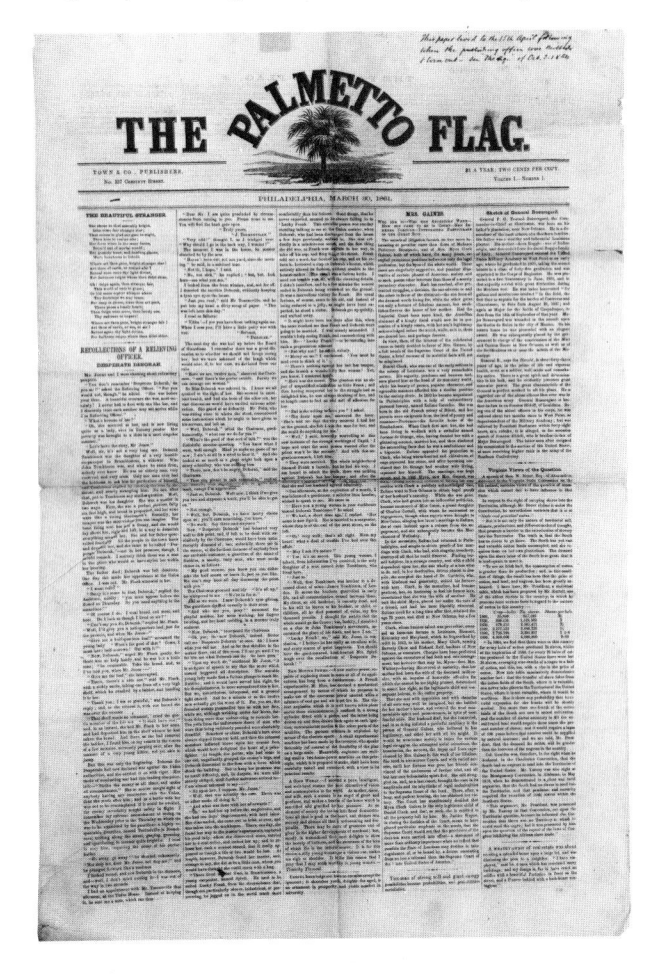

FIRST ISSUE OF THE PALMETTO FLAG

tize relief work for the soldiers during their brief pause in the city, the Union Volunteer Refreshment Saloon was organized on May 17, 1861, the first of its kind. Located near the landing place on Washington Avenue, this facility fed nearly 900,000 men prior to its closing in 1865. Much of its history is preserved in the Society's Fales Collection and some of the Society's most vivid Civil War lithographs portray its activities. By the time of the war lithographic views were beginning to lose their charm but a few in the collection were still of a high order, as well as of documentary value. Of interest is one of the Satterlee General Hospital, opened in 1862 in West Philadelphia. It accommodated 3,000 men. Another hospital view is that of the Mower General Hospital in Chestnut Hill. The largest in the Philadelphia area with 4,000 beds, it was opened in 1863.

The city cared for a great many patients, for casualties were heavy. Colonel Elmer E. Ellsworth, a popular young officer, was one of the first fatalities. He commanded a New York regiment which dressed in the colorful costume of the French Zouaves. On May 24, 1861, when Alexandria was occupied, Ellsworth saw the Confederate flag flying over the Marshall House hotel. He went in, removed the flag, and on his way out was shot by the proprietor, James W. Jackson, who, in turn, was promptly killed by one of the Zouaves. Ellsworth's death produced a profound sensation and he was honored by having his body lie in state in the White House. Shortly after his death the Marshall House's register of guests was "liberated," and subsequently was acquired by a Philadelphia collector who gave it to the Society in 1880. It contains the record of the hotel's guests from February 1 to May 24, 1861, when the hotel was taken over by soldiers of a Michigan regiment.

This early memento of a sad event is only one of a great many of the Society's manuscript records of the war. Diaries and letters of participants abound, some of them comprising large collections. General George A. McCall, who commanded a division in the Peninsular Campaign, is represented by an impressive number of letters to his wife, and Civil War documents bulk large in the papers of General

STUDY AND RELIEF BY SCHUSSELE

George Cadwalader, military commander of Baltimore at the outset of the war, and the man selected in 1863 as military commander of Philadelphia to insure against draft riots which had recently shattered New York.

Other records of the times include the minutes of the Philadelphia Committee of Public Safety for 1861, some 5,000 documents of the Citizens Bounty Fund Committee which sought to encourage enlistments through cash payments, and papers of Philadelphia's wartime mayor, Alexander Henry. Then, too, there are manuscripts which reflect the southern side. Eliza Middleton of Middleton Place near Charleston had married one of the early members of the Historical Society, Joshua Francis Fisher. Her correspondence at the Society catches the southern rage at the North of many of her friends. Most touching of all perhaps are the Society's papers of another Charleston family, the Draytons. Here we have a house divided, for in the siege of Charleston Captain Percival Drayton commanded the Union fleet's flagship, while his Confederate brother, General Thomas Drayton, commanded defense units.

Unquestionably the greatest event occurring during the Civil War in Philadelphia, one which drew to the city the President and his wife, was the Great Central Fair held in June, 1864, in Logan Square for the benefit of the United States Sanitary Commission which aided wounded service men. The Fair's buildings—long, lofty galleries with Gothic roofs—covered the square, and in them articles in infinite variety were offered for sale or for exhibition. The picture gallery eclipsed everything, bringing together, as it did, the greatest accumulation of art ever seen in America.

Of the Great Central Fair, the Society has an impressive collection. Its largest group are records gathered by the Shakespearian scholar Horace Howard Furness, who served as secretary of the Fair and who preserved much of its memorabilia. From the estate of Charles Godfrey Leland came the records of the meetings of the Fair's newspaper committee. Joseph Harrison, a locomotive and boiler manufacturer who spent some years in Russia building a railroad for the Czar, was an active member of the Fair's board. His letter books record not only data on his amassing of an enormous art collection but his work in organizing the Fair's art gallery. The correspondence of Mrs. Thomas P. James relates to the sale of autographs. She called on representatives of old families soliciting manuscripts to be sold for

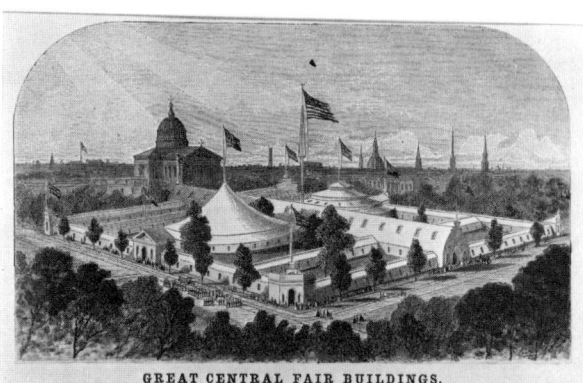

VIEWS OF BUILDINGS AND PICTURE GALLERY AT THE GREAT CENTRAL FAIR

the benefit of the Fair, and was most successful as the diary of Sidney George Fisher discloses.

One of the Society's most popular exhibits is a doll, Miss Flora McFlimsey, made by Miss Mary Kuhn, who provided Flora with an extraordinarily large wardrobe. The doll was purchased at the Fair by Mrs. Henry Drayton for her daughter, Mrs. Madison Taylor, who presented Flora to the Society in 1945. Flora is probably the most famous doll in the United States and has raised funds for charity in every war since the Civil War. She takes her name from a character in a poem, *Nothing to Wear*, written in 1857 by William Allen Butler. In his verses one learns that although Miss Flora McFlimsey of Madison Square made repeated trips to Paris, where she purchased "Dresses to sit in, and stand in, and walk in; Dresses to dance in, and flirt in, and talk in," and despite the fact that "on her last trip to Paris her goods shipped by the steamer *Arago* formed the bulk of the cargo," nevertheless whenever asked out she felt compelled to decline because she had nothing to wear!

Historian Charles J. Stillé was corresponding secretary for the Great Central Fair and had much to do with its success in raising a million dollars. Among his correspondence at the Society are papers to do with the event. Earlier, in December, 1862, when much discouraged with the progress of the war, he wrote a pamphlet, *How a Free People Conduct a Long War*, in which he drew a comparison with Great Britain's struggle against the French Revolutionary government and Napoleon. Originally issued in an edition of a mere seventy-five copies, demand for it ultimately required the printing of half a million. Stillé's papers include Lincoln's letter to him about this pamphlet, his activities as a member of the Fairmount Park Art Association in the creation of Fairmount Park's Lincoln Memorial, the work of sculptor Randolph Rogers, his career as Provost of the University of Pennsylvania, and the manuscripts of a number of his books, as well as letters relating to his presidency of the Historical Society, 1892-1899.

While one would not expect to find a major collection of papers of Salmon P. Chase of Ohio at the Society, nevertheless it owns twenty-seven boxes of them. This collection of Lincoln's Secretary of the Treasury and Chief Justice of the Supreme Court comprises his correspondence before, during, and after the Civil War, his diaries and speeches.

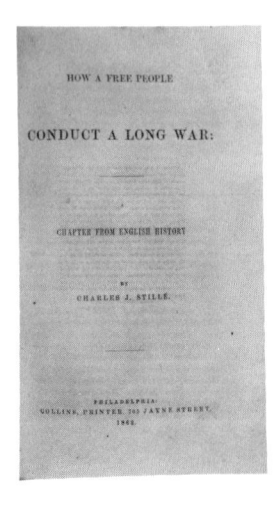

FLORA McFLIMSEY DOLL

TITLE-PAGE OF STILLÉ PAMPHLET

PART OF JAY COOKE MATERIAL

At the Treasury Chase depended heavily on banker Jay Cooke of Philadelphia, who is known as the financier of the Civil War. In 1915 Cooke's children gave the Society their father's entire correspondence which fills 106 boxes and twenty manuscript volumes. An important record of the Civil War, as well as of railroad building and other subjects, this collection contains an enormous correspondence with influential men, and also includes maps, broadsides, pamphlets, and many photographs of men and scenes of his times.

Philadelphians could well take pride in Cooke's ability to raise money to support the war effort, and they could also rejoice at the prowess of numerous local military heroes. Of these George Gordon Meade, the victor at Gettysburg, was the most prominent. His papers at the Society cover his entire career. Perhaps most interesting is his long series of letters to his wife. From Gettysburg on the morning of July 3, the last day of the battle, he wrote her: "All well and going on well with the Army. We had a great fight yesterday, the enemy attacking & we completely repulsing them. Both armies shattered. Today at it again . . . . Army in fine spirits and everyone determined to do or die." Among the gifts of the Meade family are two ceremonial swords the General received as a result of Gettysburg. The first was presented to him on Washington's Birthday, 1864, by the City of Philadelphia, and the second, extremely ornate, the work of Evans and Hassell of 418 Arch Street, contained in a magnificent box, was the gift that June of the Great Central Fair.

The transcripts of Meade's military letters from June 28, 1863, to the end of the war fill twenty-four volumes. On April 9, 1865, the day of Lee's surrender, Meade wrote Grant: "I send you a dispatch from Humphreys, his advance is now 8 or 9 miles from Appomattox C. H. . . . I also send a letter from General Lee." In another letter of April 9, Meade wrote Lee: "I have no authority to suspend hostilities unless it is with the distinct understanding that you are prepared to accept the terms indicated in the letter of Lieut Genl Grant, sent to you yesterday." Within a matter of hours the long conflict was over.

The Humphreys, mentioned above by Meade, was General A. A. Humphreys, grandson of Joshua Humphreys of Philadelphia, the shipbuilder who designed the first large warships for the Navy, and the son of Samuel Humphreys, chief constructor for the Navy from 1826 to 1846, the builder of the *Pennsylvania*, which, when launched in 1838, was the largest ship in the world. A great many of the ledgers of these shipbuilders are at the Society. A. A. Humphreys' military papers form by far the Society's largest military collection, including not only all his military correspondence but the manuscripts of his military writings after the war as well.

Active from the outbreak of hostilities as one of McClellan's staff officers, Humphreys commanded a division at Gettysburg. After the battle, Meade appointed him chief of staff of the Army of the Potomac, and in November, 1864,

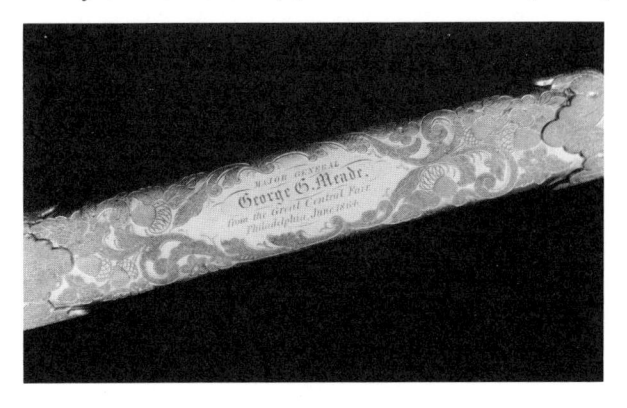

INSCRIPTION ON MEADE SCABBARD

ROBERT BROWNING AND HIS WIFE BY THOMAS BUCHANAN READ

BATTLE OF FREDERICKSBURG BY CAVADA

Grant selected him to command the Second Corps, with which he was in at the kill at Appomattox. From his headquarters near Jamestown on the Appomattox on April 7, 1865, he wrote his wife: "Yesterday my Corps had an extraordinary day. We discovered the enemy in retreat and at once pursued fighting him over twelve or fifteen miles of ground. Advancing in lines of battle. . . ." His next letter dated "near Appomattox C. H.," April 9, announced to her the end of the war. Among the Society's ceremonial swords is an elegant one presented to Humphreys by his "Fellow Citizens of Philadelphia." Inscribed on its scabbard are the names of the twenty-seven actions in which the General participated.

The Society owns a few paintings of Civil War interest. One of them is the marine artist James Hamilton's portrayal of the duel between the *Monitor* and *Merrimac*. Another depicts the Battle of Fredericksburg by Frederick F. Cavada. The son of a Cuban and a Philadelphia mother, Cavada was later to return to Cuba where he was captured by the Spaniards and executed as a rebel. A portrait of importance is Thomas Buchanan Read's painting of the cavalry commander General Philip H. Sheridan. Sheridan sat for this portrait in 1868. The Society owns a dozen portraits by Read. Among them are likenesses of literary lights Robert Browning and his wife, Oliver Wendell Holmes, and Henry Wadsworth Longfellow, as well as of Emanuel Leutze, the painter best known for his heroic "Washington Crossing the Delaware." Other Civil War participants portrayed in the collection are Matthew Wilson's General John F. Hartranft, who later served as Governor of Pennsylvania, and Bernard Uhle's Colonel Chapman Biddle.

Following the Civil War attention in Philadelphia was directed toward the erection of City Hall on Penn Square and laying plans for the 1876 Centennial celebration. Ten years of preparation preceded the Centennial, which was the first great international exposition held in America. Covering more than 450 acres in Fairmount Park, its 167 buildings housed more than 30,000 exhibitors from 50 nations. For the first time the world was given a view of America's industrial might. Attracting people in hordes from all over the nation, nearly ten million in all, the Exposition profoundly affected American taste and culture.

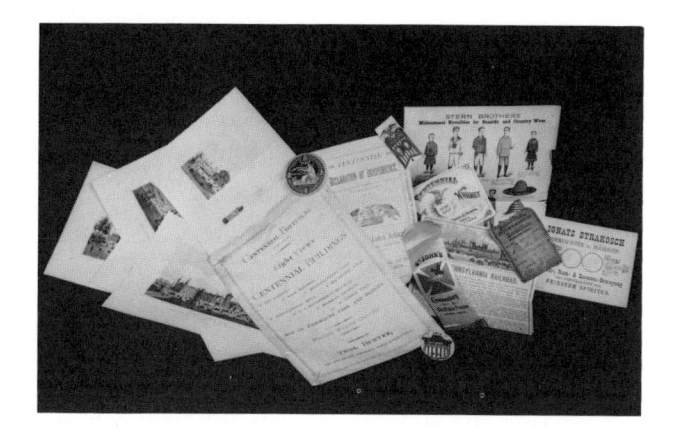

SOME CENTENNIAL ITEMS

John Welsh, who was largely responsible for organizing the 1864 Great Central Fair, managed the finances of the Centennial. Its success made his reputation and won for him the ministry to Great Britain. Welsh's correspondence at the Society deals with both these major events in his life. The Society's records of the Centennial form a ponderous collection, composed of official printings, pictures, maps, and manuscripts. Among the latter are two volumes

ANOTHER CENTENNIAL SOUVENIR

containing the signatures of the many thousands who found need to visit the Department of Public Comfort, and the register of those who called at the Women's Depot. Scrapbooks bulge with the ephemera generated by the celebration—trade cards, invitations, programs, guide books, tickets, maps, almanacs, admission cards, broadsides, announcements, form letters and labels. Eight volumes of scrapbooks document the work of the Centennial Commission in obtaining legislation, soliciting financial support, organizing the exhibits and building the huge exhibition halls. Architectural plans, both successful and unsuccessful, are included, as well as two volumes of drawings and maps collected by the Chief of the Bureau of Installation.

In views of the Centennial and Philadelphia at that time the Society's collection is unexcelled. The progress of the creation of the fair's many buildings is charted in some 1,500 stereoscopic views. And the spirit of the event is captured in Edwin S. Haley's "Streetcar Travel in Philadelphia in 1876." Haley's painting is no better than one would expect from a man who earned his living painting horse cars for the Chestnut and Walnut Street Line. It shows two of that Line's cars packed with men on their way to the Centennial grounds. Remaining to be mentioned as a final curio is a recently received bottle of Burton Ale in a state of perfect preservation. Its label bears the legend "Centennial Exhibition 1876. Continental Brewing Co. Burton Ale. Bottled under the supervision of the Co. 1920 Wash. Ave. Phila."

Visitors to the Centennial took note of the slowly rising, mammoth City Hall, whose cornerstone was laid on July 4, 1874, following seven years of planning. Designed by John McArthur, Jr. in the French Second Empire Style, it was ornamented with sculpture modeled by Alexander Milne Calder. Chief of these is his thirty-six-foot-four-inch-high colossus of William Penn, which was mounted on the tower in 1895. Penn's costume represents the research of a committee of the Historical Society, and his face is a mature version of the youthful countenance of the Society's portrait of Penn in armor. Several aluminum bronze casts in one-tenth scale were made of the colossus and one of these was presented to the Society by the widow of the builder of City Hall tower.

The Society has a splendid record of the building of City Hall, for it possesses the papers of Samuel C. Perkins, president of the commissioners for erecting it throughout the many years it took to complete the edifice. Perkins' papers include his letter books and thirty volumes of scrapbooks. In addition, the Society has a large collection of photographs of the plaster casts from which the sculpture and ornamentation were fashioned.

The appearance of Philadelphia on May 10, 1876, when President Ulysses S. Grant opened the Centennial Exposition is nowhere better seen than in the water colors of David J. Kennedy, who settled in the city in 1836 and over a period of sixty years painted, in the words of Dr. E. P. Richardson, "careful, affectionate water colors of the city's houses and streets." Two of his favorite subjects were the Reading Railroad, for which he worked, and the Centennial. His pictures of Centennial buildings, detailed studies in charming color, are unex-

PENN SQUARE BEFORE ERECTION OF CITY HALL

SOUTH SIDE OF CHESTNUT STREET AT FOURTH BY DAVID J. KENNEDY

celled. Two years after his death in 1898, the Society bought the bulk of Kennedy's work from his daughter and has since added several major lots to it. In addition to many odds and ends, the Kennedy collection contains 663 water colors by him and 326 sketches. Of his 643 Philadelphia views, 172 are of residences, 210 are of streets, and 33 are of Fairmount Park. Among 178 other American scenes, 83 are of New Jersey, 37 of them showing Atlantic City. Eleven small sketch books cover the period 1863-1885; one of these is labeled "Sketches Centennial Exhibition Buildings, etc. 1876." No other artist has equalled Kennedy in creating so large and rich a visual record of Philadelphia.

Joseph Pennell (1857-1926) was another artist who contributed to the city's iconography. He began his career as an etcher about the time of the Centennial. A number of his Germantown subjects appear as illustrations in the 1881 and 1882 issues of the Society's quarterly, *The Pennsylvania Magazine of History and Biography*, which has now completed ninety-eight years of uninterrupted publication. The Society has two of Pennell's early sketch books and a major collection of his prints and book illustrations, many of them acquired through the gift of the Sturgis collection. Yet another delineator of Pennsylvania scenes was Augustus Kollner who came to Philadelphia in 1840 and died there in 1906 at the age of ninety-four. He was prolific as a lithographer, etcher, and water colorist and the Society has a substantial number of

SKETCH BY AUGUSTUS KOLLNER

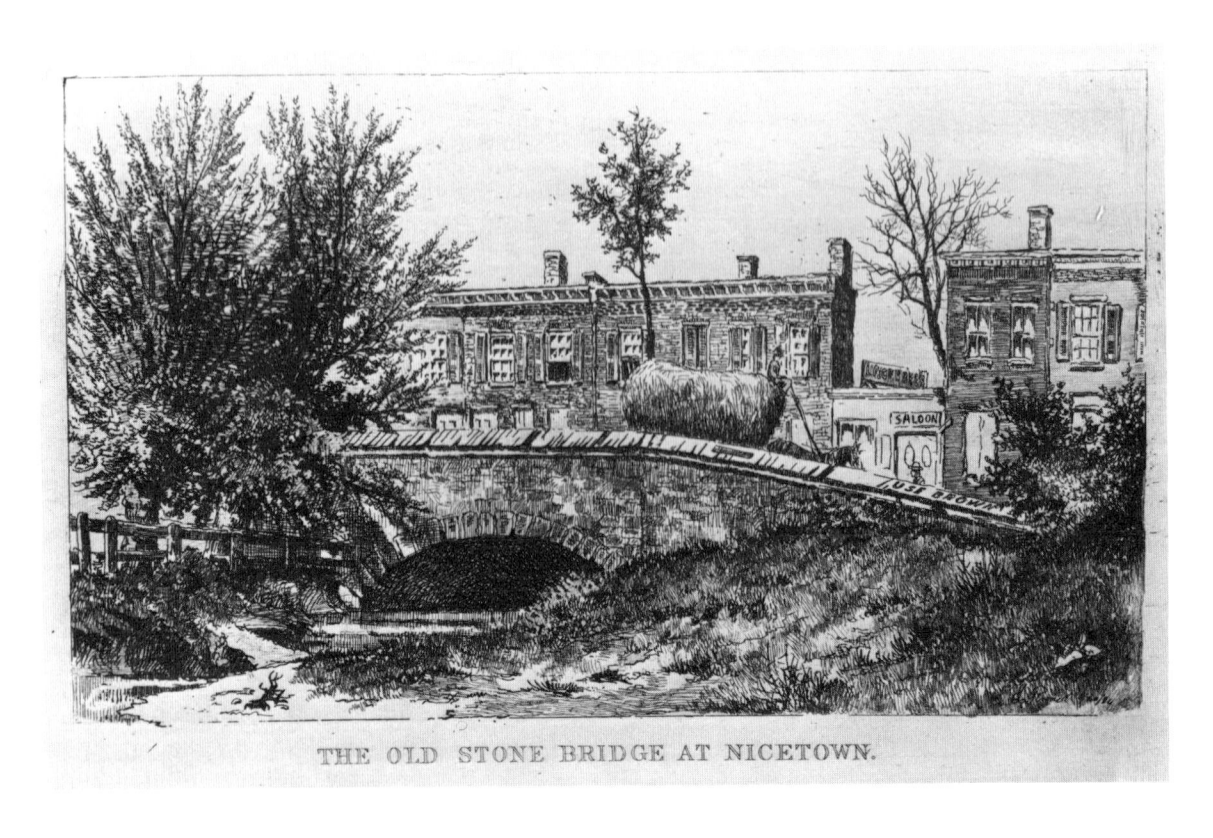

ETCHING BY JOSEPH PENNELL

his works in all these media, as well as four oil paintings of Philadelphia scenes. In yet another media, photography, the Society, thanks to the Boies Penrose fund, has an excellent collection of pictures of Philadelphia buildings and streets between 1860 and 1910.

For the post-Civil War years the painting collection has a number of representative examples. In portraits, it has likenesses of industrialists Matthias W. Baldwin and Henry Disston, the latter by J. Henry Smith in 1870. Two paintings of note by Edward D. Marchant show Edward Coles, a former governor of Illinois who settled in Philadelphia in the 1830s, and John White Geary, whose adventurous life included a term of office as mayor of San Francisco and later as Governor of Pennsylvania. Between these two events he sandwiched a valiant career in the Civil War, from which he emerged as a brigadier general. Samuel B. Waugh, probably the city's best portrait painter just prior to Eakins, is represented by his portrait of the Society's president, Charles J. Stillé, and by his likeness of Robert J. C. Walker, whose varied career included ownership of the *Saturday Evening Post*. Two newspaper men in the collection are seen in portraits by Peter F. Rothermel of Dr. Robert S. MacKenzie and, by artist unknown, of Morton McMichael, owner of the influential *North American* and Mayor of Philadelphia, 1866-1869.

In views for this period, the Society has two paintings by Antonio Jacobsen of vessels owned by the Philadelphia & Baltimore Steamship Line—the *General John Cadwalader* and the *Manna Hata*. In addition to some of his water colors, the Society has a good 1884 painting by Edmund D. Lewis of Independence Hall, and an 1875 interior scene of the Library Company, then at Fifth and Library Streets, by George B. Wood, Jr. Of Isaac L. Williams' portraits and views, the Society owns two dozen. Of these, two are interior scenes of the building occupied by the Society from 1872 to 1884 on the grounds of the Pennsylvania Hospital. Williams, who was much interested in the Society, painted these scenes just before the Society moved to its present site. The figures in these pictures are little portraits of members of the staff.

Moving from art to literature, the Society has the papers of that Philadelphia master of literary journalism, Charles Godfrey Leland (1824-1903). He earned for himself an international reputation as a humorist, poet, and essayist. His large correspondence with eminent persons and with his publishers as well as his unpublished and published manuscripts are in the collection.

Anne Hollingsworth Wharton (1845-1928) presented 80,000 of her papers a few years before her death. Member of an old Philadelphia family, she wrote books about colonial times and the Revolution, including *Through Colonial Doorways, Heirlooms in Miniature*, and *Social Life in the Early Republic*.

Mention has been made of Septimus Winner's manuscript of "Listen to the Mocking Bird," which Winner wrote in 1854 and sold for five dollars. Within fifty years twenty million copies of this song were printed. The Society has forty-one volumes of Winner's diaries, letter books, and music notebooks. A member of a talented Philadelphia family, Winner wrote more than 200 books of music for twenty-three different instruments and some 2,000 arrangements for the piano and violin. Among his many songs are "What is Home Without a Mother," "Ten Little Injuns," and "Oh where! Oh where, is my little dog gone."

Shortly before the Civil War cricket became popular and several clubs were formed. The Society has a collection of records of the Philadelphia Cricket Club, including its minutes from 1854 to 1879, and ten volumes of records of the Merion Cricket Club covering the years 1865 to 1923. To promote the game George W. Childs, publisher of the *Public Ledger*, put up two challenge cups now at the Society, both made by J. E. Caldwell. The first was for the best batsman in the Halifax Cup matches, and is engraved with the names of the winners starting in 1879. The second was for the annual competition of the local clubs and bears the names of the victorious contestants from 1880 to 1926. Indicative of the popularity of the game is *The American Cricketer, A Journal Devoted to the Noble Game of Cricket*, published by the Associated Cricket Clubs of Philadelphia. The Society has a nearly complete run of this

HISTORICAL SOCIETY LIBRARY IN 1884 BY ISAAC L. WILLIAMS

journal, starting with its first issue in 1877 and continuing to 1929. Yet another sport, for which the Society holds records from 1882 to 1902, was bicycling, as recorded in the papers of the Philadelphia Bicycling Club.

While sportsminded, Philadelphians were also charitable. Many organizations which sought to alleviate hardships have deposited their records with the Society. Among them are the Union Benevolent Association papers, 1831-1952, the Orphan Society of Philadelphia, 1815-1965, the Family Service of Philadelphia (founded in 1879 as the Philadelphia Society for Organizing Charity), and the Citizens Permanent Relief papers for 1885 to 1899. Allied to these is one of the Society's largest and most important collections, now available on microfilm, the Indian Rights Association papers. Founded in 1882 and still in operation, this organization serves as the conscience of America, focusing attention on the plight of the American Indians. It has been constantly in the forefront

CRICKET CHALLENGE CUP

of efforts to secure for the Indians the political and civil rights already guaranteed them by treaties and statutes. The collection contains correspondence up to 1968, minutes and photographs.

Among the Society's business records, which, like charitable ones, frequently begin well before the Civil War and continue long after 1900, are the Philadelphia Board of Trade papers, 1801-1942; the Baltimore & Philadelphia Steamship Company, 1844-1936; the J. C. Brill Collection of 10,000 photographs and shop records of a manufacturer of street cars and buses, 1876-1940; and, lastly, 173 volumes of Maritime Records of the Port of Philadelphia, 1766-1937, transcribed by the Pennsylvania Historical Survey in 1941.

One of Philadelphia's most dynamic post-Civil War leaders was Franklin B. Gowen, president of the Reading Railroad which hauled anthracite coal. It was he who prosecuted and broke up the Molly Maguires, a secret society which had terrified the coal regions for twenty years. In April, 1882, Gowen was preparing to go abroad when a deputation of coal barons called at his office. With them they had a chest containing the largest bowl ever made by Bailey, Banks & Biddle. Costing $2,000, it was, according to the *Philadelphia Inquirer*, "one of the handsomest silver and gold centre pieces ever manufactured in this country." Decorated with symbols of the coal mining industry, it is inscribed: "Presented to Franklin B. Gowen as a Token of our Grateful Remembrance of his Services in Suppressing Lawless Violence and Re-establishing Security for Life and Property in the Anthracite Coal Regions of Pennsylvania." The bowl came to the Society as the gift of the late James E. Gowen.

A few years before this token of appreciation was presented to Gowen, the Bell Telephone Company took root in Philadelphia. Every now and then the Society acquires one of its early phone books, but they are rare. The Society's earliest, July 1, 1883, explains why on its cover: "Destroy all other issues." Instructions on the use of the phone are entertaining: "Always give the disconnecting order and save annoyance"; "Subscribers must not permit other persons to use their Telephones."

PHOTOGRAPH FROM BRILL COLLECTION

Telephones, like other newly formed public utilities—electric companies and horsecar companies—were of interest to politicians, some of whom found ways to profit from them. Not of that stamp was Wayne MacVeagh (1833-1917), a distinguished Philadelphia politician of this period whose papers are at the Society. MacVeagh served as United States Attorney General, minister to Turkey, and ambassador to Italy. His correspondence contains letters from six presidents and many from his father-in-law, Simon Cameron.

Uriah Hunt Painter (1837-1900), who was later to promote Edison's phonograph and telephone and electric companies, was a man on the fringes of politics. A lobbyist and entrepreneur, he was Washington correspondent for the *Philadelphia Inquirer* throughout the Civil War. More than 10,000 of his papers are at the Society. Unlike Painter's part-time political career, that of Israel W. Durham was dedicated to politics. Around the turn of the century he was the Republican political boss of the city and his interests may be seen in the choice of subjects that fill thirty scrapbooks at the Society. Doubtless, he did not look with favor on the Pennsylvania Civil Service Reform League, whose papers from 1881 to 1935 form another of the Society's possessions.

Of all those Philadelphians who came into their prime not long after the Civil War, none equalled in zeal the reforming drive of Herbert Welsh. He devoted his life to worthy causes—Indian rights, anti-imperialism, Negro education, exposure of military atrocities in the Philippines, international affairs, and reform movements in politics. A son of John Welsh of Centennial fame, he published a small weekly, *City and State*, which attacked the monolithic Republican organization, and he did his unsuccessful best to unseat "Iz" Durham. A molder of liberal thought in Philadelphia, he knew that politicians were corrupt and he was not contented. The vast quantity of papers which came to the Society through Herbert Welsh express the humanitarianism of the *fin de siécle*.

BOWL PRESENTED TO FRANKLIN B. GOWEN BY GRATEFUL FRIENDS

Twentieth Century

There are those who consider the events of the present century so recent as scarcely to constitute history. To many people the chronicle of this period lacks the patina of colonial times, the heroism and romance of the Revolution, and the tragedy of the Civil War. Nevertheless, the three quarters of a century just past is a respectable length of time and much of its history is to be found in the Society's collections.

Of that somewhat forgotten conflict, World War I, the Society possesses a miscellanea of materials—letters and diaries of participants, posters, photographs, and draft records. In the papers of Albian A. Wallgren it has his record as a noted cartoonist on the A.E.F. newspaper *The Stars and Stripes*, and later for the American Legion monthly, as well as his subsequent correspondence with humorists Walt Disney and Irwin S. Cobb. Other collections contain the minutes of the Pennsylvania Committee of Public Safety, 1917-1918, the records of the Four Minute Men of the World War, an organization which promoted Liberty Loans and other patriotic activities, and also the extensive files of the Society's own War Service Committee, which entertained service men.

Between wars the country was visited by the great depression of the 1930s. This unhappy time is recorded in the collection by papers of the W.P.A. and of the Bureau of Unemployment Relief. Scarcely was the depression over before the nation was embroiled in yet another holocaust. The Society was extremely active during the World War II years in collecting materials relating to the war effort, reports of governmental agencies, broadsides, publications on defense, posters, propaganda, speeches, civilian control measures and information on scientific developments. One of its larger collections, some 40,000 documents and 78 volumes, contains financial and personnel records of the United Service Organization.

CARTOON BY A. A. WALLGREN

WPA POSTER

Perhaps Pennsylvania's most exotic offering to the war effort was embodied in the person of General A. J. Drexel Biddle, Jr. (1896-1961), athlete, sportsman, society luminary, diplomat and soldier, "Tony" Biddle was serving as Ambassador to Poland when that country was invaded by the Germans. Subsequently, he

PHOTOGRAPH OF GENERAL BIDDLE

served as Ambassador to all the overrun countries before taking on military duties. After the war, while a member of SHAEF headquarters, Eisenhower painted Biddle's portrait. His career continued with one important assignment after another, concluding with his appointment as Adjutant General of Pennsylvania and, finally, Ambassador to Spain, where he died. From his widow the Society received a large collection of General Biddle's diplomatic library, much of his correspondence and speeches, and a great many photographs illustrating his activities all over the world.

While wars raged intermittently, politics remained a constant and it appeared as if Republican control of Philadelphia was there to stay. However, Rudolph Blankenburg (1843-1918), "Old Dutch Cleanser," won election as Mayor on a reform ticket. Some of his papers and his portrait are at the Society. Although the reform movement speedily lost its momentum, Philadelphia was fortunate in a later Mayor, J. Hampton Moore (1864-1950), whose lifetime collection of papers, some 100,000, he gave to the Society. These cover his entire career in Congress from 1906 to 1920, with much on World War I, his two terms as Mayor, 1920-1924 and 1932-1936, and his other interests. Shelved next to the Moore papers are those that Joseph S. Clark presented and which fill 269 manuscript boxes and 94 volumes. Clark, a Democrat, was largely responsible for destroying Republican hegemony over Philadelphia. His papers record his political career as City Controller, 1949-1951, Mayor, 1952-1956, and United States Senator, 1957-1968.

Other political records of the times include those of a number of female organizations: the Civic Club of Philadelphia, fifty-one volumes of minute books, 1893-1959, and other records of a ladies' club devoted to good government; and the League of Women Voters of Philadelphia, 1920-1961, a nonpartisan organization. Also in this category are the papers of Constance H. Dallas who served from 1952 to 1956 on City Council, the first woman to be elected to it.

RUDOLPH BLANKENBURG BY HAESELER

Among prominent twentieth-century Pennsylvania personages whose manuscripts have been given to the Society is James T. Mitchell (1834-1915), who served on the Supreme Court of Pennsylvania from 1888 to 1910, the last seven of those years as Chief Justice. His collection of 12,000 papers document his career at the bar and on the bench where he participated in 11,580 cases. The Society is also fortunate in the papers of Joseph Fels (1854-1914), a Philadelphia soap manufacturer (Fels-Naptha), philanthropist, and ardent advocate of the single-tax movement. His correspondence includes letters from George Bernard Shaw, Woodrow Wilson, and Booker T. Washington. William B. Wilson (1862-1934) is represented by 15,000 of his papers. Wilson, a Pennsylvania coal miner, union organizer, and official of the United Mine Workers, served in Congress from 1907 to 1913, and was the Nation's first Secretary of Labor, holding that post from 1913 to 1921. His papers include his correspondence as a cabinet officer and his unpublished autobiography, "Annals of an Immigrant." Final mention is reserved for Albert M. Greenfield (1887-1967), business leader, Democratic stalwart, and philanthropist, a man engaged in so many activities that he earned the title "Mr. Philadelphia." His voluminous correspondence, the gift of his family, fills 208 transfer cases.

Wealthy Philadelphians, such as several mentioned here, lived in houses expressive of their owners' importance. Many of these magnificent mansions have since been swept away because it became impossible to staff and maintain them. Fortunately, the exact arrangements of some of the most important are preserved in the Society's architectural drawings, particularly in the Horace Trumbauer (1868-1938) collection. In his drawings is mirrored the height of luxury achieved in Philadelphia domestic architecture as expressed in the grand tradition of eighteenth-century France. The favorite architect of the Wideners and the very rich, and with clients in New York, Long Island, and Newport, Trumbauer designed Lynnewood Hall with its great art gallery for P. A. B. Widener and E. T. Stotesbury's enormous palace, Whitemarsh Hall. His architectural drawings for these mansions are in the collection as well as those for many more of the area's most stately residences, and also his plans for the Free Library of Philadelphia and other public buildings.

The earliest large lot of architectural plans at the Society are the detailed drawings submitted by the many architects who entered the Girard College competition in the 1830s. Included are the rejected plans of prominent architects John Haviland and William Strickland, and the successful ones of Thomas U. Walter. Also in the collection is a large lot, some 1,000 drawings, presented by the Philadelphia Chapter of the American Institute of Architects. While these include 68 drawings by John Notman, they are chiefly drawings made in the 1930s for the Committee on Preservation of Historic Buildings. These consist of measured floor plans and elevations of virtually all Philadelphia's most important early buildings, including Christ Church and Independence Hall, and constitute a significant historical record of artistic merit.

Yet another form of art is reflected in the Society's music and theater collection, which includes the earliest surviving Philadelphia-made piano, handsomely decorated with its

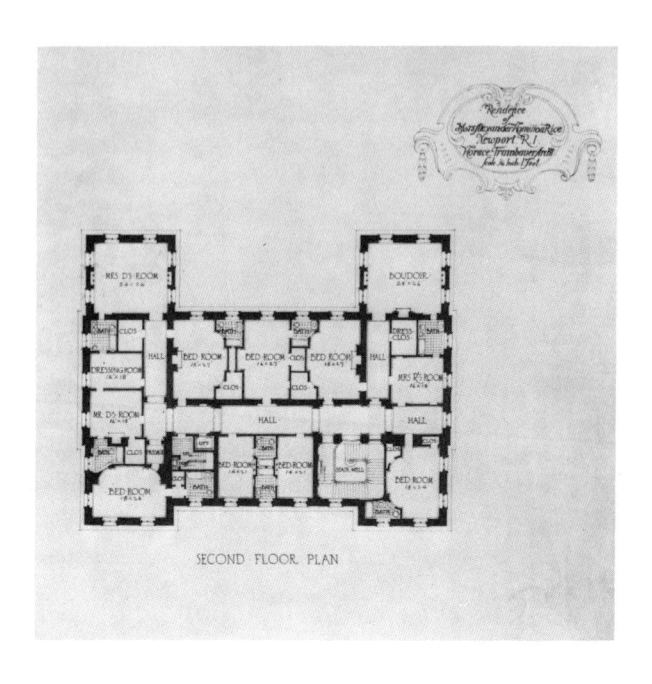

FLOOR PLAN BY TRUMBAUER

ALBRECHT'S PIANO AND DETAIL

maker's name, "Charles Albrecht Philadelphia. 1789." In manuscript, the collection has thirty-five volumes of the minutes of the Musical Fund Society, 1820-1939, as well as the minute books of the Philadelphia Musical Association, 1864-1918. For the Academy of Music, the Society has the Academy's programs from 1868 to date, and it has also the programs of the Metropolitan Opera House of Philadelphia from 1908 to 1927, as well as programs of the Philadelphia Orchestra. To these are joined a large quantity of sheet music for the piano and other instruments and an impressive collection of ballads and song sheets. The theater is principally represented by a massive accumulation of play bills dating from 1754 and by numerous theatrical scrapbooks.

The Society's interesting bookplate collection recalls literary records in its possession. Two of these are the papers of Philadelphia historians: Joseph Jackson (1868-1946), author of *Encyclopedia of Philadelphia* and of *Market Street Philadelphia*; and Harold D. Eberlein (1875-1964), a prolific writer, author of *Diary of Independence Hall* and of *Portrait of a Colonial City, Philadelphia*. In the George Horace Lorimer (1868-1937) papers there is a rich selection of that editor of the *Saturday Evening Post*'s correspondence with his authors—Will Rogers, Sinclair Lewis, F. Scott Fitzgerald and Booth Tarkington, to name but a few. Literary organizations have also deposited their records to the enrichment of the Society's resources. In such archives are the correspondence of the Society of Arts and Letters of Philadelphia, 1908-1920, and the records of the Franklin Inn and Philobiblon clubs.

Many organizations, indeed, have entrusted their records to the Society, among them the ancient and exclusive Philadelphia Assemblies, the Lawyers Club of Philadelphia, the Navy League, the Philadelphia Chamber of Commerce, the Episcopal Diocese of Pennsylvania, and the Aero Club of Pennsylvania, which was founded in 1909. In addition, the Aero Club presented its silver trophies. Business organizations have also looked with favor on the Society as a depository as evidenced by the minute books of the Autocar Company, the records of the Philadelphia Drug Exchange, and of the Philadelphia Gazette Publishing Company. Two insurance companies, the Frankford Mutual Fire Insurance Company and the Franklin Fire Insurance Company have given their sur-

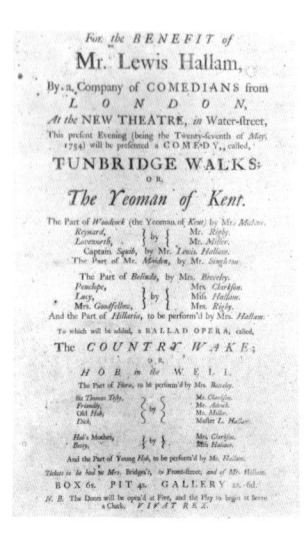

AN EARLY THEATER PIECE

veys, the Franklin's covering 42,000 properties. Fire insurance surveys are extremely interesting records since they describe in much detail the interiors of buildings and are often accompanied by maps showing the locations of outbuildings. Similar records at the Society are

AN AERO CLUB TROPHY

property atlases which map houses and their grounds, showing the locations of drives, improvements, and indicating the type of construction. These are chiefly for suburban areas. Urban sections, such as Philadelphia, were minutely mapped for insurance purposes, building by building, and the maps are contained in ponderous volumes, many of which are preserved at the Society.

These mighty tomes bring to mind equally huge bindings for newspapers. The Society has about 8,000 bound volumes of Pennsylvania newspapers. Those for which it has the best twentieth-century coverage are the *North American*, a complete run from 1839 to 1925, when the paper was absorbed by the *Public Ledger;* the *Public Ledger*, another complete run from 1836 until 1934, when the *Ledger* became part of the *Philadelphia Inquirer*; and the *Inquirer* (known until 1860 as the *Pennsylvania Inquirer*) from 1829 to 1943. Because of the brittle nature of post-Civil War wood-pulp paper, few of the Society's newspapers from that period on are allowed to be used. The alternative is microfilm, to which the Society began to turn about thirty years ago. It has the *Public Ledger* on film from 1836 to 1926 and the *Philadelphia Inquirer* from 1926 to date. The magnitude of the microfilm alternative is suggested by the fact that the *Inquirer* film takes 1,222 reels. Another newspaper of importance is the *Philadelphia Record*. The Society has this paper from 1876 to 1947, when it ceased publication. Most of the Society's *Record* was originally that newspaper's office file. It contains every edition issued each day, which helps account for the fact that 764 mammoth volumes are required to house it.

One of the Society's most valuable sources of data on the first half of the twentieth century is the *Philadelphia Record's* "morgue." Although narrowed in focus to subjects of Pennsylvania interest, it nevertheless requires 164 file drawers to contain the clippings that have been retained. Arranged alphabetically in envelopes, these clippings make readily available a wealth of material on individuals and events and are supplemented by some 20,000 photographs, which in themselves form an invaluable historical record.

The use of microfilm, as indicated by the Society's policy in purchasing the *Inquirer* on film, has burgeoned since the 1950s, when it owned only several hundred reels, to today's collection of approximately 10,000 reels. In part this is due to the microfilming of manuscript collections whenever possible for reasons of security and wider use. Thus, in recent years the Thomas Penn Papers, the President James Buchanan Papers, and the Indian Rights Papers have been filmed among many others, as well as numerous early newspapers. A large grant, just received, will make possible the filming of the Tench Coxe Papers. Where original records are issued on paper that will not long withstand handling, the Society is receptive to microfilm, such as its film of Philadelphia telephone directories from 1936 to 1954.

Another major category of films are census records. The collection includes complete census returns for the nation for 1810, 1830, and 1850, as well as returns for Pennsylvania from 1800 to 1870. These records are useful for his-

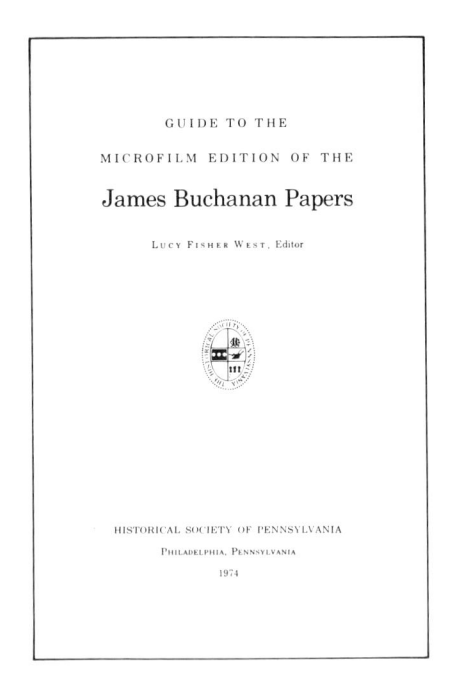

GUIDE TO THE BUCHANAN PAPERS

torians and particularly so for genealogists. In the 1890s a group of the Society's members founded the Genealogical Society of Pennsylvania to promote the collecting of genealogical data. The Genealogical Society has quarters in the Historical Society and the material it collects, according to the original agreement, automatically becomes the property of the Historical Society. Thanks to the energy and resources of the Genealogical Society, the film collection has grown rapidly, with the Genealogical Society bringing in large quantities of church and cemetery records on film. Other major targets for genealogical films include deeds, tax records, wills and inventories.

Similar records are preserved also in many volumes of transcripts, photostats, and family charts, and an extensive file contains data on individual families. Supplementing these collections is the basic one of printed books, more than 12,000 volumes of purely genealogical material, to which may be added some 8,000 more titles of secondary genealogical interest, such as church histories and other local records. The Historical Society purchases nearly every sound genealogy that is printed pertinent to its field.

Related to genealogical holdings are works on heraldry in which the Society is singularly rich.

Aside from sources on British heraldry, the library contains *Deutsches Geschlecterbuch* in 166 volumes and J. Siebmacher's *Grosses und Allgemienes Wappenbuch* in 83 volumes, as well as an interesting representation of French and Italian heraldry. Burks's *Peerage and Knightage* and similar works round out this class.

While the genealogical collections are the most often consulted by readers, the Society's general library is strong on American history with depth on the original thirteen states and most of those states contiguous to them. Coverage on colonial and Revolutionary times is heavy and the sections on the Civil War and on biography are among the Society's largest.

The uniqueness of the library consists partly in its enormous pamphlet series which include works on biography, politics, education, char-

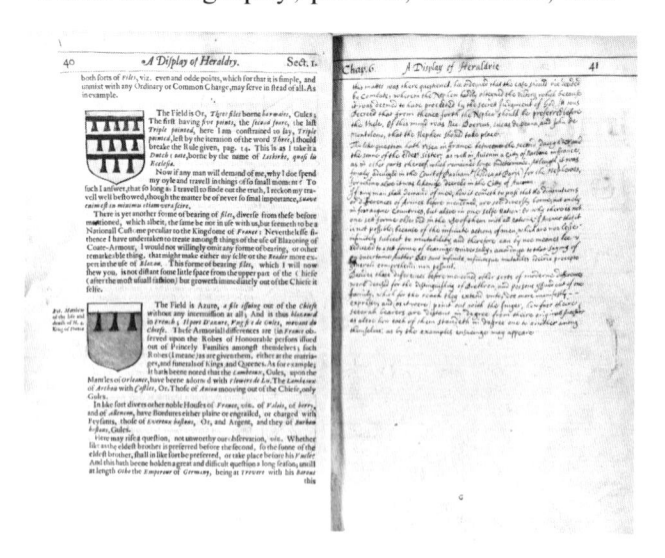

FROM THE HERALDRY COLLECTION

itable and civic establishments, and annual reports for business and religious organizations. In these areas the researcher can discover much that is not available elsewhere. Other strengths lie in long periodical runs, among them those of historical journals, on bibliography, on transportation, and on the British Isles.

Of course, the Society's greatest strength is found in its Pennsylvania holdings. Not counting Philadelphia, there is a section for each county and other sections on most conceivable subjects, such as education, religion, ethnic groups, local authors, government, and medi-

Twentieth Century

cine. For Philadelphia, nearly all of these classifications are repeated so that readers may be provided with virtually everything available in print on the history of the city. For subjects which should bring readers to its library, the Society offers a superb research collection.

To hearken back to the Society's beginnings and the expressed intention of its founders, it is evident that their ambitions have been achieved and that the Society has indeed formed "an ample library and cabinet," that it has achieved a nationally prominent collection, and that in its chosen field it has rendered extraordinary service over the past century and a half.

SCALE MODEL OF CITY HALL PENN STATUE

SIX SEASONS OF FUN!

ACTIVITIES, CRAFTS, AND MORE

Katherine A. Finegan
and
Phyllis Vos Wezeman

Augsburg Fortress
Minneapolis

INTRODUCTION
ADVENT CHRISTMAS EPIPHANY LENT EASTER PENTECOST

Welcome to Six Seasons of Fun! This resource is a collection of seasonal crafts, activities, and various resources for the church year. As a Christian education planner, you may use *Six Seasons of Fun!* to enhance classroom connections. Children and families at home may also use it to provide opportunities for them to make connections between worship, education, and the church year. *Six Seasons of Fun!* may be used with Life Together Sunday school resources or as a supplement to any curriculum.

Providing resources for learners of all ages and helping them discover that God is with them through all the seasons of life is at the heart of this book. Chapters are organized by six church year seasons: Advent, Christmas, Epiphany, Lent, Easter, and Pentecost.

The seasons begin with Advent, where we anticipate the coming of Christ both in the birth at Bethlehem and in a future coming. It is a season of preparation and waiting for Christmas. The Christmas season celebrates God taking on a human body in the person of Jesus. The Epiphany season is a bridge between the birth of Jesus and his suffering. Lent is another season of preparation, 40 days of focus on rebirth and renewal, as we get ready to celebrate Easter, the chief festival of the year. Easter in the church year lasts for seven weeks—an extended feast or season. The 50 days of Easter rejoicing culminate in the day of Pentecost when the risen Christ sends the Spirit to the church.

In each chapter you will find crafts, seasonal activities, and resources for pre-elementary, lower elementary, upper elementary, combination age groups, intergenerational groups, and worship/education/music helps.

Intergenerational learning experiences gather people of all ages together, discovering the richness of God's teachings and the implications they have for our lives today. Intergenerational events also offer peer-teaching opportunities uniting church members across all age levels.

The helps for worship/education/music provide an opportunity for cooperative activities between pastors and congregation members. Use this section to plan special programs for Sunday mornings or Sunday nights targeted at seasonal education of the entire congregation. All suggested hymns are included in either *Lutheran Book of Worship, With One Voice,* or *LifeSongs,* as well as in many other Christian hymnals.

Have fun exploring the church year!

Health/Safety Note: Many of the activities in *Six Seasons of Fun!* involve food that will be made and eaten by participants. *Before doing any activity with food it is important to find out about food allergies children may have.* Young children may not know of their allergies, so it is important to check in advance with caregivers. It is also important to make caregivers aware of any activities you will be doing that require the handling, preparing, and/or eating of food. Be prepared to provide an alternative activity for someone who has food allergies.

ADVENT

ADVENT CHRISTMAS EPIPHANY LENT EASTER PENTECOST

Advent is the season of preparation for the coming of Christ. It begins four Sundays prior to Christmas Day, December 25th. During Advent, the church prepares for the birth of Jesus as a babe in a manger as well as the rebirth of Christ's presence in the hearts of faithful people. Advent is a time to remember that we also wait for Christ's promised return to the world, called the "second coming." Scripture lessons focus on prophecy, especially Isaiah's foretelling of the Messiah and John the Baptist's announcement of the need for repentance and preparation for the one who is to come. God started preparing the world for Jesus' birth thousands of years ago. When God saw that people were not able to find their way through the darkness of sin and selfishness, God provided messengers to let people know that God had a plan! We call those people "prophets." That way, people understood that there was hope. God had not given up on human beings, but would provide a way of salvation. Even though we live in the time after Jesus came to earth, human beings still get lost in the darkness of sin and selfishness.

The blue or purple color of Advent symbolizes that we wait for the rebirth of hope, just like the prophets. We remember that God has a plan for us, too. As we prepare our minds and hearts for Jesus' rebirth, we review our need for God's salvation and open our lives to God's Messiah, the Chosen One who will show us the way through the darkness. Advent is a time to get ready on the inside so that God's love will shine through our lives and make a difference on the outside.

The color for Advent is blue or purple, representing hope. If an Advent wreath is used, people often use blue, purple, or white candles. One candle is lit each week to signify that the light of Christ is coming closer. Traditionally, some churches use a pink candle for the third candle to suggest joy. On Christmas Sunday and/or Christmas Eve, a white Christ candle is lit to announce the birth of Jesus, the Light of the world.

ADVENT SONGS

"Come, Thou Long-Expected Jesus"
(Lutheran Book of Worship [LBW] 30)

"Comfort, Comfort Now My People"
(LBW 29)

"Get Ready!" (LifeSongs 12)

"Oh, Come, Oh, Come, Emmanuel"
(LifeSongs 10; LBW 34)

"We Light the Advent Candles"
(LifeSongs 9)

All suggested hymns are included in either Lutheran Book of Worship, With One Voice, or LifeSongs, as well as in many other Christian hymnals.

ADVENT

MINI ADVENT WREATHS

(Pre-Elementary)

Materials: Blue (or pink and purple) and white birthday candles, any size canning jar rings, coasters or tiny paper doilies, foil tart pan, glue, green playdough (homemade or purchased), blue, pink and purple, or white ribbon, scissors, and toothpicks.

Preparation: Have volunteers available.

Make individual Advent wreaths to remind learners of the Savior's coming and use them to count the weeks to Christmas. As a new candle is lit each Sunday and the flames are rekindled each day, spend time reading a scripture passage, singing a song, or saying a prayer to prepare for the coming of the Christ child.

Have the learners cover an entire metal canning jar ring with green playdough. This serves as the base of the wreath. To simulate the texture of evergreen needles, have volunteers help them press lines into the dough with a toothpick.

Space four small white candles—birthday size—evenly around the ring and push them into the dough before it hardens. If small blue or pink and purple candles are available, they may be substituted for the white ones. Choose Advent candle colors according to the tradition followed in your church or family. Position the wreath on top of a paper doily or beverage coaster. Place everything on a "bottom up" foil tart pan. The foil pan will become a base for the wreath.

Roll a small ball of dough to hold the Christ candle. Push a white birthday candle into the ball and press it firmly in the center of the ring.

Cut blue or pink and purple ribbon to tie around the outside of the foil pan. If colored candles are used, tie white ribbon around the base. Since the candles for this project are small, be prepared to replace them often. Supervise closely to ensure that the candles do not ignite the ribbon. Stress the point to the children and their parents that when the candles are lit, extreme caution must be used with matches and flames!

ADVENT CANDY WREATHS

(Pre-Elementary)

Materials: Fifteen soft (gummy) or hard green circular candies with holes (such as Life Savers), scissors, shoestring licorice.

Preparation: Cut a piece of shoestring licorice about 12-15 inches (30-38 cm) long for each learner. Have helpers available. Have everyone wash hands first!

Create mini-candy wreaths for learners to share with others. Provide fifteen gummy or regular green candies for each project (include a few extras to eat)! Distribute the candy to learners and show them how to string the candies onto the licorice. When completed, help each learner gather the ends of the licorice together and tie them into a bow to form an edible wreath.

Safety Tip: If working with very young learners, use gummy candies instead of hard candy to prevent a choking hazard.

ADVENT

ADVENT

COTTON BALL WREATHS

(Pre-Elementary)

Materials: Construction paper, containers for paint, 6-8 cotton balls per learner, glue, pattern for wreaths, pencils, poster board, ribbon, scissors, green and red tempera paint, and cotton swabs.

Preparation: Cut a wreath shape from poster board; then on a piece of construction paper for each learner. Have helpers available.

Create wreaths from cotton balls by using one of two methods. Give each learner a circle and 6-8 cotton balls. Place glue and containers of green and red tempera paint between learners. Invite the learners to glue the cotton balls to the wreath shape. Give each learner an additional cotton ball. Tell the group that they will use this piece as a paintbrush to color the wreaths green, representing branches from an evergreen tree. Make sure the learners glue before they paint.

Demonstrate how to lightly dip the cotton ball into the green paint and then dab it onto the cotton balls on the wreath shape. When this step is completed, add holly berries. Supply toothpicks and have learners dip one end into the red paint and then dot clusters onto their wreaths. After the projects are dry, add a loop of ribbon to the top of each wreath to use as an ornament hanger.

Option: Trace the shape of the wreath onto construction paper or poster board for each learner. Give each person one cotton ball. Tell them to lightly dip the cotton ball into the green paint and to dab it onto the wreath shape. Then create holly berries by dipping one end of a cotton swab into the red paint and dot clusters of berries onto the wreath.

Option: Create one large wreath using either technique and display it in the class area or church building.

Leader Tip: Use old clothing as art smocks to protect the learners' clothing.

RHYTHM STORY

(Combination Age Groups)

Materials: Bibles, "God's Promised Gift" rhythm story, paper, pencils or pens.

Preparation: Practice the rhythm story before meeting with learners.

Proclaim the coming of Christ by clapping a rhythm and echoing a rhyme. In a "rhythm story," the leader says a line, and the participants repeat it back. Begin by establishing the clapping pattern: one clap on the knees and one clap of the hands; practice it several times. Chant the first line of the story to this rhythm and tell the group to echo it back. Communicate the entire message in this manner. Maintain the established rhythm throughout the activity.

God's Promised Gift
Long ago in biblical days
There was a prophet named Isaiah.
He said that a child would be born
Who would be the Messiah.
Isaiah offered many names
That told us who this child would be:
Wonderful Counselor, Mighty God,
The Prince of Peace for you and me.
Micah said that a tiny town
Would be the site of the Messiah's birth.
In Bethlehem one holy night
Would come the Savior of the earth.
This king would be from David's line
A ruler from the royal throne.
The one God promised long ago
Emmanuel: we're not alone.
Before God's great Messiah came
The prophets praised his holy name.
God's faithfulness and constant love
From age to age remains the same.

Once the activity is completed, discuss additional passages that proclaim the coming of the Messiah, including the account of John the Baptist, the New Testament prophet who prepared the way for Jesus. Select one biblical account and experiment with writing a rhythm story like the example provided. As a guideline, compose four lines per stanza with eight syllables per line. Practice the story and share the message with others.

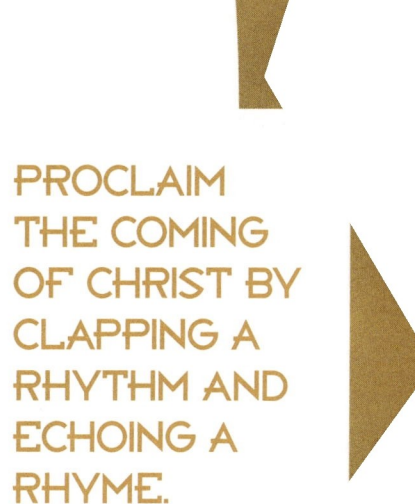

> PROCLAIM THE COMING OF CHRIST BY CLAPPING A RHYTHM AND ECHOING A RHYME.

FAITH TREE

(Intergenerational)

Materials: Coffee cans, construction paper, felt or poster board, fabric or foil, glue, hole punch, paper clips, pencils or pens, ribbon, string or yarn, scissors, stones, tree branches.

A "Jesse tree" incorporates symbols that recall important people and events that are a significant part of Jesus' ancestry. A Jesse tree is much like a family tree, and is named for the father of David, who lived about one thousand years before Jesus.

Traditionally, symbols on a Jesse tree correspond to stories recorded in Old and New Testament scripture passages.

As an Advent devotional guide, adapt the Jesse tree format from December 1 through December 24 to trace the roots of your belief in Jesus. Work together as a family unit including grandparents, mothers and fathers, as well as children; or an intergenerational group representing various ages. Add the names of 24 people who have shaped your faith and reflect on your experiences with them as you prepare for Christ's coming on Christmas Day.

Prepare a base for the "faith tree" by covering a large coffee can with a piece of fabric or foil. Tie ribbon around the top of the material to hold it in place. Set the tree branch in the center of the can and fill the container with stones to anchor the limb. Cut shapes such as circles, squares, and triangles out of construction paper or felt. Write names of significant people on your faith journey every day for 24 days. Include people such as family members, church members, teachers, friends, neighbors, and so on. Add details with marker drawings, photos and illustrations, or decorative trims.

Poke a hole at the top of each symbol and attach an opened paper clip to serve as an ornament hanger. Choose a different symbol each day—in chronological order, if possible—and connect it to the branch. Complete the activity by looking up Bible passages on faith, including Hebrews 11.

Display the tree as a reminder of your personal connection to Jesus.

ANTIPHONS
(Worship/Education/Music)

Materials: Church history books, denominational books of worship, hymnals, paper, and pencils or pens.

An "antiphon" is a type of hymn or psalm that is sung responsively, in alternating parts. In the early history of the church, monks and other religious persons sang antiphons as morning and evening prayers. One of the most familiar antiphonal hymns still sung today is "Oh, Come, Oh, Come, Emmanuel." This Advent hymn is sung as a prayer to Christ to return to earth. There were many songs of this type in the Middle Ages; so many that they are usually grouped as the "O Antiphons," and many are still related to the Advent and Christmas seasons.

Traditionally, the "O Antiphon" begins with a name for God or Jesus, and is a prayerful plea for divine presence. Many names for God are used in the antiphons. Some names that address God follow: "O Wisdom, O Creator, O Rock of My Salvation." Some address Jesus: "O Sacred Lord, O Light, O Dayspring." Any name may be chosen as long as it characterizes a quality of the divine Trinity. After naming God, the antiphon often includes a descriptive phrase that further captures the characteristics suggested by the name for God. Also the antiphon usually includes a direct request of God, beginning with the word *come.* Refer to books of church history, Christmas devotions, and prayers, hymnals, or denominational books of worship for examples.

Today, the "O Antiphons" can be used as bedtime prayers, table graces, family devotions, classroom activities, or candle-lighting sentences during Advent. As a part of Christmas preparation and celebration, write some "O Antiphons" to use this season. Include a name for God and a phrase that captures an attribute of God or that relates to the chosen name. Next develop a request of God that begins with the word *come.* For example:

(Name of God)
O Source of peace,
(Attribute of God)
Whose presence calms our restless hearts,
(Request of God)
Come to our home this Christmas
As we open our lives to your gift of Jesus.

Use original "O Antiphons" as messages for packages and cards, as table place cards, or as spoken prayers. Consider reading the "O Antiphons" aloud antiphonally, dividing phrases between two individuals or groups.

> IN THE EARLY CHURCH, MONKS AND OTHER RELIGIOUS PERSONS SANG ANTIPHONS AS MORNING AND EVENING PRAYERS.

ADVENT

CRÈCHE COLLECTIONS

(Lower Elementary)

Nativity sets are used to tell the story of the birth of the babe of Bethlehem. Try some of these suggestions for creating a crèche collection for Christmas. Suggestions for characters include the following: Mary and Joseph (Matthew 1:18-25); baby Jesus; Elizabeth, Zechariah, and John the Baptist (Luke 1:5-80); Gabriel (Luke 1:26-35); Caesar (Luke 2:1-7); innkeeper; three shepherds, three angels (Luke 2:8-20); three Wise Men (Matthew 2:1-12); Herod (Matthew 2:1-23); Anna and Simeon (Luke 2:22-38); animals.

Preparation: Set up the stable on the first day of Advent. Add a figure to the scene each day until Christmas. Some of the characters could be set around the stable rather than inside. Place the infant in the manger on Christmas Eve or Christmas Day. The three Wise Men might be added on Epiphany, January 6.

Crèche Collections

During the Christmas season, discover the variety of Nativity sets available and the various materials from which they are made. Look for crèche collections representing these methods or materials: ceramic, felt, stained glass, corn husk, nails, blown glass, cut-outs, crochet, candles, sew and stuff, needlepoint, wood, stencil, corrugated cardboard, clothespins, decorated toys, cardboard tubes, stickers, puppets, cookies, and clay.

CLAY CRÈCHE

Materials: Paintbrushes, modeling clay, evergreen branches, moss, newspaper, paper towels, plastic drop cloths, shellac, various colors of tempera paint, waxed paper (optional), glue, and water.

Create a crèche from clay. Have the learners decide which figures will be made. Show the learners how to take a small amount of clay and form it into the shape of a ball. Push and pull the clay into figures 2-3 inches (5-7 cm) high. Have the learners roll the clay into a coil to use as arms and add them to the body by using a small amount of waterlike glue. Make hair, facial features, and decorations with clay, too. Allow the clay to harden. The hardened figures may be painted in bright colors and designs and covered with shellac. Create a Nativity scene with these figures. Spread evergreen branches and moss on a table and place the characters in the middle.

CLOTHESPIN CRÈCHE

Materials: Construction paper, fabric scraps, markers, pipe cleaners, scissors, shoe boxes, straw or sand, wooden clothespins with rounded tops, and yarn.

Create a crèche to use throughout the Christmas season by constructing figures from wooden clothespins. For each figure, have learners draw a face on the head or rounded top of the clothespin. Have the learners twist a pipe cleaner around the neck to form arms. Show learners how to cut a 2 x 6-inch (5 cm x 15 cm) rectangle of fabric. Fold it in half and cut a small slit in the center. Slide the head through the opening. Arrange the material over the arms. Secure it in place by tying a piece of yarn around the middle. Hair may be formed from yarn and glued to the top of the clothespin. A small piece of cloth may be draped over the top of the head and tied in place with yarn. Have the learners construct a variety of characters.

Form the stable by covering the shoe box with construction paper. Set it on its side and sprinkle the bottom with straw or sand. Place all of the characters inside and around the stable.

COOKIE DOUGH CRÈCHE

Materials: Cookie cutters, cookie decorations; 1 egg, 2¾ cups (.6 l) of flour, ⅔ cup (.16 l) of honey, 1 teaspoon (5 ml) of lemon flavoring, 1 teaspoon of salt, 1 teaspoon of baking soda, ⅓ cup (.08 l) of shortening, and ⅓ cup of sugar; mixing and baking equipment, utensils, and ribbon. This activity requires a kitchen area with a refrigerator and a stove.

Create a cookie dough crèche, hang the pieces as ornaments on a tree, and share the results with family and friends during and after the holiday season. Form groups of four. Wash all hands! Have the learners help mix shortening, sugar, egg, honey, and flavoring thoroughly. Stir together flour, soda, and salt, and blend into the shortening mixture. Chill dough. Heat oven to 375° F. (190° C.). Show the learners how to roll dough out ¼ inch (.5 cm) thick.

Distribute cookie cutters to each group. Have the learners use cookie cutters to make the shapes, or find pictures of the characters in used Sunday school material, coloring books, or flannelgraph sets, then make patterns from them. Allow learners to poke a hole into the top of their cookie so ribbon may be strung through it later.

Place the cookies 1 inch (2.5 cm) apart on a lightly greased baking sheet. Bake 8-10 minutes. When cool, have the learners ice and decorate as desired. Learners may share the treats with others.

Option: For molasses cookies, use brown sugar in place of granulated sugar, molasses for honey, two teaspoons of cinnamon and one teaspoon of ginger for lemon flavoring.

PIPE CLEANER CRÈCHE

Materials: Paintbrushes, cardboard pieces, construction paper scraps, crayons, markers or paints, fabric scraps, glue, pipe cleaners or chenille wires, scissors, a table, and tape.

Construct and display items representing the Christmas story and present them on a tabletop model in the home or church.

Form the figures of people and animals by bending and shaping the pipe cleaners. Add fabric and construction paper scraps to the chenille wire to make faces and clothing. Create animals using the same procedure.

In keeping with the customs of many cultures, include various people who represent all walks of life and cultures in the crèche. Remember that the Christ child welcomes everyone.

Place the characters on the top of a table. Decide on the type of scene that will surround the figures and create it from materials with interesting textures and shapes. Add trees, hills, water, buildings, and anything else that would enhance the model.

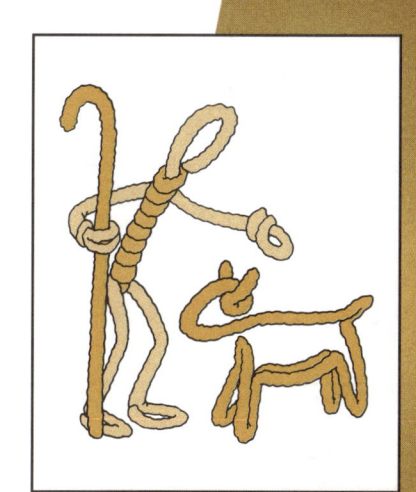

ADVENT

LEARNING CENTERS: THE FIVE SENSES

(Upper Elementary)

Many of our richest memories of the seasons are closely linked to the five senses: sight, sound, smell, taste, and touch. Arrange learning centers that explore all of the senses as a way to fully experience the seasons.

A learning center may be defined as the focal point of activity for the purpose of acquiring knowledge or skills. It must contain information on a topic and instructions for a task. A learning center needs to include the supplies and equipment necessary to complete an assignment or activity.

Learning centers may be created in many ways. They may be constructed on tabletops, desks, counters, bulletin boards, chalkboards, walls, or any other surface that will hold the essential elements. Learning centers may be extremely efficient, containing the bare essentials required for achieving the desired results, or extraordinarily elaborate with bountiful enhancements to supplement the anticipated outcomes.

DECORATED CANDLES (SIGHT)

Materials: Heavy juice glasses or tumblers, votive candles, tissue paper, gift wrap or napkins with holiday designs, scissors, white glue, paintbrushes, water, small bowls or margarine tubs, opalescent or white glitter, small foam plates, foil pie pans, and newspaper.

Preparation: Prepare the glue and water mixture in advance.

Candles glow throughout the season as a symbol for Jesus, the Light of the world. Create candles for decorations or for gifts.

Have the learners cut pictures from gift wrap or paper napkins. Be sure that the designs are in proportion to the size of the glass. Give each learner a small amount of glue in a container and thin with a little water. Have learners brush glue onto the outside of the glass and attach each paper design. Show them how to carefully position the paper shapes while the glue is wet. Then, gently brush glue over the entire surface of the paper and glass to be sure the design is fastened. Smooth away any wrinkles or bubbles.

Show learners how to place the fingers of their left hand (if right-handed) inside the glass, and spread them to hold the glass firmly. With the other hand, sprinkle glitter over the glued surface. Turn the glass to cover the sides completely. Place a pie pan or newspaper under the glass to catch the excess glitter. Tap to remove loose particles. Instruct the learners to place the glass on a foam plate or other nonstick surface to dry. Add the votive candle. If there is glitter near the bottom of the candleholder, use a coaster or other protection to keep from marring furniture. Also, when the votive burns down, add another candle to prevent the glass from getting too hot.

Leader Tip: Use caution with glass and remind everyone of candle safety!

ADVENT SONGS (SOUNDS)

Materials: Hangers, ribbon or yarn, construction paper or poster board, crayons or markers, scissors, hole punch, music for selected songs, resource materials on hymn stories.

Preparation: Cut patterns for musical shapes.

Music is a traditional part of waiting and celebrating Advent. Learn more about the songs of the season and make mobiles to symbolize their stories. Decide which carols and hymns to use and find information about them. Suggestions include "Come, Thou Long-Expected Jesus" (*Lutheran Book of Worship [LBW]* 30); "Comfort, Comfort Now My People" *LBW* 29); "Get Ready!" (*LifeSongs* 12); "Oh, Come, Oh, Come, Emmanuel" (*LifeSongs* 10; *LBW* 34); "We Light the Advent Candles" (*LifeSongs* 9).

Have the learners cut four shapes from construction paper or poster board. The shapes may help represent the message or symbolism of the music. Write the following information on three of the pieces: composer and biographical information; history of the carol; title and words. On the fourth shape, draw an illustration of the message of the song.

Punch a hole at the top of each shape and string a length of ribbon or yarn through it. Tie the four pieces to the hanger. Enjoy both the music and the message during the Advent season

LAVENDER SACHETS (SMELL)

Materials: Lavender (flowers or oil), small envelopes, poly or cotton balls, rubber stamps, purple ink pads, purple fine markers, hole punch, ribbon, and scissors.

Advent is a time of waiting for the coming of the Messiah. This period of preparation begins with quiet contemplation and progresses to the excitement of Christmas Day.

For centuries, the scent made from oils and flowers of the aromatic lavender plant has been used to calm and to soothe. Lavender is a favorite fragrance found in perfumes, bath soaps, and sachets.

Make fragrant lavender sachets with purple stamped designs as reminders to include peaceful times during the Advent season. Have each learner decorate several small envelopes (invitation size or smaller) with rubber stamps and purple ink. Choose stamps with symbols appropriate for the season, such as angels, candles, vines, stars and borders. Punch two holes in two corners of each envelope.

Distribute several poly or cotton balls for each sachet, dot with a few drops of lavender oil, and place in a prepared envelope. If dried flowers are used, place one tablespoon (15 ml) in each envelope. Have the learners seal the flap and tie a ribbon loop through the holes.

Place the sachet under a pillow or in a drawer, or hang it in the closet. Enjoy a whiff of Advent while going about the daily routine.

ADVENT

> USE "WAITING TIME" FOR LEARNERS TO DECORATE THE CONTAINERS AND GIFT TAGS.

REFRIGERATOR COOKIES (TASTE)

Materials: Recipe for cutout cookies, ingredients, work space and oven, mixing bowls and utensils, cookie cutters, rolling pin(s), baking sheets, sugar sprinkles, containers for finished cookies, art materials for decorating containers, gift tags.

Preparation: Prepare the cookie dough according to the recipe on the package. Allow the dough time to chill.

The waiting and expectation of Advent can be represented by the simple act of waiting for bread dough to rise and cookie dough to chill. We eagerly anticipate tasting the finished product. Make cutout cookies from the recipe provided, or use a favorite family recipe. Choose cookie cutter shapes to symbolize the story: an angel, star, camel, candle, and manger.

Wash hands. Roll out well-chilled dough and have learners cut shapes with floured cookie cutters. Give each learner at least two cookies to decorate. Follow the directions for baking. You could sing Christmas songs while cookies bake. Enjoy the taste of the warm cookies. Fill decorated containers with cookies to share with family and friends.

Leader Tip: Use "waiting time" for learners to decorate the containers and gift tags.

RECIPE FOR BROWN SUGAR CRISPS

Ingredients: 4 cups (1 l) sifted all-purpose flour, 1 teaspoon (5 ml) baking powder, 1 teaspoon salt, ¼ teaspoon (1.3 ml) baking soda, 2½ sticks margarine, 1½ cups (.36 l) firmly packed light brown sugar, 1 teaspoon maple extract, and 2 eggs.

Preparation: Form small groups so that each group may perform a task in cookie making.

Sift flour, baking powder, salt, and baking soda together. Cream margarine and sugar; add maple extract and eggs. Beat well. Add flour mixture, beating until blended. Cover the dough with plastic wrap and chill for several hours or overnight.

Wash hands. Lightly flour the work surface and roll out a small amount of dough to ⅛ inch (.3 cm) thickness. To prevent dough from sticking to the rolling pin, add flour as needed. Have learners cut shapes with floured cookie cutters and decorate with colored sugar. Bake at 350° F. (175° C.) for 8-10 minutes, on a greased cookie sheet. Makes 8-10 dozen.

Leader Tip: To save time, roll the cookie dough into a log and chill; cut thin slices with a sharp knife and bake according to recipe.

EVERGREEN PRINTS (TOUCH)

Materials: Paintbrushes, cleanup supplies, evergreen branches, heavy books, newspaper, paint (fabric paint for sweatshirts or other cloth projects), paper or cloth items, heavy white paper, pencils, scrap paper.

Preparation: Cut and fold heavy white paper for notes and greeting cards.

Preparations for Christmas would not seem complete without the varied textures and distinctive fragrance of evergreens. In advance, gather small cuttings from evergreens. Blue spruce, cedar, or juniper will work well for this project.

Have the learners decide what the finished project should be: greeting cards, notepaper, place mats, sweat- or T-shirts, or wrapping paper. To make wrapping paper, separate sheets of tissue paper and place over newspaper before printing. For printing on sweatshirts or other cloth articles, follow directions on fabric paint containers. Choose evergreen boughs that are small enough to print on the paper or fabric that has been prepared. Flatten branches of evergreens between several sheets of newspaper that are weighted down with heavy books or irons.

Experiment on scrap paper to find the right color and the correct amount of paint. Brush paint on one side of the evergreen branch; firmly press onto the paper or fabric. After printing, lift the branch carefully to prevent the lines from smudging. Make fingerprint dots for berries or paint tiny pinecones for added interest. Allow the paint to dry. Enjoy the textured evergreen prints and make extras to give as gifts.

CHRISTMAS
ADVENT CHRISTMAS EPIPHANY LENT EASTER PENTECOST

Christmas is the 12-day season from December 25 until January 6. As carols are sung, the Christmas story read, and the birth of Christ celebrated, Christians rejoice that God sent us the promised Messiah in the form of a baby named Jesus. Jesus is the fulfillment of a promise that God made hundreds of years earlier. God, who formed the universe and who was saddened to see creation fall, designed a plan for redemption through the birth, life, death, and resurrection of Jesus.

We learn in Advent that the prophets told people to get ready because a Messiah was coming, the chosen one of Israel who would lead God's people to find hope and peace. In the 12 days of the Christmas season, we have the opportunity to share again and again the joy of knowing that God faithfully kept the promise to send a Savior—and we know him to be Jesus! Jesus, God-in-flesh, came to earth to bring hope, to show us the way, and to be the way.

Scripture passages related to the story of Jesus' birth and the events that preceded and followed it include Matthew 1:1-2; Luke 1 and 2; and John 1:1-14. Each reading or telling of the Christmas story invites us to recognize anew that we are the ones who need the Savior, we are the ones whom "God so loved." At Christmas God opens our hearts to the rebirth of the joy of knowing that Christ came to be our Savior. The color for Christmas is white, representing holiness.

CHRISTMAS SONGS

"Away in a Manger"
(With One Voice 644)

"Go Tell It on the Mountain"
(LifeSongs 23)

"Joy to the World"
(Lutheran Book of Worship [LBW] 39)

"Oh, Come, All Ye Faithful"
(LBW 45)

"Silent Night, Holy Night!"
(LBW 65)

All suggested hymns are included in either Lutheran Book of Worship, With One Voice, or LifeSongs, as well as in many other Christian hymnals.

YULE LOG TREATS

(Pre-Elementary)

Materials: One stick of butter or margarine, cinnamon red-hot candies, 6 cups (1.4 l) of crispy rice cereal, decorator tubes, frosting, green food coloring, knife, 4 cups (1 l) of miniature marshmallows, 1 teaspoon (5 ml) of vanilla, waxed paper, measuring cups, frying pan, platter, wooden spoon, and stove.

Preparation: Have the learners thoroughly wash their hands. Assemble the equipment and the ingredients. Tear off one piece of waxed paper for each learner. Have enough measuring cups for learners to share.

Foods give a special flavor to the Christmas season. They can be used as the focal point of a gathering at church, home, or school; or can be given as gifts. This simple Yule log recipe is easy to make and could serve as a festive treat or a fantastic gift.

Create a batch of treats with a group of pre-elementary learners. Learners may be involved in measuring the ingredients, but one or more adults should be responsible for the portion of the project that involves the use of the stove. After the cooking process, the children may shape the Yule logs and decorate them.

Have the learners gather at the worktable. Guide the learners as they measure 4 cups of miniature marshmallows and 6 cups of crispy rice cereal. Show learners how butter is melted in a pan. Have the learners watch as an adult melts the butter in a large frying pan. Add marshmallows and continue stirring until they are melted. Remove from heat. Add vanilla. Stir in the cereal. Mix well and let cool to room temperature. Place a small mound of the mixture on each learner's piece of waxed paper. Monitor the temperature before the children touch the mixture. Show the learners how to form the crispy rice cereal into the shape of a log. Assist the learners as needed.

Fill the decorator tubes with green frosting and show the learners how to form holly leaves across the top of each log. Have the learners place cinnamon red-hot candies to add as the berries. Place the completed logs on a platter to share with others or offer a prayer and eat the treats together.

Leader Tip: When melting the butter and marshmallows, adjust the heat so that it does not splatter or burn.

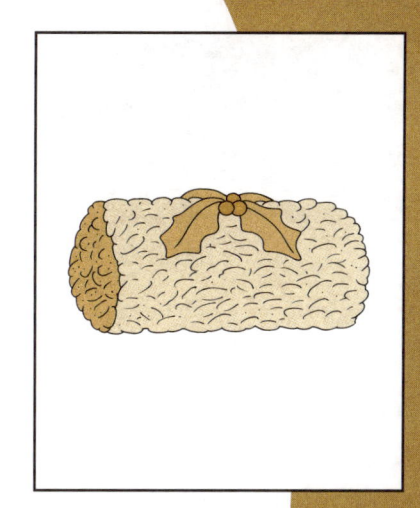

CHRISTMAS

ANGEL ORNAMENTS

(Lower Elementary)

Materials: Glitter, rickrack or sequins, pipe cleaners, glue, paper clips, ribbon or yarn, white paper doilies, small paper plate halves, pattern for angel, photographs of learners, 8½ x 5-inch (22 x 13 cm) white poster board for each learner, scissors, stapler, and staples.

Preparation: Take an individual head shot photo of each learner in advance. Cut out the head shots and have angel patterns available for each learner.

Angels announced the birth of the baby Jesus in biblical times. Use angel ornaments as reminders that it is everyone's responsibility to spread the message of the Messiah today.

Distribute angel patterns to each learner and have them trace the pattern on the poster board, then cut the angel out. Show the learners how to glue their photos to the head of the angel. Fold the paper plate half into a cone shape, staple it shut and attach it to the bottom of the angel shape. Add glitter, rickrack, sequins, or pipe cleaners around the head to form a halo. Back the poster board, especially the wing area, with pieces of paper doilies. Punch a hole in the top of the head. Use an opened paper clip or a piece of ribbon or yarn, placed through the hole, to attach the angel to the tree.

Have the learners keep the ornaments as keepsakes or give them to someone special in their lives.

> HAVE THE LEARNERS KEEP THE ORNAMENTS AS KEEPSAKES OR GIVE THEM TO SOMEONE SPECIAL IN THEIR LIVES.

CHRISTMAS

Reproducible Page, for use with "Angel Ornament," *Six Seasons of Fun! Activities, Crafts, and More* © 2002 Augsburg Fortress. May be reproduced for local use.

21

CHRISTMAS

SCRIPTURE SCRIPTS

(Upper Elementary)

In Christian congregations and communities throughout the world, the Christmas story is retold through programs and pageants. Children of all ages are involved in playing parts and singing songs that proclaim the good news of the Savior's birth.

Experience the story of the Nativity through the use of drama. Create an easy script from the words of Luke 2:1-20 by following four simple steps. The goal is to break the Bible verses into character parts so that the passage will be more understandable to those hearing it. The object is not to embellish the text and to add details that are not suggested, but to adhere as closely as possible to the words of the Bible.

SCRIPTURE SCRIPTS STEPS

Step One: Identify the characters in the passage and make a list of these people.

Step Two: Find all of the quotes in the passage. Match a character to each of them. Write the person's name on the left side of a paper, and write the words of the quote next to it. Try to break long passages into several parts.

Step Three: Write lines for any portion of the passage that could be assigned to a specific person. Clues to look for are verbs. These words suggest that the narrative could be written in dialogue form.

Step Four: Add a narrator, or several, to provide information between the speaking parts.

A sample script, based on Luke 2:1-20, is provided. Take turns playing the parts: Narrator, Caesar Augustus, Joseph, Mary, Angels, and Shepherds. Drape pieces of fabric over the actors' heads and shoulders to create simple costumes. If additional costume suggestions are needed, refer to page 41 of the Epiphany section of this book for ideas.

SAMPLE SCRIPT

Caesar Augustus:
A census must be taken of the entire Roman world. Everyone must go to his or her own town to register.

Joseph:
Mary, we must go from Nazareth to Bethlehem, because I am of the house and line of David.

Mary:
It will be a long journey for me since my baby is due to be born very soon.

Narrator:
Upon arriving in Bethlehem, Joseph and Mary discovered that there was no room for them in the inn.

> CREATE AN EASY SCRIPT FROM THE WORDS OF LUKE 2:1-20 BY FOLLOWING FOUR SIMPLE STEPS.

Reproducible Page, for use with "Scripture Scripts," *Six Seasons of Fun! Activities, Crafts, and More*
© 2002 Augsburg Fortress. May be reproduced for local use.

Joseph:
We will stay in the stable where the cattle are kept.

Narrator:
While they were there, the time came for the baby to be born, and Mary gave birth to her firstborn, a son.

Mary:
Let us wrap the baby in cloth to keep him warm.

Joseph:
We can place him in the manger.

Narrator:
There were shepherds living out in the fields nearby, keeping watch over their flocks.

Shepherd One:
One night an angel of the Lord appeared to us, and the glory of the Lord shone around us, and we were terrified.

Angel:
Do not be afraid, I bring you good news of great joy that will be for all people. Today in the town of David, a Savior has been born to you; he is Christ the Lord. This will be a sign to you: You will find a baby wrapped in cloths and lying in a manger.

Shepherd Two:
A great company of the heavenly host appeared with the angel, praising God, saying:

Angels:
Glory to God in the highest, and on earth peace to God's people.

Narrator:
When the angels returned to heaven, the shepherds said to one another:

Shepherd One:
Let's go to Bethlehem and see this thing that has happened, which the Lord has told us about.

Shepherd Two:
We hurried and found Mary and Joseph and the baby, who was lying in the manger.

Shepherd One:
After we worshiped the baby, we spread the word concerning what had been told to us about this child. All who heard it were amazed at what we said to them.

Mary:
I will treasure all of these things and ponder them in my heart.

Narrator:
The shepherds returned, glorifying and praising God for all that they had heard and seen, which was just as they had been told.

> THE SHEPHERDS RETURNED, GLORIFYING AND PRAISING GOD FOR ALL THAT THEY HAD HEARD AND SEEN.

Reproducible Page, for use with "Scripture Scripts," *Six Seasons of Fun! Activities, Crafts, and More*
© 2002 Augsburg Fortress. May be reproduced for local use.

CHRISTMAS

BASIC BULLETIN BOARD SUPPLIES:

- STAPLER AND STAPLES
- PUSHPINS OR DRESSMAKER PINS
- CUT OR PRECUT LETTERS
- CONSTRUCTION PAPER
- MARKERS
- SCISSORS

BULLETIN BOARDS
(Combination Age Groups)

Bulletin boards provide an excellent way to reinforce a seasonal theme and to decorate wall space. Displays can be simple, as well as elaborate, with handmade or purchased components. Try cooperative or interactive arrangements that allow for many learners to contribute to the final results.

Simplify the preparation of bulletin board backgrounds by using large rolls of paper such as wallpaper, gift wrap, or paper from a paper supply store. A bulletin board can be made quickly by covering framed areas with paper tablecloths, fabric, or poster board. Keep captions short in order to get the attention of the viewers and avoid cutting dozens of letters. Investigate craft shops, teaching materials stores, or office supply centers for die-cut and pin-back letters. Check with local schools or resource centers for a machine that cuts several letters at once. Add three-dimensional items for special interest; place a border around the edge to give the project a finished look.

Try any or all of these five bulletin board suggestions to help people experience the Christmas message through sight, smell, sound, taste, and touch.

INSPIRATIONAL BULLETIN BOARD (SIGHT)

Materials: Old Christmas cards, greeting cards, magazines, velvet fabric, gold paper lace place mats, gold ribbon, gold lace doilies, letters, pushpins or dressmaker pins, and letters for a theme.

Make use of beautiful old Christmas cards, pictures from curriculum packets or old issues of magazines for a simple and inspirational bulletin board.

Cover the bulletin board with velvet fabric for a look of elegance. Secure the fabric in place using dressmaker pins or pushpins. Use gold ribbon to make a border. Have the learners cut various pictures or scenes from Christmas cards, magazines, and so on. Show the learners how to mount larger pictures on gold paper lace place mats or frame the pictures with wide gold ribbon. Pictures from greeting cards can be mounted on gold lace doilies to resemble ornaments or medallions. Allow ample space for a caption and scripture reference. Do not place pictures too close together so the beauty of each one can be appreciated separately.

Choose a caption and cut out letters or write on paper the caption. It should relate to the theme of the pictures featured. For example, write "See Christ's Star" if most of the illustrations include Bethlehem, stars, and Wise Men; "Behold, I bring you good news" would be appropriate for pictures of the angels and the shepherds.

Option: Use reproductions of paintings by famous artists for a holiday theme.

GRAFFITI BOARD (SMELL)

Materials: White paper from a large roll, garland of evergreens, candy canes or round peppermints, red ribbon, a red bow, stapler and a black marker, 3- or 4-inch (7-10 cm) red letters that spell: "Christmas smells like...."

Think of how many Christmas memories are associated with a particular scent: pine, citrus, peppermint, spices, fresh baked goods, special holiday foods, and bayberry candles.

Cover a bulletin board with white paper. Arrange a garland of real or artificial evergreens around the frame. Real evergreens will smell great, but might shed. Attach small wrapped peppermint candies or candy canes to the garland for color as well as for a sweet scent.

Cut or purchase 3- or 4-inch red letters for the caption: "Christmas smells like...." Use a long red ribbon to tie on a red marking pen. Invite the learners to write Christmas scent memories on this graffiti board. Top off the board with a big red bow.

MAKE A JOYFUL NOISE UNTO THE LORD (SOUND)

Materials: Large roll of red paper or fabric, artificial evergreens or green construction paper, musical instrument ornaments, construction paper, pushpins or stapler and staples, letters that spell: "Make a Joyful Noise unto the Lord!"

Cover a bulletin board with red paper or fabric. Form artificial evergreens into a large wreath, covering most of the board. Another option is to have learners trace their handprints on green construction paper and then cut them out to form a wreath. Fasten the wreath securely to the center portion of the board using stapler or pins. Decorate the wreath with musical instrument ornaments.

Position the scripture from Psalm 100: "Make a Joyful Noise unto the Lord!" in the center of the wreath, directly on the red paper or on a separate sheet of paper. Use a marker with a wide tip, a calligraphy pen, or small cutout letters. Have the learners cut small musical notes from construction paper for a border or to scatter in the open areas.

Option: Use the bulletin board as a backdrop for announcements of church musical events or community concerts. Make the wreath smaller and staple the announcements around the edges.

RECIPE EXCHANGE (TASTE)

Materials: Red and white checkered tablecloth or one with a Christmas design, construction paper; dressmaker pins; stapler; large white, green, or red paper plate; foam or paper cup; plastic knife, spoon, and fork; a holiday napkin; baskets of index cards, pens, pencils, and tacks.

Cover the bulletin board with a red and white checkered tablecloth or one with a Christmas design. In the center of the cover, fasten a table setting: large white, red or green paper plate; foam or paper cup; plastic knife, spoon, and fork; holiday napkin. Use long dressmaker pins to attach items that cannot be stapled.

Print or cut letters for "Holiday Favorites" or "A Taste of Christmas" with a subtitle:

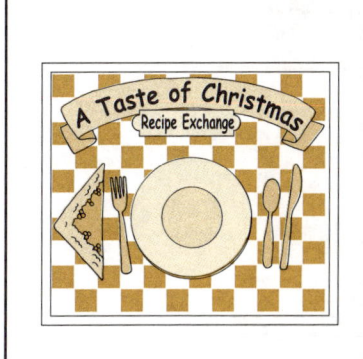

"Recipe Exchange." Place a table for supplies under the bulletin board. Provide baskets of index cards, pens, pencils, and tacks. Invite learners and church members to write out a favorite family recipe, sign their names, and add it to the display. When the bulletin board fills up with a variety of recipes, gather up the cards and have photocopies made.

Option: For a true "Taste of Christmas," plan to have samples of the foods as well as recipes available at a special holiday event! Assign several families to create this arrangement and to duplicate and distribute the recipes.

CHRISTMAS STORY IN TEXTURES (TOUCH)

Materials: Light or dark blue roll of paper, traditional Nativity picture, feathers, blankets, burlap fabric, fleece or wool, straw or hay, wood slats, satins, brocade and velvet fabric, jewels, a book about the Christmas story, duct tape, and staples.

Preparation: Have learners bring in squares of cloth from old clothes in advance. Group the cloth by textures.

Experiment with a tactile display that encourages everyone to "Please Touch!" Cover the bulletin board with light or dark blue paper and in the center staple a traditional picture.

Create a random collage or "crazy quilt" of textures surrounding the picture. Choose textures that relate to the Christmas story: feathers for angels; soft blanket for the baby Jesus; rough fabric for the clothing of Joseph and the shepherds; fleece or wool for the sheep; straw or hay and wood slats for the crib; satins, brocades, velvets, and jewels for the kings.

Read the Christmas story to the learners and ask them to think of different types of materials. Have the learners contribute to the display by bringing in a square of cloth from old clothes. Use duct tape or staples to fasten materials so that there are no sharp points to injure exploring fingers!

The collage will have a balanced look if materials, colors, and textures are repeated across the board. Add the words: "Please Touch!" Place the caption under the bulletin board frame or write the words on a band of wide ribbon and fasten it diagonally across one corner.

CHRISTMAS CUSTOMS AROUND THE WORLD

(Intergenerational)

Celebrate Christmas with an event to help the entire Sunday school—and the congregation—explore and experience some of the ways in which Christ's birth is commemorated around the world. Use this unique framework—Gather! Explore! Celebrate! Share!—during one or more church school sessions, as a special children's or intergenerational program, or as an exciting educational event during Christmas break.

Gather!

Gather the participants in the sanctuary for music and an explanation of the program. Sing carols with international origins, such as: "From Heaven Above to Earth I Come" (Germany); "Infant Holy, Infant Lowly" (Poland); "Joyful Christmas Day Is Here" (Japan); "O Holy Night" (France); "The First Noel" (England); and "Silent Night, Holy Night!" (Austria). Besides congregational singing, music may be presented by choirs, soloists, small groups, and instrumentalists.

Explore!

Continue the event in a large room, such as a social hall, or individual classrooms, where a variety of "Christmas around the World" learning activities have been prepared in advance. Displays related to international customs may also be exhibited.

FLANNELGRAPH FIGURES (AUSTRALIA)

Materials: Bible storybooks, felt, flannelgraph background, glue, markers, *The Nativity* (Vivas, Julie, illustrator. San Diego: Harcourt Brace Jovanovich, 1986), paper, interfacing, pencils, sandpaper, and scissors.

Preparation: Have two flannelgraph figures available.

Australian illustrator Julie Vivas captures the spirit of the Christmas story in a lovely picture book, *The Nativity*. Read the story aloud and show learners the pictures. Have the learners make felt renderings of some of the characters and use them to retell the story using the flannelgraph. Have older learners prepare patterns for the main characters of the book by drawing them freehand or tracing the illustrations.

Show the learners how to copy the figures onto the interfacing material. Have learners color and highlight the pieces and cut them out. Show the learners how to back the shapes with small pieces of sandpaper or felt so they will adhere to the background material. Place the figures on the background at the appropriate times in the story.

Option: Allow learners to make individual sets of characters to retell the story at home or as a witnessing tool to someone they know in their neighborhood.

CHRISTMAS

TISSUE PAPER FLOWERS (BRAZIL)

Materials: Green floral tape, 12 inches (30 cm) of florists' wire, paper, pencils, petal patterns, scissors, various colors of tissue paper, green floral tape.

Preparation: Enlarge or reduce petal pattern to desired size and cut them out. Cut florists' wire for each learner. Have four different ready-made flowers in various colors available.

Crafts from Brazil reflect the influence of the country's native, European, and African inhabitants. Tissue paper flowers serve as a reminder of the culture and the customs of Brazil. The flowers suggest the bright blossoms that bloom during the Christmas season. The flowers can be used as table decorations or tree ornaments.

Distribute the petal patterns and have the learners cut them out and trace them on tissue paper. For a fuller flower, have the learners cut two or three of each petal. Show the learners how to put the decorations together in order, with the largest as the base of the flower. Distribute florists' wire.

Show learners how to place the wire underneath the base of the flower, and run the wire up through the center of all the petals. Then, run the wire back down in the center to form a small loop. Twist the two pieces of wire together and cover the stem with green floral tape.

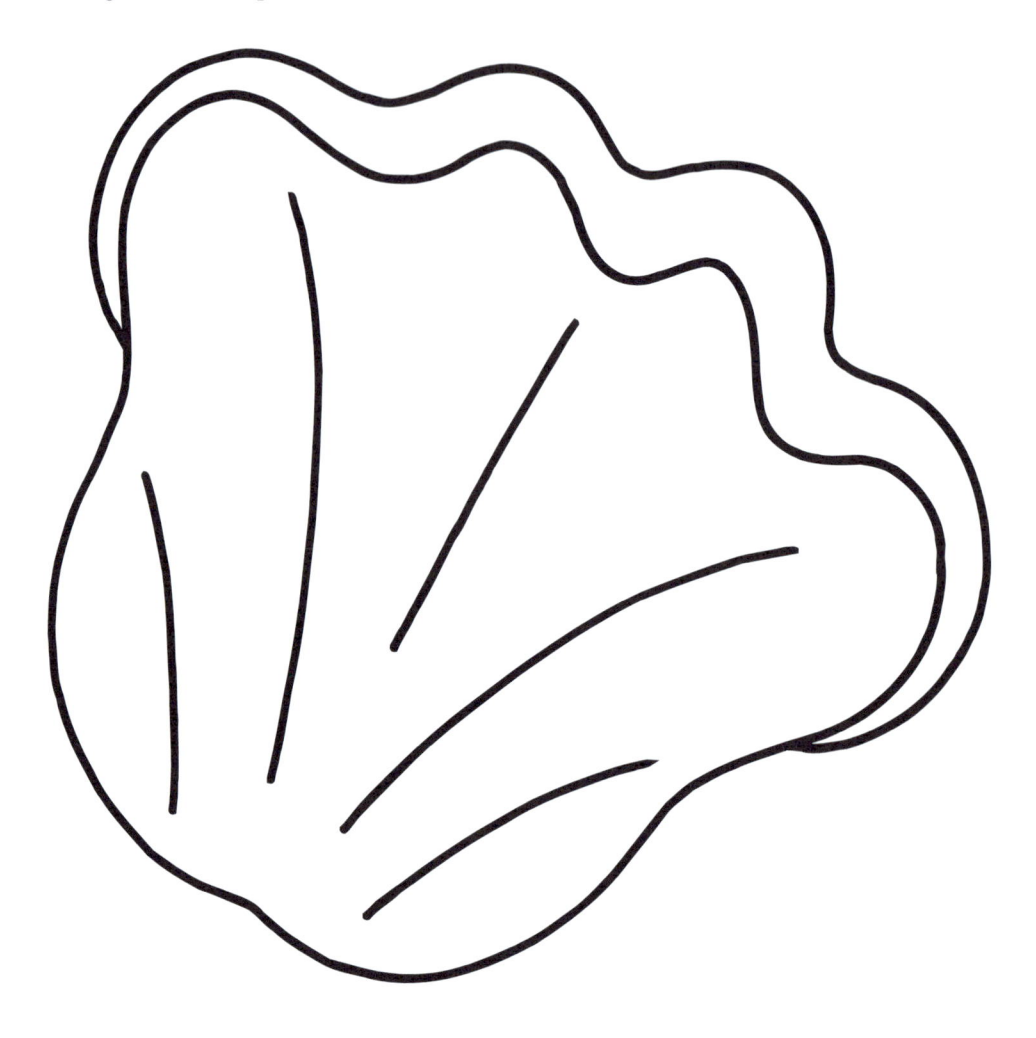

Reproducible Page, for use with "Tissue Paper Flowers," *Six Seasons of Fun! Activities, Crafts, and More*
© 2002 Augsburg Fortress. May be reproduced for local use.

CHRISTMAS

CHRISTMAS

STAINED-GLASS WINDOW DESIGN (FRANCE)

Materials: Various colors of construction paper, glue or glue sticks, markers, scissors, tape, and colorful tissue paper.

Preparation: Cut each learner a 4 x 4-inch (10 cm x 10 cm) square of black construction paper.

Stained glass is an art form in which pieces of tinted glass are assembled in a lead frame to form a picture or design. Daylight or artificial light that passes through the glass is transformed into an array of color. Stained-glass windows often depict scenes from Bible stories. Use the directions below and make a Christmas card that resembles a stained-glass window.

Begin with a 4 x 4 square of black construction paper. Have the learners fold it corner to corner to form a triangle. Show learners how to cut a circle out of the paper. With the black paper still folded into the triangle shape, or smaller, cut a design such as a star or a snowflake. Tell the learners to cut on the folds as well as on the edge of the black paper. Have the learners unfold the paper and glue or tape colored tissue paper pieces behind each opening of the design. Show the learners how to fold a piece of construction paper in half and glue the stained-glass piece to the front of it. Have the learners write a message on the inside of the card before it is delivered or mailed.

TUBE PUPPET (MEXICO)

Materials: Craft sticks or dowel rods, fabric scraps, felt, glue, any size cardboard tubes for each learner, scissors, yarn, or fake fur.

In Mexico small gifts for children are left at the manger scene on Christmas morning. The real gifts are given by the three kings on Epiphany, January 6. On the night of January 5, children fill their shoes with straw from the manger and leave it as an offering for the camels. In the morning, the straw is gone and the shoes are buried in mounds of gifts. Make a wise old puppet and tell the story of the gift giver of Mexico.

Distribute cardboard tubes. Show the learners how to form the puppet face by cutting a piece of felt and gluing it to the top one-third of the tube. Have the learners make facial features from felt scraps and glue them in place. Tell the learners to glue yarn or fake fur for hair and attach to the top of the tube.

Show the learners how to glue a piece of felt around the remainder of the tube to serve as the undergarment. Layers of fabric in contrasting or complementary colors can be added as clothing. Make arms from strips of cloth or felt, and glue them to the sides of the tube.

Apply a craft stick to the inside back of the tube to serve as the rod by which the puppet is operated. Leave about 2 inches (5 cm) of the craft stick exposed.

Options: If felt is not available, use construction paper instead. The facial features may be drawn on with marker. Substitute tissue paper for fabric to form the outer garments.

VIDEO BOX MURAL (NIGERIA)

Materials: Cardboard box, cardboard or wood scraps, dowel rods, knife, markers, paper, and tape.

Preparation: Note the video box mural pictured on the cover of this resource. Cut the flaps off the cardboard box and cut a large square out of the center of the bottom of the box. Leave a 2- or 3-inch (5-7 cm) border around the entire area. Turn the box on its side, so that the bottom now becomes the front, the viewing area.

The birthday of the Savior is an occasion for great joy and celebration in Nigeria. Church services on Christmas involve large pageants with many scenes. Worship services and programs provide wonderful ways to celebrate the gospel story and to share the good news with relatives and friends. Singing and dancing are part of all festive occasions in Africa, and Christmas is no exception.

Use a video box to share some of the Christmas customs of Nigeria. A video box combines a series of drawings that tell a story with a method for showing them that is similar to a television screen. The box may range in size from a tiny matchbox to a huge cardboard carton. The instructions below are for a large box that can display many drawings.

Make a set of parallel holes in the top and bottom of the box on both sides of the window. Place a dowel rod through each set of holes. Secure them in place with tape, or a cardboard or wooden stop. Have learners use markers to illustrate each custom on individual sheets of paper, or use a roll of paper. If using individual sheets, tape them together to form a long roll. Attach the beginning of the mural to one dowel rod and the end to the other. Wind the mural through the box to tell the story.

CHRISTMAS HEART BASKETS (SWEDEN)

Materials: Three-inch x eight-inch (8 cm x 20 cm) rectangles of red and green construction paper, glue, pencils, and scissors.

Christmas heart baskets are a traditional Swedish decoration as well as a gift. Have learners fold the construction paper pieces in half. Show learners how to use a pencil to draw a dotted line 1 inch (2.5 cm) from the unfolded end of each rectangle. Hold both pieces together and cut a rounded arch on the open end above this line. Be sure both pieces are the same size.

Beginning at the fold, show learners how to cut two slits 1 inch from each side of each paper. Cut up to the dotted line on each slit, being careful not to cut all the way through. The paper will be divided into three equal strips.

Have learners weave the three strips of each paper through each other to form a heart shape. Carefully open the basket and smooth out the weaving.

Each learner should cut a ½ inch (1 cm) wide strip of construction paper and glue it to the top of the basket to form a handle. The complete Christmas heart basket may be filled with candies and hung on the tree or given as a gift as a reminder of God's loving gift of Jesus.

Option: Use blue and yellow construction paper for the colors of Sweden.

CHRISTMAS

Celebrate!

At the conclusion of the activity time, form a procession, and journey from the social hall to the sanctuary for a time of worship including carols, scripture reading, prayers, and a brief devotion.

Share!

Following worship, invite the participants to the social hall to share refreshments or a meal. Provide desserts and dishes from around the world.

GO TELL IT ON THE MOUNTAIN

(Worship/Education/Music)

Materials: Markers, music to "Go Tell It on the Mountain," and poster board.

Share the story of the Christmas carol "Go Tell It on the Mountain," with your entire congregation. This could be led by the pastor, a director of Christian education, or a Sunday school teacher. Add movements to interpret each phrase and engage the congregation in singing the song and adding the gestures.

The Christmas carol "Go Tell It on the Mountain" is an African-American spiritual. A spiritual is a religious song that expresses deep emotion, and contains a combination of rhythmic music and words.

John Wesley Work II arranged and published the music for the song in the early 1900s. He was a Latin and Greek professor at Fisk University in Nashville, Tenn. Add simple movements to "Go Tell It On The Mountain" and proclaim the Christmas story through music and gestures. Use these or make up your own!

GESTURES

Go
(Extend hands, palms up, in front of body)

Tell it
(Cup hands to mouth)

On the mountain
(Extend hands over head to form a triangle)

Over the hills
(Move hands up and down in front of body in a ripple motion to form hills)

And everywhere.
(Extend arm in front of body, palm up, and then to mouth)

(Then repeat the motions for the first three lines and add:)
That Jesus Christ is born.
(Mimic movement of rocking a baby)

EPIPHANY

ADVENT CHRISTMAS EPIPHANY LENT EASTER PENTECOST

Epiphany begins on January 6 and immediately follows the 12 days of Christmas. In many churches, Epiphany is celebrated until the beginning of Lent, although some congregations observe a season of "ordinary time" between the festival of the Epiphany and the first day of the Lenten season, Ash Wednesday.

Epiphany means literally "appearance" or "revelation." Other words to describe this time in the church year include "manifestation" or "showing forth." At this time, Christians celebrate the visit of the Wise Men from the East to the Christ child in Bethlehem, signifying that God has been revealed to all the nations in Jesus. The magi, or Wise Men, saw the star that foretold this birth and they followed its light until they found the special child God had sent. The fact that they came from far away and from different cultures was God's way of revealing that the Savior was for everyone who believes and follows, not just a chosen few.

Epiphany also celebrates that Jesus didn't remain a small child, but grew to be a man who had a mission to fulfill for God. At Jesus' baptism, God revealed that Jesus was the Son of God. Epiphany reminds us that Jesus was born to save the world. The season of Epiphany is a time of celebrating new revelations of God's presence among us.

For the festival of Epiphany, the appropriate color is white, although gold is sometimes used as the color of the star and the gift brought the Christ child. Those churches that designate part of this season as ordinary time often use green as the interim color prior to Lent.

EPIPHANY SONGS

"As with Gladness Men of Old" (Lutheran Book of Worship [LBW] 82)

"Brightest and Best of the Stars of the Morning" (LBW 84)

"Shine, Jesus, Shine" (LifeSongs 38)

"This Little Light of Mine" (LifeSongs 32, 33)

"We Three Kings of Orient Are" (With One Voice [WOV] 646)

All suggested hymns are included in either Lutheran Book of Worship, With One Voice, or LifeSongs, as well as in many other Christian hymnals.

EPIPHANY

FOLLOW THE STAR

(Pre-Elementary)

Materials: Dowel rod or pole, and a star.

Play a game similar to "Follow the Leader." Provide a large star on a dowel rod or pole for one learner to carry. The group can pretend to be the Wise Men who followed the star. As the leader guides the group through the room, he or she should direct the participants in many different gestures and movements. Be sure everyone willing has a turn to be the leader.

Younger children may enjoy wearing crowns during the activity while older children might like to create their own headpieces to display.

Option: As the children are following the star, softly play the music to "We Three Kings of Orient Are" from *LifeSongs* 30.

SCAVENGER SEARCH

(Pre-Elementary)

Materials: Bible(s) and items associated with Epiphany stories.

Preparation: Read and review Bible passages and children's books related to Epiphany in advance.

Refer to the account of the visit of the Wise Men, Matthew 2:1-12, the description of Jesus' baptism, Matthew 3:13-17, or the narrative about the miracle at the wedding at Cana, John 2:1-11.

Select a story and make a list of items associated with it. For example, symbols connected with the story of the magi would be a crown, a map, and a star. For Jesus' baptism they might include a baptismal font, a bowl of water, or a dove. The wedding at Cana miracle could be represented by a clay jar, a pitcher of water, and a wedding picture.

Explain that as a story is read or told, the leader will stop, call out an object, and ask the group to search for the item in the room. The leader could also share the entire story in which the items to be found would be named; then the learners would be instructed to find them. Before the game begins, review the guidelines such as time limit, location boundaries, number of items per person, safety issues such as walking instead of running, and so forth. Answer any questions that will clarify the procedure.

Once the items are located, gather the group and discuss each object's connection to the story of Epiphany. Older children with reading skills may enjoy sharing the story, or verses of it, with the class.

GLASS AND FOIL LANTERN

(Lower Elementary)

Materials: Baby food jars, glue, heavy duty foil, hole punches, matches (optional), pencils, ribbon, tape, tissue paper, and votive candles.

Preparation: Clean jars thoroughly and remove the labels. Cut foil and tissue paper for each learner, depending on the size of the jar.

Since light is an important symbol of the season of Epiphany, make a unique candle to use at church, home, or school, or to give as a special gift.

Distribute baby food jars and a strip of bright-colored tissue paper long enough to wrap around the jar. Guide the learners in cutting the foil so it is about 1 inch (2.5 cm) taller than the container; fold under ½ inch along the top and bottom edges. Show the learners how to draw simple pictures or symbols, such as a crown or a star, across the foil using a blunt pencil. Follow along the pattern with a hole punch to create a see-through design.

Show the learners how to wrap the tissue paper around the jar and fasten with a little white glue. Cover the tissue with the punched foil and tape it at the seam to keep it from slipping. Tie ribbon around the neck of the jar to keep the materials in place. Place a votive candle in the bottom of the lantern. Tell the learners to light the candle only if adult supervision is available. The candlelight will shine through the colored tissue and highlight the pattern formed by the dots.

Option: Adapt the project for older children by using larger jars and forming words, such as *Epiphany, reveal,* or *world,* with the dot designs.

> SINCE LIGHT IS AN IMPORTANT SYMBOL OF EPIPHANY, MAKE A UNIQUE CANDLE TO GIVE AS A SPECIAL GIFT.

EPIPHANY

"WE THREE KINGS" STAR-SHAPED POEM

(Upper Elementary)

Materials: Music for "We Three Kings of Orient Are," paper, pattern for six-pointed star, pencils or pens, gold markers, poster board, and scissors.

Preparation: Make copies of the six-pointed star pattern for each learner. Cut poster board into 8½ x 5-inch (20 x 13 cm) rectangles, one per learner.

One of the most familiar Epiphany carols is "We Three Kings of Orient Are." The verses of the song describe the gifts that the Wise Men brought to the Christ child: gold, frankincense, and myrrh.

Their three gifts help us understand even more about why Jesus was born. Gold was a gift for Jesus our king. Frankincense was a gift for Jesus our priest. Myrrh was a precious gift for Jesus our Savior.

Sing the song "We Three Kings of Orient Are" together, and then write a star-shaped poem as an offering to Jesus. Take turns talking about the gifts that each person could offer to our Savior: hands, heart, love, obedience, special belongings, talents, time, and voice.

Give each learner a six-pointed shaped star and a piece of poster board. Tell the learners to cut the star out and trace it on poster board. Have the learners write a poem reflecting the gift(s) one might bring to Jesus like those that the magi brought at the first Epiphany. Use the rhyme of the carol's lyrics to compose a new stanza for the poem.

For example:
I am small with little to bring,
But this song of praise I sing:
Alleluia! Alleluia!
Worship the newborn king!

Write the words of the poem around the shape of the poster-board star. Take time to share the shape poems with others in the class.

Younger children might enjoy talking about a gift that they could give to Jesus, such as love, and printing the letters around the edges or in the center of the star (or having an adult do it for them). All of the stars, from any age group, could be combined into a bulletin board display of "Epiphany Gifts."

> TAKE TURNS TALKING ABOUT THE GIFTS THAT EACH PERSON COULD OFFER TO OUR SAVIOR.

EPIPHANY

I am small / with little / to bring. / But / this song / of praise / I sing: / Alleluia! / Worship / the newborn / king!

Reproducible Page, for use with "Star Shaped Poem," *Six Seasons of Fun! Activities, Crafts, and More*
© 2002 Augsburg Fortress. May be reproduced for local use.

37

GIANT PUPPET KINGS

(Combination Age Groups)

Materials: Cardboard poles, construction paper, duct tape, glue, masking tape, newspaper, paper plates, paper tablecloth, fabric or crepe paper, large plastic garbage bags, large scissors, yarn, and fake fur or fiberfill.

Preparation: Note the giant puppet kings pictured on the cover of this resource. Make giant puppets of the three kings and use them in worship during the children's message, or as the characters in a program or pageant.

Construct the head of the puppet from a large plastic garbage bag. To make it stronger, use several bags inside of each other. Hold open the bags. Unfold the newspaper and stack it on a pile. Crumple the newspaper, one sheet at a time, and stuff it into the open bag. It is important to unfold it one sheet at a time, or the weight will not be evenly distributed. When the bag is approximately half full, insert the pole into the middle of the newspaper. Continue stuffing the bag. When the bag is full, gather the top of it around the pole and tape it securely. Turn the puppet upside down. Continue to hold the puppet while the features and costume are added.

Use duct tape to attach the features to the puppet. Cut two eyes from construction paper or paper plates and attach them to the face. Cut a nose, ears, and a mouth and affix them to the head. Make hair from yarn, fake fur, fiberfill, or another material and affix it to the top of the stuffed bag.

Construct a simple costume from packaging material, a paper tablecloth, or lightweight fabric, such as an old sheet. Snip a hole in the center of the piece, and slide it up the pole. Tape it into place around the neck of the puppet. Attach trimming, such as a crown, to add character to the puppet. Use the tube to carry and operate the puppet.

Leader Tip: The puppets are made from recyclable materials, and will be easier to construct if several people of varied ages, or teams work on the project.

EPIPHANY DRAMA: THE KINGS VISIT A KING

(Intergenerational)

Present the story of the magi, Matthew 2:1-12, in a dramatic way. In Sunday school classes or worship services, a simple choral reading may be done with stools for actors and music stands to hold scripts, or readers may be scattered throughout the congregation and speak from the pews. A more elaborate production with costumes and memorized parts would make a meaningful seasonal program or devotion.

Materials: Biblical costumes, props, and script.

Characters: Narrator, Herod, King One, King Two, King Three, Chief Priest One, and Other Chief Priests.

THE KINGS VISIT A KING

Narrator *(Facing congregation)*:
Now, when Jesus was born in Bethlehem of Judea in the days of King Herod *(Herod stands, smiles, and gestures in a "kingly" way)*, behold, Wise Men from the East came to Jerusalem saying:
(All three kings stand.)

King One:
Where is he who has been born king of the Jews?

King Two:
For we have seen his star in the East,

King Three:
And have come to worship him.

Narrator:
When Herod the king heard this, he was troubled *(Herod stands and grumbles)* and all Jerusalem with him. And assembling all the chief priests and scribes of the people *(Priests stand)*, he inquired of them:

Herod:
Where is the Christ supposed to be born?

Chief Priests:
In Bethlehem of Judea; for so it is written by the prophet:

Chief Priest One:
"And you, O Bethlehem, in the land of Judah, are by no means least among the rulers of Judah; for from you shall come a ruler who will govern my people, Israel."

> PRESENT THE STORY OF THE MAGI, MATTHEW 2:1-12, IN A DRAMATIC WAY.

Reproducible Page, for use with "Epiphany Drama," *Six Seasons of Fun! Activities, Crafts, and More*
© 2002 Augsburg Fortress. May be reproduced for local use.

EPIPHANY

WHEN THEY SAW THE STAR, THEY REJOICED EXCEEDINGLY!

Narrator:
Then Herod summoned the Wise Men secretly and ascertained from them what time the star appeared *(Herod gestures and Wise Men turn toward Herod)*, and he sent them to Bethlehem, saying:

Herod:
Go and search diligently for the child, and when you have found him bring me word, that I too may come and worship him.
(Wise Men bow and nod agreement.)

Narrator:
After they had heard the king, they went on their way. *(Herod and priests sit.)*

Kings:
Let's go—follow that star! There it goes!

Narrator:
And lo, the star that they had seen in the East went before them, till it came to rest over the place where the child was.

King One:
In that stable?

Narrator:
When they saw the star, they rejoiced exceedingly!

Kings:
Yes!

Narrator:
And going into the stable they saw the child with Mary his mother, and they fell down and worshiped him. *(Kings kneel)* Then, opening their treasures, they offered him gifts.

King One:
Gold!

King Two:
Frankincense!

King Three:
And myrrh!

Narrator:
And being warned in a dream not to return to Herod... *(The kings make a "sh-h-h-h!" sign and pretend to tiptoe away as Herod stands)*, they departed to their own country by another way. *(Kings sit as Herod looks around, then shrugs and sits.)* Let those who are wise still listen to the angels' voices and follow the light of the Bethlehem star! *(Narrator sits.)*

Leader Tip: To involve more people, create acting groups—any number of people of any age—to represent the three kings and the chief priests.

Reproducible Page, for use with "Epiphany Drama," *Six Seasons of Fun! Activities, Crafts, and More*
© 2002 Augsburg Fortress. May be reproduced for local use.

BACKDROPS/MURALS

Add scenery to the drama by finding one or more illustrations to enhance the story such as the court of Herod, a star-lit path, or the town of Bethlehem. Make an acetate transparency of the drawing on a copier or at a copy store. Tape a background, such as a large piece of art paper, cardboard, or poster board to a wall. Set up an overhead projector, place the transparency on the stage, and position the picture to fit the background on the wall. Adjust the size by moving the projector closer to or farther away from the background. Sketch the scene onto the paper or the sheet. Remove it from the wall and complete the scene by filling in the details with markers or paints.

COSTUMES

Costumes may be as elaborate or as simple as budget and time allow. Keep in mind that the main purpose of dramatic presentations is to "tell the story" and costumes are to enhance the message. Gather information about biblical costumes from reference books. Costumes for the Wise Men may require some research to learn about African, Oriental, or Persian clothing styles.

PROPS

Suggestions: Jewelry boxes, baskets, or hinged boxes *(Paint gold or trim with jewels)*; urns, bottles with stoppers, and vases *(Paint gold or cover with florists' foil; add jewels)*.

> COSTUMES MAY BE AS ELABORATE OR AS SIMPLE AS BUDGET AND TIME ALLOW.

EPIPHANY

PRAYER PROCESSIONAL
(Worship/Education/Music)

Materials: Candles, chalk, container of water, cross, evergreen branch, gifts, incense, incense container, and matches.

Preparation: Have adults light candles and incense before the prayer walk begins. Have leaders for the blessing of the rooms selected in advance.

Among the special customs celebrated on Epiphany is the blessing—imploring God's protection in the coming year—of rooms of a church, home, or school.

Invite children, the congregation, and specific members of the community to participate in this ritual: walking a path that will lead them closer to Christ. Organize the event by deciding which rooms will be blessed, and the order in which they will be done. In a large building, select at least five different locations; while in a small facility include as many places as possible.

Select a leader, such as the pastor, and invite a different person to offer the prayer in each place. Show the children the items that will be used on the journey. These include candles, incense, a cross, symbolic gifts, water in a bowl, and an evergreen branch. Invite each child to choose something to carry on the walk. Be sure that the item is appropriate for the age of the participant, having adults and older youth carry candles and incense for safety concerns.

Proceed through each room. Sing Epiphany carols, if desired. *LifeSongs* contains many options including "Bring Forth the Kingdom" (35); "Come to the Mountain" (40); "I Am the Light of the World" (34); "I Want to Walk As a Child of the Light" (36); "Jesus Brings a Message" (39); "Open Our Eyes, Lord" (31); "Shine, Jesus, Shine" (38); "The Virgin Mary Had a Baby Boy" (29); "This Little Light of Mine" (32, 33); "We Are Called" (37); and "We Three Kings of Orient Are" (30). Many traditional Christmas carols also include verses about the Wise Men, for example: "Angels from the Realms of Glory" (verse 3); "Silent Night, Holy Night!" (verses 3 and 4); "The First Noel" and "There's a Song in the Air."

Bless each room by saying the following or something similar:

In the Classroom: May this classroom be a place of listening to and learning more about God.

In the Church Office: May this room be a place for doing God's work in our world.

In the Kitchen: May this kitchen be a place of nourishment for our relationships as well as for our bodies.

In the Nursery: May this nursery be a place where our youngest members experience God's love through nurturing caregivers.

In the Sanctuary: May this space be a place where true worship of Jesus takes place.

> INVITE EACH CHILD TO CHOOSE SOMETHING TO CARRY ON THE WALK.

EPIPHANY

THE BLESSING

Use the evergreen branch to sprinkle water around each space. Take turns having different people participate in this ritual.

Chalk the frame of the door of each room with the initials of the traditional names of the three Wise Men: *G* for Gaspar; *M* for Melchior; and *B* for Balthasar. In addition to the three initials, include the current year's date. Crosses between each letter and number implore God's protection in the year ahead. Conclude with a prayer surrendering the space to God and thanking God for the assurance of safekeeping through the coming year.

Option: As an additional Epiphany activity, gather the group and celebrate "Three Kings Day" with a crown cake. See the recipe for a crown cake on page 44.

EPIPHANY

> TRADITIONALLY THE PERSON WHO FINDS THE PRIZE WILL HAVE A VERY GOOD YEAR.

CROWN CAKE

Materials: Candy gumdrops, mini baby doll, mixer, bowls, baking equipment, tube pan, oven, knife, plates, napkins, forks, cups, and juice. For cake—1¼ cups (.3 l) softened margarine, 2¾ cups (.6 l) sugar, 5 eggs, 1 tablespoon (15 ml) freshly squeezed lemon juice, 3 cups (.7 l) flour, 1 teaspoon (5 ml) baking powder, ¼ teaspoon (1.3 ml) salt, 1 cup (.24 l) evaporated milk, and 2 teaspoons (10 ml) grated lemon peel. For glaze—⅓ cup (.08 l) softened margarine, 2 cups (.5 l) powdered sugar, 2-3 tablespoons (30-45 ml) freshly squeezed lemon juice, and hot water.

Preparation: Preheat the oven to 350° F. (175° C.). Wash the mini baby doll.

If the participants make the cake before the prayer processional begins, explain that they will be making a cake symbolizing a crown that might have been worn by one of the Wise Men. Invite learners to measure and mix ingredients, and later share the results.

Combine margarine, sugar, eggs, and lemon juice in a large mixer bowl on low speed for one minute, scraping the bowl constantly. Beat five minutes on high speed. Mix in flour, baking powder, and salt alternately with milk on low speed. Add lemon peel. Place the washed mini baby doll in the batter.

Pour the batter into a greased and floured tube pan. Bake for one hour and fifteen minutes. Cool the cake in the pan for twenty minutes. Remove it from the pan and allow it to cool.

Make the glaze by melting ⅓ cup (.08 l) margarine, and stirring in 2 cups (.5 l) powdered sugar and the lemon juice. Beat until smooth. Add one tablespoon (15 ml) of hot water at a time until the mixture reaches the desired consistency. Pour over the cake. Decorate the cake with candy gumdrops of various colors and sizes to represent jewels.

Share the cake with the participants. Remind them to eat carefully as one piece contains the mini baby doll. Traditionally, the person who finds the prize will have a very good year.

LENT

ADVENT CHRISTMAS EPIPHANY LENT EASTER PENTECOST

Lent is another season of preparation focusing on repentance, renewal, and rebirth. Traditionally, Lent began as a time of preparation for baptism. For the 40 days prior to Holy Saturday, church candidates for baptism fasted and were educated in the teachings of the church.

This time of penitence was gradually embraced by the whole congregation as a period of preparation for Easter. Historically, it was a time of denying the body by going without meat or rich foods, and instead focusing on the spirit. People were encouraged to acknowledge and repent of their sinful ways and embrace the reality of God's love in Christ in their lives.

The word *Lent* is derived from the Anglo-Saxon word for "springtime." In the northern part of the world, it is also the time when the days begin to lengthen, and we look forward to warmer days.

Lent is marked at its beginning by Ash Wednesday and it ends on Holy Saturday, the day before Easter Sunday. It is 40 days long, not including Sundays, which are considered resurrection celebrations. The number of 40 days recalls the 40 days Jesus was tempted in the wilderness, the 40 years that the Israelites wandered in the wilderness, and the 40 days that Moses stayed on Mt. Sinai.

The day before Ash Wednesday is Shrove Tuesday. The word *shrove* is the past tense of *shrive* and has to do with confession, penance, and absolution. In an effort to prepare for confession on Ash Wednesday, Christians rid their homes of all food that was tempting and rich. The Tuesday before Ash Wednesday, Christians enjoyed the last opportunity for feasting and fun before the more somber season of Lent began. This day has also become known as Mardi Gras, which means "fat Tuesday." The celebration was first known as *Beouf Gras* to acknowledge the last feast of meat before the spare meals and various abstinences expected in Lent.

After Shrove Tuesday comes Ash Wednesday. The spirit of this day is solemn and reverent. The suggested liturgical color is black. Ash Wednesday marks the beginning of 40 days of repentance and confession that will climax in the absolution and peace offered at the Maundy Thursday worship of Holy Week. As participants in worship receive a cross of ashes on their forehead, they are reminded that "you are dust and to dust you shall return." We are reminded of our mortality, of our identity as finite creatures dependent upon God for our lives. Ashes also suggest the renewal to come. Just as farmers burn a field to prepare and enrich the soil for planting, so do we die in this life and rise to new life in Christ. Ashes were also once used as a kind of soap. They serve to remind us of our baptism, and how we are washed clean of our sin.

The days of Lent deepen our faith and our relationship with God. These 40 days are brought to a passionate end during the last 7 days of this time of spiritual discipline. The observance of Holy Week is a journey in which Christians move through the last dramatic days of Jesus. The liturgical color for Lent is purple. Through participation in worship and liturgy, Christians relive the events that are central to the Christian faith and recommit themselves to share in the death and resurrection of Christ.

LENTEN SONGS

"Jesus, Remember Me" (With One Voice [WOV] 740)

"Glory Be to Jesus" (Lutheran Book of Worship [LBW] 95)

"There Is a Balm in Gilead" (WOV 737)

"Were You There" (LBW 92)

"Jesu, Jesu, Fill Us with Your Love" (LifeSongs 146)

All suggested hymns are included in either Lutheran Book of Worship, With One Voice, or LifeSongs, as well as in many other Christian hymnals.

JONAH GELATIN

(Pre-Elementary)

Materials: Blue gelatin squares, gummy worms and fish, clear plastic cups and spoons, the story of Jonah as told from a Bible storybook.

Preparation: Make the gelatin in advance, cut into squares, and place in a large bowl. Have the learners gather around you. Begin reading the story of Jonah, showing the learners pictures as you read the story. After reading the story, give each child a clear plastic cup and spoon. Show the learners how to fill their cups with gummy fish, blue gelatin, and gummy worms.

As the learners are eating, discuss the following:

Jonah was saved by the fish from drowning; we are saved from our sins by Jesus.

It was three days before Jonah came out from the darkness of the fish's belly; it was also three days before Jesus came out of the darkness of the tomb.

Option: Tell the story using a flannel board and flannel board figures.

BIRD FEEDERS AND RIBBONS

(Lower Elementary)

Materials: Pinecones, unsalted peanut butter, craft sticks or plastic knives, paper plates or bowls, a bucket of birdseed, ribbon, zipper lock sandwich bags, newspapers, and wet wipes.

Preparation: Cover your workspace with newspaper. (This can be a messy project.) Lent is a time when we prepare for Easter and the joy of new life in the risen Christ. Spring is a season when birds prepare for the new life of eggs by building nests.

Give each learner a paper plate or bowl, a pinecone, and a ribbon. Show the learners how to tie the ribbon securely to the bottom of the pinecone. Give each learner a glob or two of peanut butter on her or his paper plate. Have each learner smear the peanut butter all over the pinecone using a craft stick or a plastic knife.

Have the learners roll their pinecone in a bucket of birdseed. Place each completed bird feeder in a plastic bag to take home.

"JOURNEY WITH JESUS" GAME

(Upper Elementary)

Materials: Game board, cards, one die, and a game marker for each child.

Preparation: Reproduce and enlarge the game board on page 48. Reproduce card questions on pages 49 and 50 and those for page 51 onto two different colors of cardstock paper and cut them apart.

Place "Jesus and You" questions in order if you wish the game to move chronologically through the ministry of Jesus. "Bible Break" questions need not be in any order. The objective of this game is to travel the way of the cross. Learners may place game markers in any of the "Rest Stop" areas at the center of the cross and follow the arrows accordingly. Since this game has no end, children may play as long as time allows or interest holds.

Learners roll the die and move the number of spaces indicated. Each space offers a direction. A description of each possibility follows:

Jesus and You: Gives a brief biblical reference and then asks the child a question out of that context. There are no right or wrong answers.

Bible Break: Asks a Bible trivia question. The person to the player's left draws the card and asks the question for the person who has landed on the "Bible Break" space. The answer to each question is in the lower portion of the card. The "Bible Break" square will indicate what the player should do in the event of either a correct or an incorrect answer. A "don't know" answer counts as incorrect.

Rest Stop: Offers an opportunity for players to get up and stretch or do some physical activity.

Fun for the Road: No doubt Jesus had a sense of humor. These squares are opportunities for children to share some laughter.

If you have a learner who has physical limitations, think of alternate "Rest Stop" activities where necessary.

JOURNEY WITH JESUS

START HERE

		JESUS AND YOU Pick a card.	**FUN FOR THE ROAD** Tell a knock-knock joke.		
		BIBLE BREAK **Right:** Move forward two spaces. **Wrong:** Move back one.	**JESUS AND YOU** Pick a card.		
FUN FOR THE ROAD Make a funny face.	**JESUS AND YOU** Pick a card.	**REST STOP** Hop on one foot ten times.	**REST STOP** Do five jumping jacks.	**BIBLE BREAK** **Right:** Move forward one space. **Wrong:** Try again.	**JESUS AND YOU** Pick a card.
JESUS AND YOU Pick a card.	**BIBLE BREAK** **Right:** Move forward three spaces. **Wrong:** Stay out until next turn.	**REST STOP** Run around a chair five times.	**REST STOP** Flap your arms like a bird and jump ten times.	**JESUS AND YOU** Pick a card.	**FUN FOR THE ROAD** Make up and do a cheer for Jesus.
		JESUS AND YOU Pick a card.	**BIBLE BREAK** **Right:** Trade places with any player. **Wrong:** Move back one space.		
		FUN FOR THE ROAD Pat your head and rub your tummy at the same time.	**JESUS AND YOU** Pick a card.		
		JESUS AND YOU Pick a card.	**BIBLE BREAK** **Right:** Move to any other space for next turn. **Wrong:** Stay here one more turn.		

FINISH HERE

Reproducible Page, for use with "Journey with Jesus," *Six Seasons of Fun! Activities, Crafts, and More* © 2002 Augsburg Fortress. May be reproduced for local use.

"JESUS AND YOU" CARDS

LENT

1. Jesus was a king, but he was born in a barn instead of a palace. His coming was not what people expected. Tell about a time when something happened that wasn't what you expected.

2. The angels sang to the shepherds when they were out in the fields. What is your favorite song? What is the most beautiful music you have ever heard?

3. Luke 2:25-26 tells the story about Simeon who waited his whole life to see the Messiah. Name three things that you would like to see or do before you grow old.

4. John the Baptist came to prepare the way for the Lord. He asked that people repent. Name one thing that people do that you think Jesus doesn't like.

5. When Jesus was baptized, the Holy Spirit was present in the form of a dove. Do you know who was present at your baptism? Who? If you're not sure, ask your mom or dad.

6. Jesus chose 12 to travel with him and learn what he had to teach. They were his closest friends. Name three of your closest friends.

7. Jesus healed many people who were sick or hurt. Tell about a time when you were sick or hurt. Who helped you? How?

8. Jesus taught us that we should treat others as we would like to be treated. What do you think this means?

9. Once when Jesus and his disciples were in a boat, a huge storm came. The disciples were frightened. Tell about a time when you were frightened.

10. Once Jesus fed thousands of hungry people because a boy was willing to share all he had: five loaves of bread and two fish. What do you have that you are willing to share?

11. Jesus told the story of the good Samaritan. In this story one man helped another man who was robbed and hurt. Tell about a time when you were hurt and someone helped you, or someone else was hurt and you helped them.

12. Jesus taught his disciples to pray the Lord's Prayer. Teach the others playing this game another prayer that you know.

13. Luke 12:8 reads, "If you tell others that you belong to me, the Son of Man will tell God's angels that you are my followers." Have you ever told anyone what you know about Jesus? When—or why not?

14. In Luke 12:22-23 Jesus tells his disciples not to worry about what you're going to eat or wear. "Life is more than food and clothing." Name one thing that you worry about sometimes.

15. Jesus says that he is like a shepherd, and if you are lost, he will come find you because you are his sheep. Tell about a time when you were lost or tell about what you would do if you became lost.

Reproducible Page, for use with "Journey with Jesus," *Six Seasons of Fun! Activities, Crafts, and More* © 2002 Augsburg Fortress. May be reproduced for local use.

LENT

"JESUS AND YOU" CARDS

16. Jesus tells the story of two sons. One ran away and spent all his money. The other stayed with his father and helped him work. When the son who ran away was welcomed back, the other son was angry. Have you ever been angry with a brother, sister, or parent? Why?

17. Jesus once healed ten people who were sick, but only one thanked him. Why do you think it's important to thank people when they do something for you or give you something? Why do you like to be thanked?

18. Zacchaeus was a short man who wanted to see Jesus so badly that he climbed a sycamore tree to get a better look. Do you have a tree that you like to climb? Tell about it.

19. Jesus rode into Jerusalem on a donkey and people waved palm branches as he went by. Have you ever been horseback riding or sat on a donkey? Have you ever been to or been in a parade? Tell about it.

20. Jesus saw a poor woman put all the money she had in the offering. Why do you think it's important for people to share what they have?

21. In the Gospel of John, Jesus washed the feet of his disciples to show them how to serve each other. What are some things people your age can do to serve others?

22. Jesus went to a garden to pray. When do you pray? Tell about a time when prayer helped you feel better.

23. When Jesus was on trial, some people told lies about what Jesus had said and done so that Jesus would get into trouble. Tell about a time when you got into trouble for something that you did not do.

24. Soldiers made fun of Jesus and hit him. Have you ever seen someone make fun of someone else? How do you think it feels to have someone make fun of you?

25. Jesus died a very painful death. He was hit so hard that he was bleeding. And he had huge nails pounded through his hands and feet. Tell about a time when you or someone you loved was hurt.

26. When Jesus died, the sky grew very dark even though it was the middle of the day. Have you ever seen the sky grow dark during the day? What happened?

27. When Jesus died, his friends cried very hard. Has anyone in your family, a pet or a person, died? What happened? How did you feel?

28. Jesus died so that we might know how much God loves us. Think of the people you love the most. Who are they?

29. On Easter morning, some of Jesus' friends went to the tomb and found it empty! Angels said that he had risen from the dead. Tell about one of the happiest times that you can remember.

30. Because Jesus rose from the dead, we believe that after we die, we will still be alive with God. What do you think heaven will be like? Who will you see there?

Reproducible Page, for use with "Journey with Jesus," *Six Seasons of Fun! Activities, Crafts, and More* © 2002 Augsburg Fortress. May be reproduced for local use.

"BIBLE BREAK" CARDS

LENT

What city was Jesus born in? Bethlehem	What was the name of the mother of Jesus? Mary	Who prepared the way for Jesus to come, baptized people, and ate bugs? John the Baptist	When Jesus was baptized, the Holy Spirit was present in the form of a what? dove
When Jesus fed the 5000, who gave his five loaves and two fish to help? a boy	How many days was Jesus in the tomb? three	At Communion, what do people eat and drink that they can taste? bread and wine	Where is the baptismal font at your church?
What happened on Good Friday? Jesus died	On Palm Sunday, what did Jesus ride on? donkey	How many disciples did Jesus have at first? 12	Who was the disciple who betrayed Jesus? Judas
Whom did Jesus raise from the dead? Lazarus	What do we celebrate on Easter Sunday? that Jesus rose	What is the church season when we prepare for Easter? Lent	Who was the disciple who said that he didn't know Jesus? Peter
Who was the man who climbed a tree to see Jesus better? Zacchaeus	Fill in the blank: Jesus said, "I am the _____ of the world." light	Who built the ark? Noah	Who had a dream about ladders and angels? Jacob
Who doubted that Jesus had risen from the dead? Thomas	How many days was Jonah in the belly of the fish? three	Who were the first two people in the garden of Eden? Adam and Eve	Whose descendants will be more in number than the stars in the sky? Abraham

Reproducible Page, for use with "Journey with Jesus," *Six Seasons of Fun! Activities, Crafts, and More* © 2002 Augsburg Fortress. May be reproduced for local use.

LENT

"SERVING HANDS" PLASTER

(Combination Age Groups)

Materials: Rolling pins, plastic knives, clean workspace, salt clay (see recipe), paint (optional). For salt clay—1½ cups (.36 l) of salt, 4 cups (1 l) of flour, 1½ cups of water. Optional: 1 teaspoon (5 ml) of alum (for a preservative if you do not wish to bake the clay).

Preparation: Mix salt and flour (and alum) together in a large bowl. Add water gradually.

Mix dough to the size of a large ball. Knead well, adding water if too crumbly, or flour if too wet. Shape the dough into tennis-ball-sized portions.

Form pairs or small groups. Give each learner a tennis-ball-size portion of clay. Have learners take turns using the rolling pin to flatten the clay until it is 1 inch (2.5 cm) in thickness. Show the learners how to press their hand into the center of the clay for a handprint. Have learners use the plastic knife to trim the edges of the handprint. Using the knife again, around the edge of the circle, participants can write, "My Hands Serve Jesus" and the date. Air dry or bake at 300° F. (150° C.) for 30-40 minutes or until hard.

Option: Learners can decorate the hand with tempera paints.

Many people prefer not to use foodstuffs that will not be eventually consumed in art projects. As the above recipe uses flour, you may prefer to purchase modeling clay for the activity.

> LEARNERS CAN DECORATE THE HAND WITH TEMPERA PAINTS.

"SERVING HANDS" T-SHIRT

(Combination Age Groups)

LENT

Materials: White T-shirt for each learner, variety of fabric paint, pie tins, washtubs of soapy water, cardboard or large cereal boxes for each learner, newspaper, permanent markers, and long tables.

Preparation: Prepare washtubs of soapy water in advance. Cover the tables with newspaper. Have each learner bring a white T-shirt from home.

Have learners place their T-shirt over a piece of cardboard or a flattened cereal box. Lay the T-shirt on the table. Show learners how to write "Hands in God's Service" or "Hands Are for Serving" with a permanent marker in the middle of each T-shirt. Allow each learner to pick a fabric paint color and have them squirt 1-2 tablespoons (15-30 ml) in a pie tin.

Have learners place one of their hands into the paint, making sure the entire palm is covered. Then, place their palm on their shirt. Tell the learners they will walk from shirt to shirt, placing their handprint on the learner's shirt next to them, working around the central message written on the shirt. Learners may press their hand into the paint as needed, being careful to remove any excess from the edges of their hands.

After the learners have placed their handprint on each other's shirts, have them wash their painted hand as their T-shirts dry. Once dry, turn the shirts over and do another set of handprints on the other side.

Leader Tip: Leaders should replenish paint often.

Option: Have learners wear their shirts to a service project. Some service project suggestions are listed on page 56.

LENT

MARDI GRAS MYSTERY MEAL

(Intergenerational)

Materials: Menu, cooked meal, thematic decorations, a spirit of fun and adventure.

Offer people of all ages a Mardi Gras mystery meal on Shrove Tuesday, the evening before Ash Wednesday. Each participant receives a menu that is written in secret code. This menu contains 9-12 items from which each participant orders 3 items to make a 3-course meal. Each course should offer 3-4 items.

The menu for a Mardi Gras mystery meal might look like this:

Name of Guest _____

FIRST COURSE

CAJUN CATFISH _____
KING'S CAKE DELIGHT _____
PARADE PARADISE _____

SECOND COURSE

KREWE CREATIONS _____
JOKING JESTERS _____
BEADS GALORE _____

THIRD COURSE

FRENCH QUARTER FRENZY _____
CANAL STREET SURPRISE _____
FLOATS FANTASTIC _____

Each participant indicates on their menu which items they would like for each course. However, they have no idea what they are ordering. Each menu item stands for something else that they will actually receive.

Explain to the participants that each course will be completely cleared away before the next one is served and also that eating utensils are included in the menu. Waiters should be watchful to clear away everything as someone might be sneaky and try to hold onto a spoon.

There is flexibility in deciding what your Mardi Gras menu will be. While Mardi Gras is celebrated in many cities in the United States, Canada, and Europe, the festival in New Orleans may be the one participants know best, so you may wish to have foods that reflect that part of the country; or consider French foods in recognition of the people who brought Mardi Gras to New Orleans. Some food suggestions include gumbo or jambalaya, Cajun or Creole chicken, grits, baked bananas, barbecued chicken, biscuits, French fries, French onion soup, and so on. If you would like to search for authentic Mardi Gras recipes, try searching the public library or the Web for recipes. Another possibility appropriate to Shrove Tuesday would be pancakes and sausages.

What you are serving might look like this:

pancakes	syrup
fruit	sausages
milk	muffin or hot crossed bun
knife	drink
knife	fork
spoon	napkin

Assign one real item from this list to each mystery menu item. The two don't have to have anything to do with each other; such is the mystery of the meal. The menu translation should be kept secret from everyone except the kitchen staff and waiters.

Notice that two knives are on the menu. This allows for the chance, however remote, that some fortunate person will order just the right things in such a way as to receive a knife with their pancakes or a knife to butter their muffin.

If you are feeling merciful at the end of the meal, allow participants "seconds" complete with the appropriate eating utensils.

Decorate your meal area in Mardi Gras colors: green (faith), yellow (power), and purple (justice). Add a festive touch by placing beaded necklaces on the table and having a costume parade, face painter, games, jokes, and silly songs.

At the end of the meal, invite participants to think about what they might abstain from as individuals or families during Lent. Some ideas are fast food, movies, ice cream or chocolate, and meat on Fridays. Have them write down their decisions on note cards and take them home as a reminder. Close with a Lenten prayer.

LENT

> DENYING OURSELVES A FOOD OR ACTIVITY KEEPS US AWARE THAT WE ARE LIVING IN THE LENTEN SEASON.

IDEAS FOR OBSERVING LENT
(Worship/Education/Music)

Lent is a wonderful opportunity to refocus our lives on the spirit and actions that strengthen our faith and provide a witness of that faith to others. Here are some ideas that can be adapted to individual, family, or congregational life to enrich the spiritual discipline of Lent.

FASTING (ABSTINENCE)

Denying ourselves a food or activity keeps us aware that we are living in the Lenten season. Whatever an individual or family decides to fast should not be so difficult that it becomes a temptation, or overwhelming, but not so easy as to make it unnoticeable. Fasting from a particular food, not going out for meals, or not watching television as much are a few ideas.

Another alternative is to choose to set aside time: a time of prayer in the morning or evening, family devotions, talking to someone new every day. These things can help keep us mindful of Lent and deepen our participation.

SERVICE PROJECTS

Every community offers opportunities to serve at food shelves, shelters, or through other service organizations. Offer to paint, put together meals, visit, play bingo at the nursing home, pick up trash, or clear out a vacant lot. Check the phone book for volunteer opportunities.

You could also arrange for a worship day when people of all ages could meet at church, worship, and have a fellowship meal. Plan this event with various church departments, especially the church musicians.

Option: Make "Serving Hands" T-shirts ahead of time and wear them on your outing. See page 53 for this activity.

CLASS COLLECTIONS

Sunday school classes might collect items for a specific goal during Lent. Some established organizations can help you access the needs in your community. Contacting Lutheran Social Service, the Salvation Army, Catholic Charities, or other similar groups can provide valuable connections and resources.

Some ideas follow:

A school kit, including an eraser, paper, markers, crayons, pencils, a ruler, a pencil sharpener, paints, a scissors, and a pencil box.

A toiletry kit, including a toothbrush, toothpaste, mouthwash, a washcloth, dental floss, shampoo, soap, and deodorant.

A cleaning kit, including a bucket, cleaning fluids, sponges, a mop, a broom, and a scrub brush.

A kit for a children's shelter or group home, including books, toys, games, stuffed animals, and clothing (including underwear). Personalize it further and find the names, ages, and sizes of specific children in those situations.

A crisis nursery kit, including diapers, formula, baby food, clothing items, baby bottles, and baby blankets.

Churches can also sponsor different drives that are unusual enough to spark community interest. A few are listed below:

> Peanut butter and tuna fish. Food shelves value these items because of their ease of use and high protein.
>
> Underwear, socks, shaving lotion, razors, face cream, combs, brushes, shampoo, and other basic clothing and toiletry items for men's and women's shelters.
>
> Children's books for overseas orphanages.
>
> Bibles for overseas and local outreach or missions.
>
> Sleeping bags for foster children.

CHURCHES CAN ALSO SPONSOR DIFFERENT DRIVES THAT ARE UNUSUAL ENOUGH TO SPARK COMMUNITY INTEREST.

EASTER

ADVENT CHRISTMAS EPIPHANY LENT EASTER PENTECOST

EASTER SONGS

"Alleluia, Alleluia, Give Thanks"
(LifeSongs 58)

"Halle, Halle, Hallelujah" (With One Voice [WOV] 612)

"Thine the Amen, Thine the Praise"
(WOV 801)

"Halleluia! We Sing Your Praises"
(WOV 722)

"Alleluia! Jesus Is Risen!"
(LifeSongs 62)

All suggested hymns are included in either Lutheran Book of Worship, With One Voice, or LifeSongs, as well as in many other Christian hymnals.

Easter celebrates the single most important event in the Christian faith: the resurrection of Jesus Christ. Scripture records the emphatic testimony of those first witnesses: "He is risen!" As modern Christians, we add our own witness to the saving love of God in Christ Jesus, and our voices answer with "He is risen indeed, Alleluia!"

Traditionally, the Easter vigil service contained the first Easter celebration. Christians would gather after midnight hours of Holy Saturday and pray together in the darkness. The dark night was a stark reminder of the grief of the disciples and the darkness of the cold tomb. But as the rays of dawn spilled over the horizon, the vigil of prayer and waiting would become a celebration of joy. Those gathered would hear the proclamation "He is risen!" and share the meal at Holy Communion, beginning their Easter morning.

The Easter vigil service moves from darkness to dawn, from the contemplation of death to the joy of new life. It is a service in which, historically, many were baptized into the community of faith. Candidates, having completed their Lenten instruction, were received into the body of Christ. Today, a baptism at the Easter vigil service is a wonderful reminder of our identity as children of God and inheritors of eternal life. The service of baptism calls us to confess our faith. Recalling our baptism also reminds us that we are empowered through the work of the Holy Spirit to be workers in the kingdom of God.

Easter is a time of joy and new life. After 40 days of spiritual discipline, Christians are renewed. We celebrate our new life in Christ and recommit ourselves to following the example of Jesus. Because of Jesus, we know our present suffering is not the end. As children of God, we too shall rise to new life, and it is this future hope that transforms our present reality.

Easter is the central celebration of the Christian church. The Easter season of the church lasts 50 days to celebrate and deepen our understanding of the resurrection. The fiftieth day of the Easter season is also the same day we celebrate the birth of the church, Pentecost, when the spirit of Christ was poured out on those waiting to receive it.

The color for Easter is white: the color of bright glory, of purity, and of high holy days.

COFFEE FILTER BUTTERFLY

(Pre-Elementary)

Materials: Coffee filters, spring clamped clothespins, fuzzy pipe cleaners, magnets (available at craft stores), glue, newspaper, watercolor paints, markers, paintbrushes, and water.

Preparation: Cover the workspace with newspaper. Glue small magnets to one side of the clothespin for each learner.

Butterflies are a symbol of new life. Just as Jesus came out of the tomb to new life, caterpillars emerge from cocoons to a new life as butterflies.

Give each learner a coffee filter. Have the learners decorate the filter using watercolor paints or markers. If learners use markers, have them dip a paintbrush in water and wet the places where they have drawn to allow the colors to run. Allow the filter time to dry.

When the filter is dry, help the learners crinkle the filter into the clothespin, clamping its middle, allowing the sides to fan out to create wings. Show the learners how to clamp a small piece of pipe cleaner to the end of the clothespin for antennae.

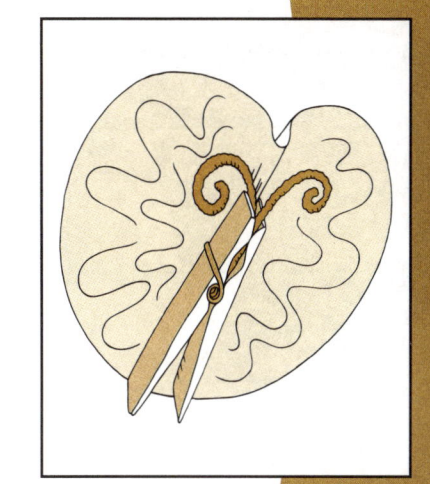

EASTER EGG PIÑATAS

(Lower Elementary)

Materials: Balloons (balloon size should be 9-11 inches [23-28 cms]), papier-mâché paste (see recipe below), newspaper, colorful tissue paper (optional), shallow bowls or pie tins, acrylic or tempera paint and brushes, yarn or string, ribbons, broom handle, candy (optional).

Preparation: Make papier-mâché paste and check for latex allergies in advance. Tear newspaper into 1-inch (2.5 cm) strips, about 6 inches (15 cm) long.

PAPIER-MÂCHÉ PASTE RECIPE

Mix one part wallpaper paste with three parts water.

Distribute balloons to each learner and have learners blow them up, assisting with tying. Pour papier-mâché paste into a shallow container for each child. Show the learners how to dip one strip at a time into the paste. Have the learners rub a finger and thumb down each strip to remove excess paste and carefully place on the balloon, smoothing out the crinkles and bumps. Have learners continue applying strips in a crisscross fashion to the balloon until there are 2-3 layers of paper covering the balloon, but leaving the tie of the balloon accessible.

Allow the balloon to dry overnight, adding 2-3 more layers of pasted strips. An optional final layer is to add strips of colorful tissue paper. Allow the piñata to dry completely and have the learners decorate with acrylic or tempera paint.

EASTER

Show the learners how to pop the balloon at the tie after it is completely dry. The opening should be small, but large enough to allow candy to be stuffed into the piñata. Poke three small holes about 2 inches from the end opening. Thread colorful ribbons through the holes and gather in a knot. Tie string to the knot and hang. Learners may take their piñatas home, and hang them from the ceiling at about 6 to 10 feet (2-3 m) high.

Learners can have lots of fun taking turns trying to hit the egg with a broom handle while blindfolded, releasing a shower of candy.

Option: If there are children who are allergic to latex, have them make a papier-mâché bowl. Cover the outside of a medium-sized plastic bowl with petroleum jelly. Following the same instructions as above, cover the outside of bowl with strips of newspaper that have been dipped into paste. Allow it to dry. Add another layer. When it is completely dry, separate it from the bowl. Paint and decorate.

> ITEMS WILL BE VERY FRAGILE AND FLAT AFTER PRESSING TAKES PLACE. HANDLE WITH CARE.

PRESSED FLOWERS AND HOMEMADE PAPER

(Upper Elementary)

PRESSED FLOWERS

Materials: Flowers, leaves, ferns, grass, petals, fuzzy dandelion seeds, waxed paper, heavy books.

Preparation: Try to gather flowers 3-4 weeks before Easter. If you live in a climate where snow is still on the ground, pick up what you need from a florist or grocery store.

Have the learners pick several items they would like to press. Give each learner a sheet of waxed paper that is large enough to fold in half, but still fits between the pages of one of the heavy books. Show the learners how to place the flowers and petals on the waxed paper so that the center of the flower is visible when it dries. Items should not touch each other.

Have learners fold the waxed paper over the items and place them carefully between the pages of a heavy book. Stack the books on top of each other to add weight. Monitor the progress of the items by checking on them in seven days. Items will be very fragile and flat after pressing takes place. Handle with care.

HOMEMADE PAPER

Materials: Blender, water, sponge, paper headed for recycling (computer printouts, construction paper, colorful envelopes, and so on), smooth cotton toweling cut into 10 x 12-inch (25 x 30 cm) pieces, wooden block (or book) in a freezer bag, dishwashing tub or storage container, cookie sheet with a small lip around the edge, iron and ironing board. Optional: dried petals, grasses, dryer lint.

Hand Mold Materials: Light diffuser board (ceiling grid used for suspended ceilings). It usually comes in a 2 x 4 foot (61 x 122 cm) sheet and can be found at the hardware store.

Plastic Screen Materials: Plastic canvas material found in fabric stores in the cross-stitching aisle. This plastic canvas generally comes with so many squares per inch, for example 7 or 14. Get the 14 or higher. You will also need a deckle frame; it provides the border for the paper pulp. You may use an old 8 x 10 (20 x 25 cm) or 5 x 7 inch (13 x 18 cm) frame or just make one out of wood.

To Make a Deckle Frame: The measurements for the frame are dependent on the tub you will be using. The frame should be able to rest completely on the bottom of the tub and be lifted up without difficulty. Check out your hardware store in the molding department. Simple pine molding should come in approximately 1 x 1-inch square pieces. Cut two pieces 6 inches (15 cm) long and two pieces 10 inches (25 cm) long. Nail or staple together to make a rectangle. This is your deckle.

Cut the ceiling grid a ½ inch (1 cm) bigger than the inside measurement of your deckle so that the deckle can rest securely on the grid. Cut the plastic screen material and the plastic canvas to the same dimensions. Place the grid on a flat surface. Place the plastic canvas on top of the grid and the deckle frame on top of that. This is your hand mold.

DIRECTIONS FOR PAPER

Preparation: Have the learners tear up individual sheets of paper in advance. In a blender, put one torn up sheet of paper and 4 cups (1 l) water. Run blender for approximately 30 seconds, until paper is shredded. This is your pulp. The making of pulp allows for a lot of creativity. Have the learners add some of the following: dryer lint, glitter, bits of brown paper bags, colored construction paper, and dried pressed flower petals. Pour the pulp into the dishwashing tub. This is the vat.

Help the learners repeat the first step four or five times until the pulp in the vat is at least 2 inches deep. Stir the vat to break up any clumps and to be sure that the pulp is not resting on the bottom. Pick up the hand mold and keep the three pieces together. Holding it vertically over one side of the vat, dip the mold under the surface of the pulp and rest the mold on the bottom of the tub. Allow the pulp to cover the surface of the vat.

Have the learners submerge pieces of ferns, pressed flowers, or whatever sparks their imagination directly above the deckle. Or place flowers on the surface after the water has drained a little in the next step.

Keeping the mold level, lift it out of the vat and allow it to drain for 10 seconds. Place mold on cookie sheet.

1. Carefully lift the deckle off the mold. Place the sheet of gray plastic screen material on top of the pulp. Using a sponge, press on the screen to remove as much water as possible. Wring out the sponge as necessary.

2. Peel off the screen. Lay one toweling piece over the wet paper. Pick up the mold, and invert onto a flat workspace. Carefully remove the grid and the plastic canvas from the pulp. Place another towel on top of the wet paper.

EASTER

> THE MAKING OF PULP ALLOWS FOR A LOT OF CREATIVITY.

EASTER

> PAPER CAN BE FOLDED TO MAKE EASTER CARDS OR DRIED FLOWERS ADDED TO MAKE A PRETTY PICTURE.

3. Using a wooden block (or a book) in a plastic bag, press on the toweling to flatten paper and remove more water. Remove the wet toweling and replace with dry toweling.

4. Carefully pick up the two pieces of toweling with the new paper in between and lay them on the ironing board.

5. Using the iron without steam, iron damp toweling with paper in between until the top one is dry. Turn over and repeat. Remove the dry toweling and iron directly on paper until it is completely dry. If one side of the new paper has added pressed flowers, iron through the toweling to protect it. You may iron directly onto the other side of the paper.

Each vat will yield 2-3 sheets of paper. Add more pulp by repeating step 1 except blend a sheet of paper with 3 cups (.72 l) of water instead of 4 cups.

Option: Dried flowers can also be added after the paper dries. Use a small paintbrush with some slightly watered down glue and paint glue on the dried flowers to adhere them to the paper. When completed, spray with aerosol hairspray or a fixative from the craft store.

Paper can be folded to make Easter cards or dried flowers added to make a pretty picture.

EASTER TREE

(Combination)

The Easter tree celebrates the symbols of new life and the colors of spring. The tree can be gathered from the backyard. With permission, small branches can be harvested from flowering trees, brought inside, and put in water—ideally to bloom in time for Easter. Large dead twigs that have fallen during the winter can be brought inside, arranged in a jar or vase, and brought to life with the help of silk flowers and the decorations described in this activity.

BLOWN EGGS

Materials: Uncooked eggs (have extras!), thread, buttons, skewer or sharp poker, plastic bowls, markers, egg dye, fingernail polish, and enamel and watercolor paint. Egg holders or egg cartons would be helpful to steady eggs while decorating.

Preparation: Leaders should blow out the eggs of younger learners in advance. Show the older learners how to poke a hole in the top and bottom of a raw egg. Have the learners blow the raw egg into a bowl. Gently rinse egg and blow out excess water.

DECORATING THE EGGS

Dye: Follow instructions on the dye kit. Eggs are now hollow and will float. Gentle pressure will be necessary to keep the egg in the dye.

Markers: In the Ukraine, Easter eggs are decorated with elaborate designs. Children can use their imaginations to fill their eggs with color and style.

Fingernail Polish or Watercolor, Acrylic, or Enamel Paint: Can be bright, pearly, or glossy. They come in a variety of colors and are easy to work with.

HANGING THE EGGS

With a long needle and thread, yarn, or ribbon, tie one end to a button and poke the other end through the hollow egg through the other hole. The button or a large yarn knot will keep the end secure and allow the egg to be hung.

Some people prefer not to use foodstuffs that will not be consumed in art projects. If you share that concern, you may wish to use polystyrene, plastic, or wooden eggs from a craft supply store.

OTHER SYMBOLS

Materials: Thin sheets of flexible foam (such as Fun Foam) in different colors, or heavy cardstock paper or poster board, and stencils made from the patterns on page 64.

EASTER

Using the stencils below as patterns, cut out shapes from foam or heavy paper.

If you are using foam, symbols can be decorated using permanent markers, or you can glue other bits of colorful foam to the symbol. If you are using heavy cardstock, symbols can be decorated with regular markers, or you can glue colorful pieces of tissue paper on to add variety.

Using a hole puncher or needle, poke a hole in the top of the symbol and thread it with yarn or ribbon to hang from the Easter tree.

Reproducible Stencil Page, for use with "Easter Trees," *Six Seasons of Fun! Activities, Crafts, and More*
© 2002 Augsburg Fortress. May be reproduced for local use.

64

EASTER STORY COOKIES

(Intergenerational)

Materials: Two sets of the following—One cup (.24 l) whole pecans, 3 egg whites, 1 cup sugar, 1 teaspoon (5 ml) vinegar, pinch salt, mixer, wooden spoon, tape, cookie sheet, waxed paper.

Preparation: This activity should be done the Saturday afternoon before Easter Sunday, or another time when you can prepare the cookies in the afternoon or evening and then come back together the next day. Plan to make two batches of cookies, with one batch prepared through the beating of the egg whites to stiff peaks, when participants arrive. When telling the story, begin the second batch and proceed as directed through the adding of the egg whites. Then switch to the batch that you prepared earlier, so that those in attendance do not have to wait for 12-15 minutes while you beat egg whites.

Preheat oven to 300° F. (150° C.). Make copies of the recipe for learners to take home. Break pecans into small pieces.

READ JOHN 19:16-18.

"Then Pilate handed Jesus over to be nailed to a cross. Jesus was taken away, and he carried his cross to a place...called Golgotha. There Jesus was nailed to the cross" (CEV).

Let each child smell the vinegar. Put 1 teaspoon vinegar into mixing bowl. Explain that when Jesus was thirsty on the cross, he was offered vinegar to drink.

READ JOHN 19:28-30.

"Jesus knew that he had now finished his work. [To fulfill the scripture] he said, 'I am thirsty!' A jar of [vinegar] was there. Someone then soaked a sponge with the vinegar and held it to Jesus' mouth on the stem of a hyssop plant. After Jesus drank the [vinegar], he said, 'Everything is done!' He bowed his head and died" (CEV).

Add egg whites to the vinegar. Tell the learners that eggs represent life. Explain that Jesus gave his life to give us life.

READ JOHN 10:10-11.

"A thief comes only to rob, kill, and destroy. I came so that everyone would have life, and have it in its fullest. I am the good shepherd, and the good shepherd gives up his life for his sheep" (CEV).

Sprinkle a little salt into each learner's hand. Let learners taste it and brush the rest into the bowl. Explain that salt represents the salty tears shed by Jesus' followers when Jesus died.

> SALT REPRESENTS THE SALTY TEARS SHED BY JESUS' FOLLOWERS WHEN JESUS DIED.

EASTER

> **DISCOVER FOR YOURSELF THAT THE LORD IS KIND.**

READ LUKE 23:27.

[When Jesus was being led to the cross], "a large crowd was following Jesus, and in the crowd a lot of women were crying and weeping for him" (CEV).

Add sugar to the mixture. Explain that the sweetest part of the story is that Jesus died because he loves us. He wants us to know that we belong to him.

READ PSALM 34:8.

"Discover for yourself that the LORD is kind. Come to him for protection, and you will be glad" (CEV).

ALSO READ JOHN 3:16.

"God loved the people of this world so much that he gave his only Son, so that everyone who has faith in him will have eternal life and never really die" (CEV).

Beat the mixture with a mixer on high speed for 12-15 minutes or until stiff peaks form.

READ JOHN 3:1-3.

"There was a man named Nicodemus who was a Pharisee and a Jewish leader. One night he went to Jesus and said, 'Sir, we know that God sent you to teach us. You could not work these miracles, unless God were with you'" (CEV).

Fold in broken nuts. Drop by teaspoons onto a cookie sheet covered with waxed paper. Explain that each mound represents the rocky tomb where Jesus' body was laid.

READ MATTHEW 27:57-60.

"That evening a rich disciple named Joseph from the town of Arimathea went and asked for Jesus' body. Pilate gave orders for it to be given to Joseph, who took the body and wrapped it in a clean linen cloth. Then Joseph put the body in his own tomb that had been cut into solid rock and had never been used. He rolled a big stone against the entrance to the tomb and went away" (CEV).

Put the cookies in the oven, close the door, and turn the oven OFF. Give each child a piece of tape to seal the oven door. Explain that Jesus' tomb was sealed.

READ MATTHEW 27:65-66.

"Pilate said to them, 'All right, take some of your soldiers and guard the tomb as well as you know how.' So they sealed it tight and placed soldiers there to guard it" (CEV). Explain that they may feel sad to leave the cookies in the oven overnight. Jesus' followers were in despair when the tomb was sealed.

READ JOHN 16:20 AND 22.

"I tell you for certain that you will cry and be sad, but the world will be happy. You will be sad, but later you will be happy" (CEV).

"You are now very sad. But later I will see you, and you will be so happy that no one will be able to change the way you feel" (CEV).

On Easter morning, gather again to open the oven and pass out the cookies! Notice the cracked surface, and take a bite. The cookies are hollow! On the first resurrection day, Jesus' followers were amazed to find the tomb open and empty.

READ MATTHEW 28:1-9.

"The Sabbath was over, and it was almost daybreak on Sunday when Mary Magdalene and the other Mary went to see the tomb. Suddenly a strong earthquake struck, and Lord's angel came down from heaven. He rolled away the stone and sat on it. The angel looked as bright as lightning, and his clothes were white as snow. The guards shook from fear and fell down, as though they were dead.

"The angel said to the women, 'Don't be afraid! I know you are looking for Jesus, who was nailed to a cross. He isn't here! God has raised him to life, just as Jesus said he would. Come, see the place where his body was lying. Now hurry! Tell his disciples that he has been raised to life and is on his way to Galilee. Go there, and you will see him. That is what I came to tell you.'

"The women were frightened and yet very happy, as they hurried from the tomb and ran to tell his disciples. Suddenly Jesus met them and greeted them. They went near him, held on to his feet, and worshiped him. Then Jesus said, 'Don't be afraid! Tell my followers to go to Galilee. They will see me there'" (CEV).

He is risen! He is risen, indeed! Alleluia!

> **HE IS RISEN! HE IS RISEN, INDEED! ALLELUIA!**

EASTER

PIÑATA PROCESSIONAL

(Worship/Education/Music)

Materials: For each child: an almost complete Easter egg piñata, paste, ribbons, streamers and feathers (optional), a broom handle or dowel.

Preparation: Have each learner take a 3 foot (91 cm) length of ribbon and dip the middle of the ribbon into the paste. Apply to a completed piñata (see page 59), wrapping from the tie end around the bottom (opposite end) and back up to the tie end. Repeat this process 2 to 3 times with additional ribbon, always being sure to wrap ribbon around the bottom end of the balloon, which is the opposite end from the tie. This will help ensure that as the children carry their piñatas, the weight of the piñata will be held securely by the ribbons. Allow to dry.

The piñata procession is an opportunity for the children to be involved in Easter worship and display Easter items they have made. Show the learners how to gather the ends of the ribbon and tie them in a knot. Tie to the end of a dowel or broom handle and allow ribbons to cascade down the pole. Have the learners wrap the pole with streamers, feathers, and more ribbons as decoration for the piñata procession. Just before worship, gather the learners together with their Easter egg piñatas and have them line up to proceed into church during the opening hymn.

PENTECOST

The word *Pentecost* is derived from the Greek word for "the fiftieth." Originally, the day was called Pentecost because it fell 50 days after Passover. Jews celebrated Pentecost, also known as the "Festival of Weeks," as a celebration of the wheat harvest. But what happened on the fiftieth day after Christ was raised from the dead changed the meaning of Pentecost and the world, forever. Jesus promised to send his Spirit, and on the day of Pentecost, that promise was fulfilled.

As we read in Acts 2, the followers of Jesus were gathered together in one place when suddenly a great noise filled with wind and fire swept over the assembly. Tongues as of fire appeared over their heads and they were filled with the Holy Spirit. Since it was Pentecost, Jerusalem was full of Jews who had come from all over to observe the festival of harvest. They came rushing toward where the disciples were gathered to investigate the commotion. And then they heard the disciples, who were not particularly educated men, speaking in each of their own languages. They were amazed, excited, and full of wonder.

The word used for "spirit" in Hebrew is also the same word for "breath" and "wind." The Hebrew word *ruah* can be translated three different ways. Putting these translations together gives the word a greater dimension. The Spirit (wind, breath) of God moved over the waters of the deep in Genesis. God breathes (spirit, wind) life into Adam. And at Pentecost, a mighty rushing wind (breath, spirit) breathes new life into believers, filling them with the Holy Spirit and giving life to their efforts to give witness to the truth of God in Christ Jesus. The church is created, but more than that, life is transformed because the Spirit continues to be active and present in the world.

The work of the Spirit is not easy to describe. Just as we can only see the wind as it moves through the trees, we are surer of the Spirit's activity when we observe evidence of its presence. It is the Spirit that brings us to belief, binds our community in faith, nurtures us, sustains us, and ultimately keeps us as disciples of Jesus. It is through the Holy Spirit that we are washed clean of our sins at baptism, and adopted into the family of God. It is through the Spirit that we receive the body and blood of Jesus in the bread and wine. And it is through the Spirit that we are empowered to "Go make disciples of all nations" (Matthew 28:19). Just as the first disciples were on fire with the good news of the life, death, and resurrection of Jesus, we too are called to share what we know to be the truth.

The color for the day of Pentecost is red, recalling the tongues of fire and the presence of the Holy Spirit. The season after Pentecost continues through the summer and extends into the fall until Christ the King Sunday just before the beginning of Advent. In this longest season of Pentecost, the red color of Pentecost day changes to green to reflect the growing season of summer and the Spirit's activity in the growth of the church.

PENTECOST SONGS

"Spirit, Spirit of Gentleness" (With One Voice [WOV] 684)

"Holy, Holy Spirit" (LifeSongs 70)

"Lord, Listen to Your Children Praying" (WOV 775)

"Spirit of the Living God" (LifeSongs 72)

"O Day Full of Grace" (Lutheran Book of Worship 161)

All suggested hymns are included in either Lutheran Book of Worship, With One Voice, or LifeSongs, as well as in many other Christian hymnals.

HOLY SPIRIT HATS

(Pre-Elementary)

Materials: Bible storybook; white painter hats or large bandana-sized handkerchiefs; orange, yellow, and red fabric paint; paper plates or plastic lids; paint smocks; large brushes (½–1 inch [1-2.5 cm] in width) or 1 inch [2.5 cm]) sponge brushes; tape; cardboard; small jars of water; pie tins; and newspaper.

Preparation: Cover your workspace with newspaper. Crumple sheets of newspaper to stuff hats.

Read the story of Pentecost in Acts 2 to the learners and talk about how people knew the Holy Spirit was present due to what appeared to be tongues of fire on people's heads.

Have the learners put on paint smocks and explain that they are going to make hats or head coverings that will remind them of the Holy Spirit. Give each learner a handkerchief or hat. Fill the hat with crumbled newspaper to make hats easier to paint.

To make the handkerchiefs easier to paint, staple them to cardboard or tape them to a table.

Give each child a quarter-sized blob of yellow, red, and orange fabric paint on a paper plate or plastic lid. If orange fabric paint is unavailable, show the children how to mix red and yellow. Also give them a blob of iridescent gold to add a few sparkling brush strokes.

Allow learners to decorate their hats or handkerchiefs with the paint. Let the hats and handkerchiefs dry completely, then let the learners wear them.

SAND CANDLE

(Lower Elementary)

Materials: Sandbox, a tub or gallon bucket full of damp sand, wicks, wax or old candles, long pencils to hold the wicks. Optional: shells, pebbles, glitter, or other decorative items.

Preparation: Have an adult helper melt wax or old candles in advance.

Making and lighting candles can help us remember the fire of the Holy Spirit that appeared at Pentecost. Have children make a depression in damp sand. It can be a handprint, the underside of a small bowl, or a free-style creation.

Have the leader or an adult helper pour melted wax into the depression. Show the learners how to wrap one end of the wick around a long pencil. Allow the wick to dangle to the bottom of the hot wax at the center of the candle. Straddle the pencil across the depression over the cooling wax so that the wick stays in place. Allow wax to cool completely.

Show the learners how to carefully remove the wax from the depression in the sand, and brush off any excess sand. Trim the bottom of the candle wherever necessary so that it will sit level and not tip over or burn unevenly. Cut the wick to a ½ inch (1 cm) and light the candle, saying a prayer to thank God for the gift of the Holy Spirit!

Option: Decorate the sides of the depression with shells or pebbles.

PENTECOST

WIND CHIMES
(Upper Elementary)

Materials: Small 3 or 4 inch (8 or 10 cm) terra-cotta plant pots, oven dry craft clay (available at craft stores), plastic knives, cooking parchment, toothpicks, fishing line, one 1½ inch (3.8 cm) large metal washer, one ½ inch (1.3 cm) washer, additional small and large washers, one 8-inch (20 cm) metal wreath frame (available at craft stores), and one key chain ring.

Preparation: Write the learners' names on cooking parchment and place the names on a cookie sheet.

If a metal wreath frame is unavailable, cut a plastic ring from a cottage cheese container or something similar. Ring should be about 4 inches (10 cm) in diameter and 2 inches (5 cm) from top to bottom. Simply cut off the 2 top inches of the container. The presence of the Holy Spirit is accompanied by a mighty wind. Wind chimes let us know when the wind is blowing and remind us of the activity of the Holy Spirit.

Distribute a tennis-ball-sized portion of clay to each learner. Have the learners make balls, snakes, little bells, and flat shapes out of the clay. Give learners a toothpick and have them poke holes in each item, place them on a cookie sheet, and follow the instruction on the clay for drying.

While the clay is drying, give each learner a terra-cotta pot, some fishing line, a large and small washer, a wire wreath frame, and a small key ring. Show the learners how to tie two 1-foot (30 cm) pieces of fishing line to the small washer. Thread one line through the drainage hole in the inside of the pot, and tie it loosely to the small ring. The height of this string may need to be adjusted, so wait to tie it securely. Tie the other end to the large washer. As you pick up the pot by the small ring, the large washer should still be inside the pot. You have now made a bell with the pot, and the washer is the ringer.

Show the learners how to take the larger 8-inch wreath frame, (or your homemade plastic ring) and tie six 1-foot (30 cm) pieces of line at regular intervals around the ring. Gather the 6 lines together and tie in a knot about 6 inches (15 cm) above the ring. Place the ring/wreath frame over the pot and tie a secondary knot to the key chain. The large ring/wreath frame is now attached to the small ring and hangs like an umbrella over the bell-like pot.

Hang dried clay pieces and additional washers too if you like, with fishing line from the larger ring. Items can be hung from various lengths of line. Keep in mind, the idea is for them to hit each other or the pot when the wind blows.

Hang the key ring from a hook as the children work to better gauge the length of line needed to add clay pieces. Once all the clay pieces have been added, hang the chimes in the wind. As you listen for the wind to do its work, remember to listen also for the work of the Holy Spirit!

Options: Hang an additional large washer from the large washer that acts as the bell ringer. This will provide additional movement for the "bell" and will give the clay pieces something else to hit. Decorate all the clay pieces and the terra-cotta pot with a high gloss latex paint.

PRAYER MAT
(Intergenerational)

Materials: Copies of prayers and pictures on pages 74-75, scissors, roll of clear contact paper, and 11 x 14-inch (28 x 36 cm) paper.

Preparation: Copy prayers and pictures for each learner in advance.

The prayer mat is like a large place mat. It can be used for the center of a table, or room, or wherever you would like to pray. One side of the mat is for table prayers and the other side is for evening or bedtime prayers. Families should work on one mat together.

Give each family or learner making a mat an 11 x 11-inch (28 x 28 cm) piece of paper. (Some paper comes larger. Trim off the excess with a paper cutter.) Have available a copy of the list of prayers for each mat being made. Also provide a copy of the mat center and decorative pictures.

Option: Copy a mat center design (see pages 74 and 75) onto the center of the 11 x 11 paper first so that it's already there when you hand it out.

Have families or learners choose which prayers they want on their mat and arrange the prayers as they like around the mat's center, putting mealtime prayers on one side and bedtime or evening prayers on the other. If a prayer is not listed that they would like to include, invite them to write it on the mat. Have the families or learners decorate the mat with pictures.

Option: Copy each side of the completed mat on two sheets of 11 x 14-inch paper. This eliminates the raised tape edges and makes for a cleaner look. Make the mat square in shape by trimming the excess inches.

Decorate the mat with markers. Finish the mat by laminating the two sides of mat between two sheets of clear contact paper. Trim contact paper so edges are even, but allow for at least a ½ inch (1 cm) margin of contact paper only so that the two sides of the mat are secured between the contact paper.

> THE PRAYER MAT CAN BE USED FOR THE CENTER OF A TABLE, OR ROOM, OR WHEREVER YOU WOULD LIKE TO PRAY.

PENTECOST

PENTECOST

MEAL PRAYERS

Bless this food to our use and
Our lives to your service,
Through Jesus Christ our Lord.
Amen

God is great; God is good.
Let us thank God for our food.
By God's hand we all are fed.
Give us, Lord, our daily bread.
Amen

Our Father in heaven
Hallowed be your name,
Your kingdom come,
Your will be done,
On earth as it is in heaven.
Give us today our daily bread.
Forgive us our sins as we forgive those
Who sin against us.
Save us from the time of trial
And deliver us from evil.
For the kingdom, the power, and the glory
Are yours, now and forever.
Amen

The Lord's Prayer from *A Contemporary Translation of Luther's Small Catechism, Pocket Edition*, trans. Timothy J. Wengert.

Bless us O Lord and these thy gifts
Which we are about to receive from thy bounty,
Through Christ our Lord. Amen

Before the meal:
Come Lord Jesus be our guest
And let these gifts to us be blessed. Amen

After the meal:
O give thanks unto the Lord for he is good.
And his mercy endures forever. Amen

For health and strength and daily food
We praise thy name, O Lord. Amen

ADDITIONAL GRAPHICS

O, the Lord is good to me
And so I thank the Lord,
For giving me the things I need
The sun and the rain and the apple seed.
The Lord is good to me. Amen

Be present at our table Lord
Be here and everywhere adored,
These mercies bless and grant that we
May feast in paradise with thee.
Amen

Reproducible Page, for use with "Prayer Mat," *Six Seasons of Fun! Activities, Crafts, and More* © 2002 Augsburg Fortress. May be reproduced for local use.

PENTECOST

God, who made the earth and heaven,
Darkness and light:
You the day for work have given,
For rest the night.
May your angel guards defend us,
Slumber sweet your mercy send us,
Holy dreams and hopes attend us,
All through the night.

God only is the maker
Of all things near and far.
God paints the wayside flower,
God lights the evening star.
The winds and waves obey him;
By God the birds are fed.
Much more to us, his children,
God gives our daily bread.
All good gifts around us are sent
From heaven above.
We thank the Lord,
Yes, thank the Lord for all his love.

BEDTIME PRAYERS

Now I lay me down to sleep.
I pray the Lord my soul to keep,
Angels guard me through the night,
And keep me safe 'till morning light.
Amen

Praise God from whom all blessings flow,
Praise him all creatures here below.
Praise him above ye heavenly hosts.
Praise Father, Son, and Holy Ghost. Amen

Now all the woods are sleeping,
Through fields the shadows creeping,
And cities sink to rest;
Let us, as night is falling,
On God our maker calling,
Give thanks to him who loves us best.

Text © 1978 *Lutheran Book of Worship*.

Dear God,
Bless me as I sleep this night.
Keep me from all harm and fright.
Thank you for the now done day.
Love and rest have come my way.
Amen

Lord Jesus, since you love me,
Now spread your wings above me
And shield me from alarm.
Though evil would assail me,
Your mercy will not fail me;
I rest in your protecting arms.

My loved ones, rest securely,
For God this night will surely
From peril guard your heads.
Sweet slumbers may he send you
And bid his hosts attend you
And through the night watch o'er your beds.

SAMPLE PRAYER MAT

Reproducible Page, for use with "Prayer Mat," *Six Seasons of Fun! Activities, Crafts, and More* © 2002 Augsburg Fortress. May be reproduced for local use.

75

PENTECOST

DECORATED CANDLE JAR

(Upper Elementary)

Materials: Small jars, craft paint for glass, brushes, water, stencils shown below.

Preparation: Cleanse the jars thoroughly.

The prayer mat center is the perfect place for a candle to be lit during devotions and other times of prayer.

Paint the jar as you like, using the stencils or free hand. To get a stained glass effect, outline each image in black paint. Allow the paint to dry. Place a candle in the jar and light at prayer times.

> THE PRAYER MAT CENTER IS THE PERFECT PLACE FOR A CANDLE TO BE LIT DURING DEVOTIONS AND OTHER TIMES OF PRAYER.

Reproducible Stencil Page, for use with "Decorated Candle Jar," *Six Seasons of Fun! Activities, Crafts, and More*
© 2002 Augsburg Fortress. May be reproduced for local use.

PENTECOST: A RETELLING

(Worship/Education/Music)

Materials: Long poles such as broom handles, banner poles, or dowels, streamers of paper or cloth. Optional: add some sparkling gold, orange, or red to the streamers or cloth.

Preparation: Have many volunteers available and have a dress rehearsal before the actual event.

PENTECOST SCRIPT

This is a dramatic retelling of the Pentecost event within a context that is more familiar to our own. It follows the story as recorded in Acts 2 closely, but offers an alternative reading that includes a wide variety of nationalities, emphasizing the Holy Spirit's power to move in and speak to the lives of all people everywhere.

A reader from the lectern begins.

Reader: On the day of Pentecost all the Lord's followers were together in one place. Suddenly there was a noise from heaven like the sound of a mighty wind!
(Volunteers with streamers on poles make rushing, blowing noises as they sweep into the congregation. Additional volunteers with rain sticks and fans may be used to add to the effect. The streamers should be over 10 feet [3 m] long and connected between two or more poles so that when the volunteers take their places, the congregation will have streamers crisscrossing over their heads. This will require some practice and organization ahead of time to decide where volunteers will stand and what route they will take to get there.)

Reader: Then they saw what looked like fiery tongues moving in all directions…
(Volunteers shake their poles.)

Reader: … and a tongue came and settled on each person there.
(Streamers are still.)

Reader: The Holy Spirit took control of everyone, and they began speaking whatever languages the Spirit led them to speak.
(Simultaneously, each volunteer will say the phrase "Peace be with you" in another language, twice. Some possibilities are presented phonetically on page 78. Greater possibilities may exist within the membership of your congregation. The more languages represented, the better.)

> **HAVE MANY VOLUNTEERS AVAILABLE AND HAVE A DRESS REHEARSAL BEFORE THE ACTUAL EVENT.**

Reproducible Page, for use with "Pentecost: A Retelling," *Six Seasons of Fun! Activities, Crafts, and More*
© 2002 Augsburg Fortress. May be reproduced for local use.

PENTECOST

SHALOM. PEACE BE WITH YOU.

English:	Peace be with you.
Chinese:	Joo nee ping ahn
Korean:	Pyung hwa pah-duh-say-yo
Arabic:	Salaam mel-a-coom
Hebrew:	Shalom
Spanish:	Paz a usted
Norwegian: (Norway)	Fred vere med deg *(spelled)* Frayed var-eh may die *(pronunciation)*
German: (Germany)	Friede zie nit euch Freeda zy nit oych
Swedish: (Sweden)	Frid var med dig Freed var med deeg
Akan: (Ghana)	Asomdwoe nka mo Asomjway unka mo
Malagasy: (Madagascar)	Ho aminao anie ny fiadanana Hoo ameenow ah-nee-ay nee feeah-dah-nah-nah
Hindi: (India)	Shanti aapke sath ho Shawn-tee op-kay soth ho
Latvian: (Latvia)	Miers lai ir ar jums Meers lie eerda arda yooms
Setswana: (Botswana)	Kagiso ya morena Kaheeso ya moe-ray-na

Reproducible Page, for use with "Pentecost: A Retelling," *Six Seasons of Fun! Activities, Crafts, and More*
© 2002 Augsburg Fortress. May be reproduced for local use.

Reader: Many people from every country in the world were living in *(your city)*. When they heard this noise, a crowd gathered. But they were surprised, because they were hearing everything in their own languages. They were excited and amazed and said, "Don't all these who are speaking come from *(your neighborhood)*? Then why do we hear them speaking in our own languages? Some of us are from Judea, Mesopotamia, and Egypt. Some are from Namibia, Tanzania, and other parts of Africa. Others are from India, China, and Japan. Still others come from Norway, Sweden, Denmark, Finland, and Russia. There are those, too, from Great Britain, Germany, France, Spain, Italy, Greece, Poland, and Afghanistan. And still others come from Canada, the United States, Mexico, Brazil, Chile, and Argentina. These are but a few of the places from which we come, because we come from *all* over the world. Yet, we hear them using our own languages to tell the wonderful things that God has done."
(Volunteers speak their phrases again, in unison, two times.)

Reader: Everyone was excited and confused. Some of them even kept asking each other, "What does all this mean?"
(Volunteers speak their phrases again, in unison, two times. Then they say together in the language in which they regularly worship, "Peace be with you.")

*If the peace is shared here, the **Reader answers:** And also with you.
(Volunteers may move out of the way as people share the peace with each other.)

If sharing the peace here is too crowded with the streamers and volunteers, go directly into an appropriate Pentecost hymn while the volunteers place their streamer poles out of the way for the rest of the worship. Think about how streamers and poles could be left in the worship space to add some Pentecost color, perhaps along the sides of the sanctuary.

Also, the phrases could be reproduced in your worship folder so the congregation can be aware of what is being said and even listen for the various phrases.

> EVERYONE WAS EXCITED AND CONFUSED.

Reproducible Page, for use with "Pentecost: A Retelling," *Six Seasons of Fun! Activities, Crafts, and More*
© 2002 Augsburg Fortress. May be reproduced for local use.

PENTECOST

> THE RAIN STICK SHOULD MAKE AN EXTENDED SHUSHING NOISE AS THE PEBBLES AND SAND CASCADE FROM ONE END TO THE OTHER.

RAIN STICK

(Combination Age Group)

Materials: Drill, one mailing tube (2 x 24 inch [5 x 61 cm]) with stoppers for the end for each learner, toothpicks, sand, small pebbles, tissue paper, decoupage gloss such as Modge Podge (available at craft stores).

Preparation: Drill small toothpick–sized holes in mailing tubes. Make sure the holes are spaced every inch or so around the circumference and down the length of the tube.

Have the learners place toothpicks in the holes and cut off any part that extends outside the tube. The toothpicks will crisscross inside the tube creating a lattice.

Show the learners how to place one stopper on the end of the tube and fill the tube with pebbles and sand. When the tube is filled, have them place the other stopper in the other end. Have the learners try to see if the rain stick works by turning it upside down. The rain stick should make an extended shushing noise as the pebbles and sand cascade from one end to the other. Adjust sand and pebbles as desired. Glue tissue paper on the entire tube and add a coat of decoupage gloss for a nice finish.

The shushing noise of the rain stick can remind us that it is good to take time to listen for the Holy Spirit speaking in our lives.

The Amazing Animals of Latin America

Have you ever heard of a Capybara, the biggest rodent alive? Did you know that it sometimes weighs more than 200 pounds, but can be taught to eat peanuts out of your hand and to come when you call its name?

Only a few of the animals of Latin America can be tamed. Most, like the Puma or the Jaguar, are savage and very dangerous.

William Wise, in his first book about amazing animals, makes them all become excitingly alive.

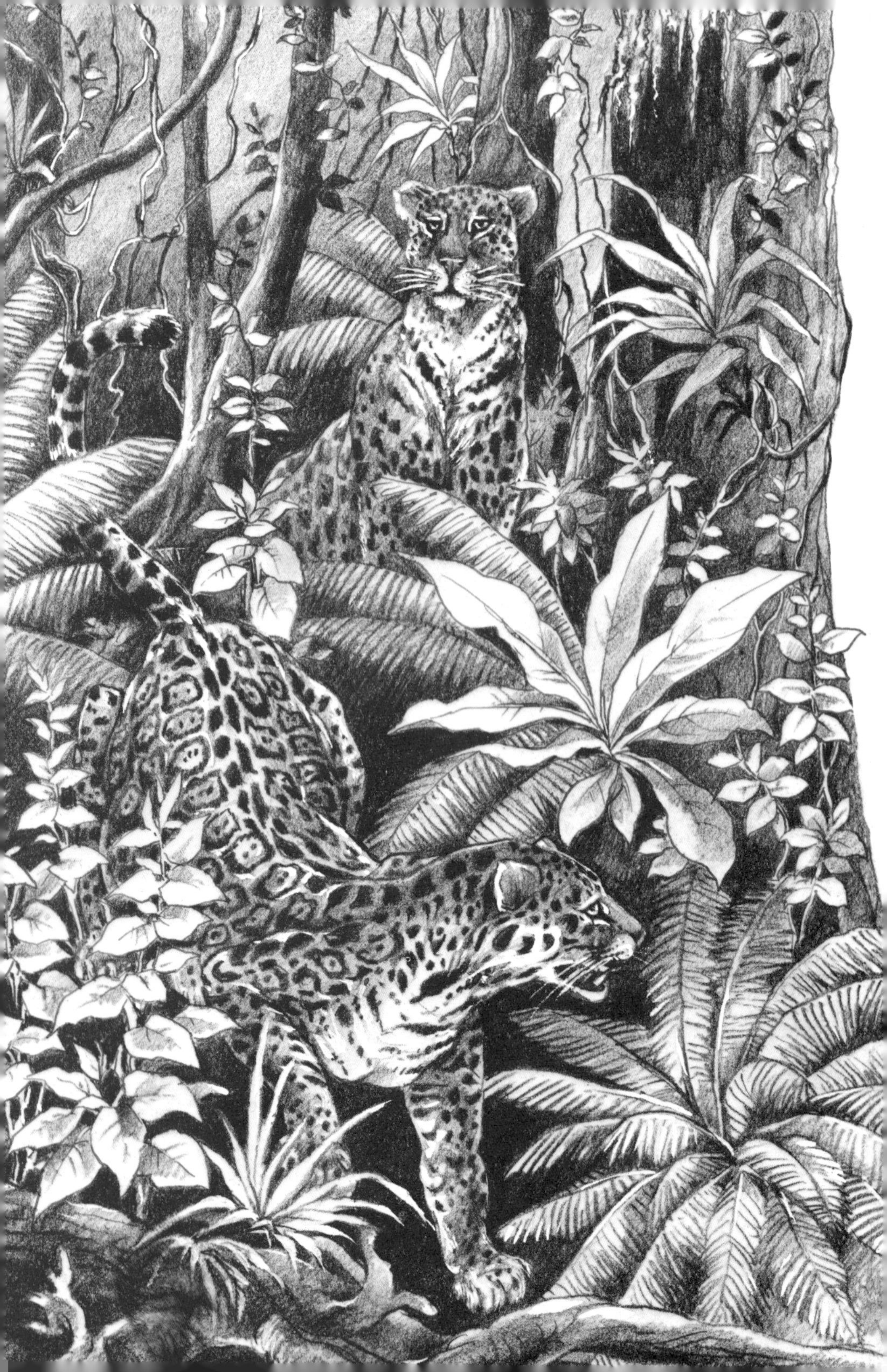

The Amazing Animals of Latin America

by William Wise

Illustrated by Joseph Sibal

A SEE and READ BEGINNING TO READ BOOK

G. P. Putnam's Sons   New York

Text copyright © 1969 by William Wise
Illustrations copyright © 1969 by Joseph Sibal
All rights reserved. Published simultaneously in the
Dominion of Canada by Longmans Canada Limited, Toronto.
Library of Congress Catalog Card Number: 70-77758
PRINTED IN THE UNITED STATES OF AMERICA
07209
6928

We live in a part of the world called North America. To the south of us there is another part of the world.

It is a wonderful place to live.

It is a wonderful place to visit.

It is a part of the world called Latin America.

Most people who visit Latin America come by airplane. From an airplane you can see the highest mountains of Latin America. They are called the Andes. There is snow on top of the Andes all year round.

From an airplane you can see the wide plains of Latin America. They are called the Pampas. You can see the great rivers and jungles of Latin America, too.

But there are some things you cannot see from an airplane. You cannot see the animals of Latin America.

Some of them live in the mountains.

Some live on the plains. Some live in the jungles.

To find them, you must ride in a boat far up one of the great rivers. Or you must climb on foot, high up into the mountains.

The Alpaca is a large animal that lives in the Andes. He is one of the strangest-looking animals in all Latin America.

His wool coat is very thick. He needs a thick wool coat to keep him warm.

The Alpaca is not a wild animal, though. He is a domestic animal, like the cow or the horse. Because he is very strong, people make him carry things along the mountain roads.

The Llama is another domestic animal that lives in the Andes. He is a very useful animal. The people of the mountains take wool from his thick coat. They use it to make their own clothes.

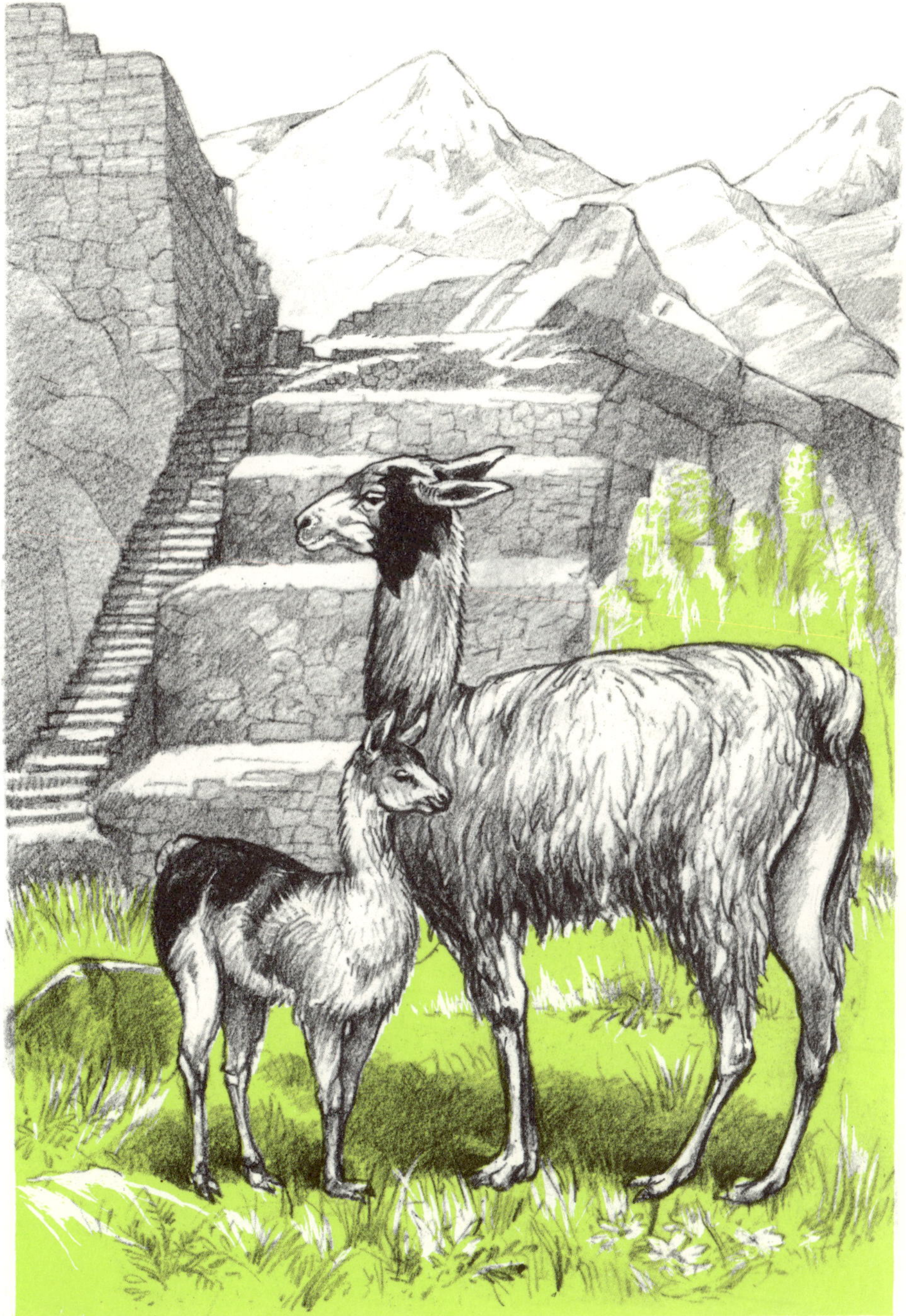

They drink Llama's milk as we drink cow's milk. And they make the Llama carry heavy things along the roads. The Llama is such a useful animal that it would be hard for people to live in the Andes without him.

All the same, the Llama is not a very friendly animal.

He often grows angry. When he does, he picks up little stones with his teeth. Then he spits the stones at you. And spitting stones is not a friendly thing for an animal to do.

You can live for a long time in the Andes and never see the Chinchilla. He is a small, wild animal. He sleeps in the day. He looks for his food at night.

The Chinchilla belongs to the rodent family. He is one of the many rodents in Latin America.

We have many rodents in North America, too. The squirrel is one of our North American rodents. So is the house mouse, and so is the rat.

The Chinchilla has soft, warm fur. Because his fur is so soft and warm, people have always liked to wear it. Long ago in Latin America, Indian kings liked to wear Chinchilla fur.

Then, in our own time, men began to catch the Chinchilla to make fur coats. They caught so many Chinchillas that today almost none are left in Latin America.

The smallest deer in the world lives in the Andes. He is called the Pudu. He is only about as big as a small dog. At first, most people who see a Pudu think that he *is* a small dog.

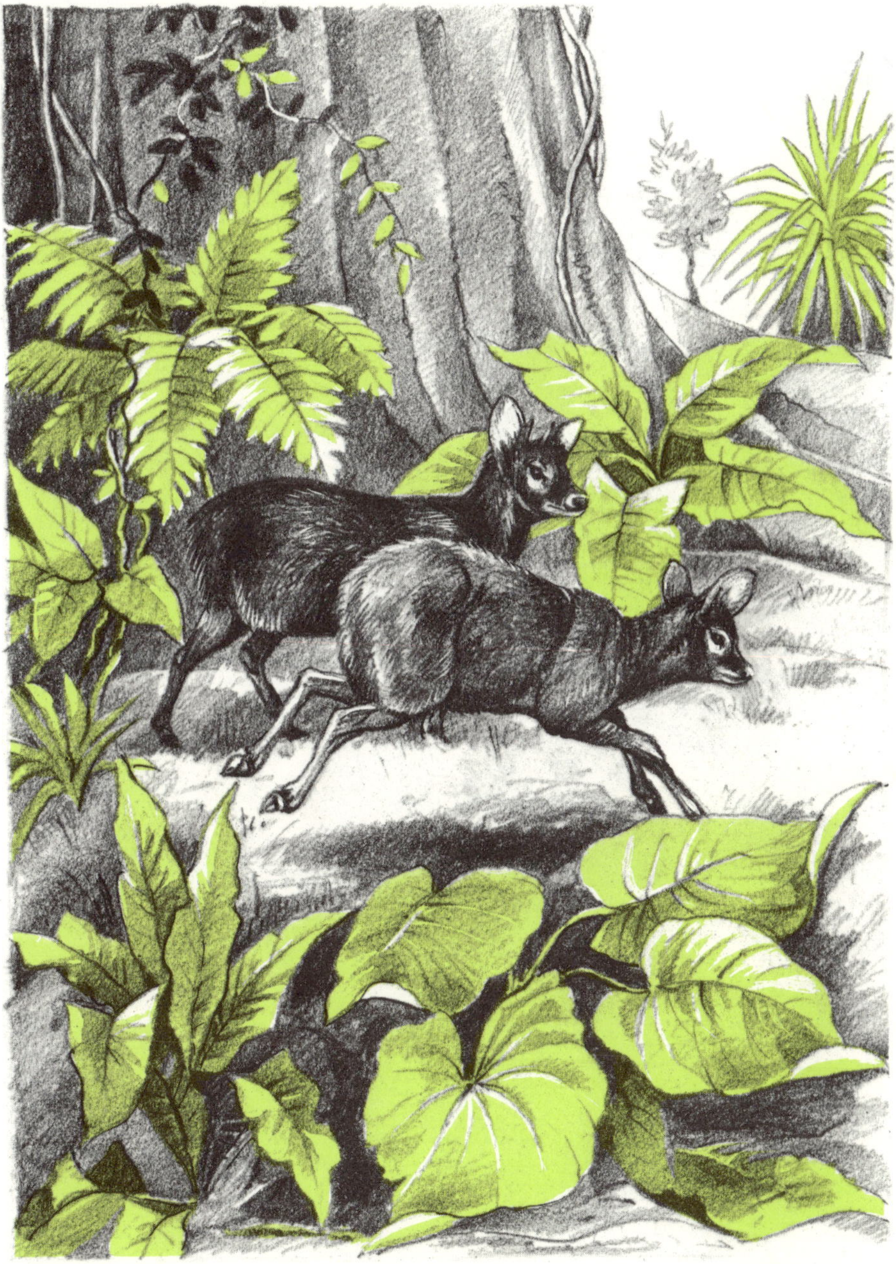

Once a man came to the Andes and found two Pudus. He took them home to Paris, far away from the Andes. He gave them to his children for pets.

The children loved the Pudus. When they took the Pudus for a walk, no one else knew what the little animals were.

"Are they dogs?" people asked.

The children laughed and said, "No, they are not dogs. They are Pudus. They are the smallest deer in the world."

There would be more Pudus in the Andes if it were not for another animal. He is a big cat. In North America he is called the mountain lion. In Latin America he is called the Puma.

Like all big cats, the Puma eats other animals. He eats the Pudu when he can catch him. He eats almost any smaller animal he can catch.

You will find the Puma in the Andes. You will find him on the plains and in the jungle. He is one of the few animals in the world that can live where it is cold and where it is hot.

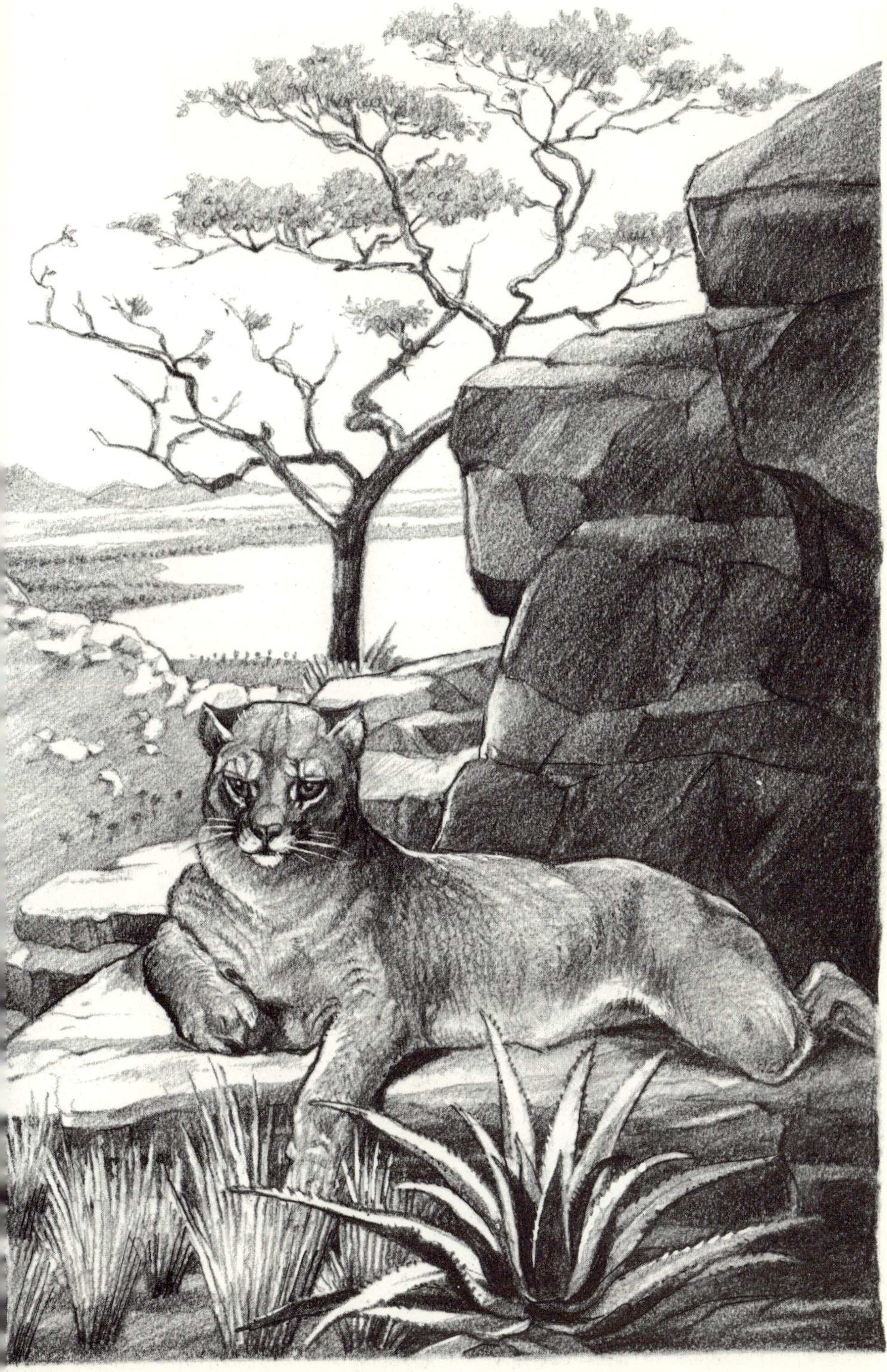

The Coypu lives on the Pampas. He is a large rodent that makes his home near the water. He often swims in the rivers of the Pampas.

A mother Coypu may have six or seven babies at a time. When she goes for a swim, she takes her family along. Then you can see her in the water, with all her babies riding on her back.

The Vizcacha is another rodent of the Pampas. Counting his tail, he is almost three feet long.

Vizcachas like to live together in a big family. They dig large, deep holes in the ground. They live together in the holes. They dig such large, deep holes that even birds and snakes find room to live there, too.

Before you have been on the Pampas very long, you will see the Rhea. He is not an animal, though. He is a giant bird that never leaves the ground.

The Rhea is so heavy that he cannot fly. But he can run very fast. He also can kick very hard.

The biggest animals know how hard he can kick, so they do not come near the Rhea if they can help it.

Some of the most amazing animals in Latin America live in the jungles. You will find the Howler Monkey there.

He is a large monkey, with a long tail. He has many big teeth. But the amazing thing about the Howler Monkey is not his long tail. It is not his teeth.

It is the noise he makes in the tops of the trees.

The Howler Monkey really *howls*. You can hear him far, far away. Of all the animals in Latin America, the Howler Monkey makes the most noise.

There are other amazing animals in the jungle trees. One of them is the Sakiwinki.

He is smaller than the Howler Monkey. He is stranger-looking, too.

The Sakiwinki has long, thin legs. He has big hands, almost like a man's. He has a long, thick tail and a very, very sad face.

When you see the Sakiwinki sitting in a tree you know one thing. You know that you are looking at one of the strangest animals in the world.

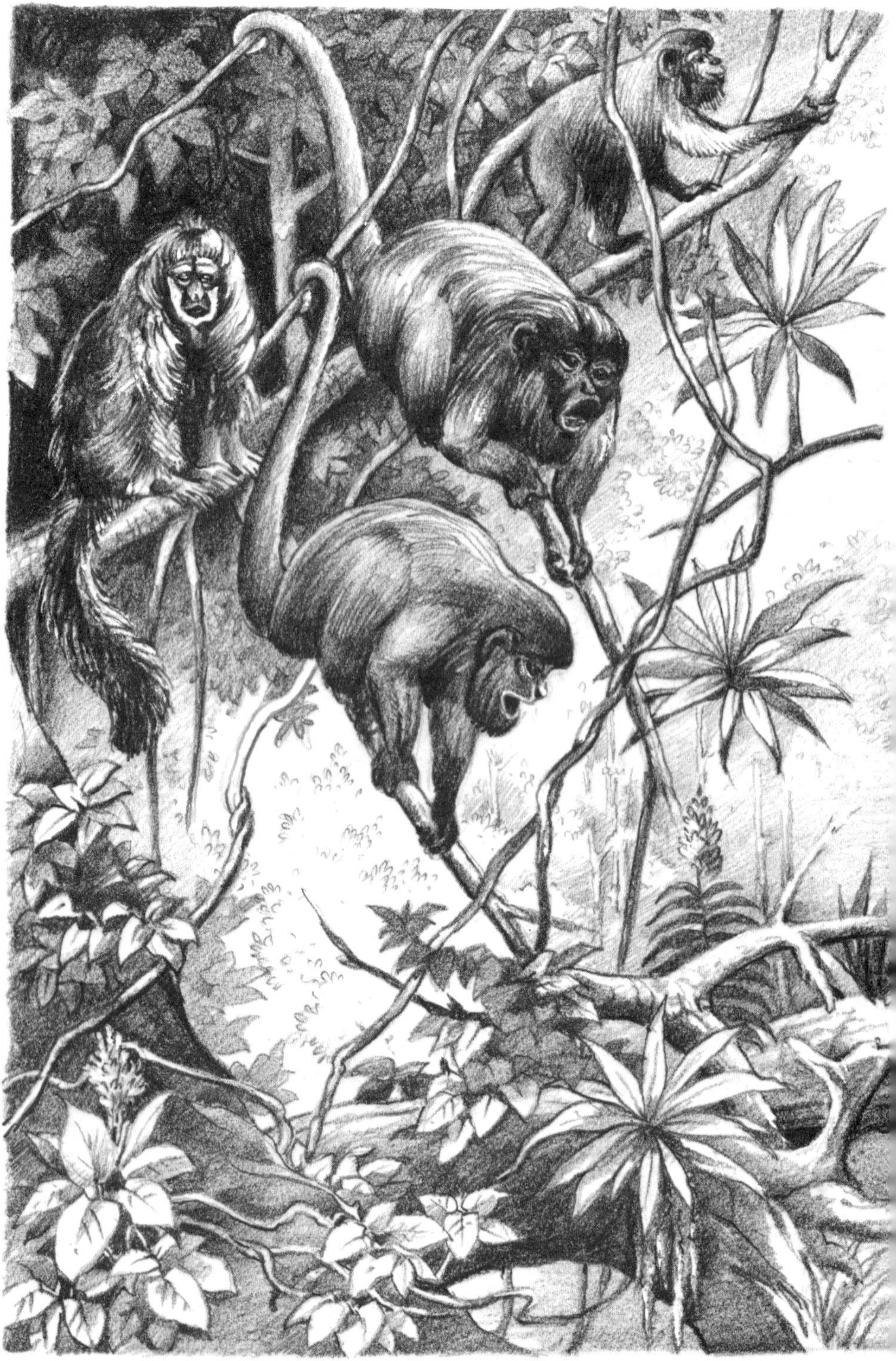

The Sakiwinki and the Howler Monkey have to watch out for another animal. He is called the Jaguar. He is a big cat. He is even bigger than the mountain lion. The Jaguar is so big and strong that some people in Latin America call him the king of the jungle.

The Jaguar likes to eat many other animals. He likes to eat the Sakiwinki and the Howler Monkey. But the Jaguar must be very, very hungry before he will try to eat the Giant Anteater.

From nose to tail, the Giant Anteater is more than six feet long. He has strong legs and big claws.

When the Giant Anteater fights, he stands on his back legs and waves his claws around. He can fight very well, and the Jaguar knows he can.

The Giant Anteater does not have any teeth. So he cannot eat other animals. Instead, he uses his long, sticky tongue to catch insects in the jungle.

When the Giant Anteater finds the home of some jungle insects, he breaks it open with his claws.

He puts out his long tongue. The insects run over his tongue and stick to it. Then the Giant Anteater pulls in his tongue and eats the insects for his dinner.

One of the most amazing animals in the jungle is the Sloth. You will find him among the trees, hanging upside down. Most of the time he looks as though he were asleep.

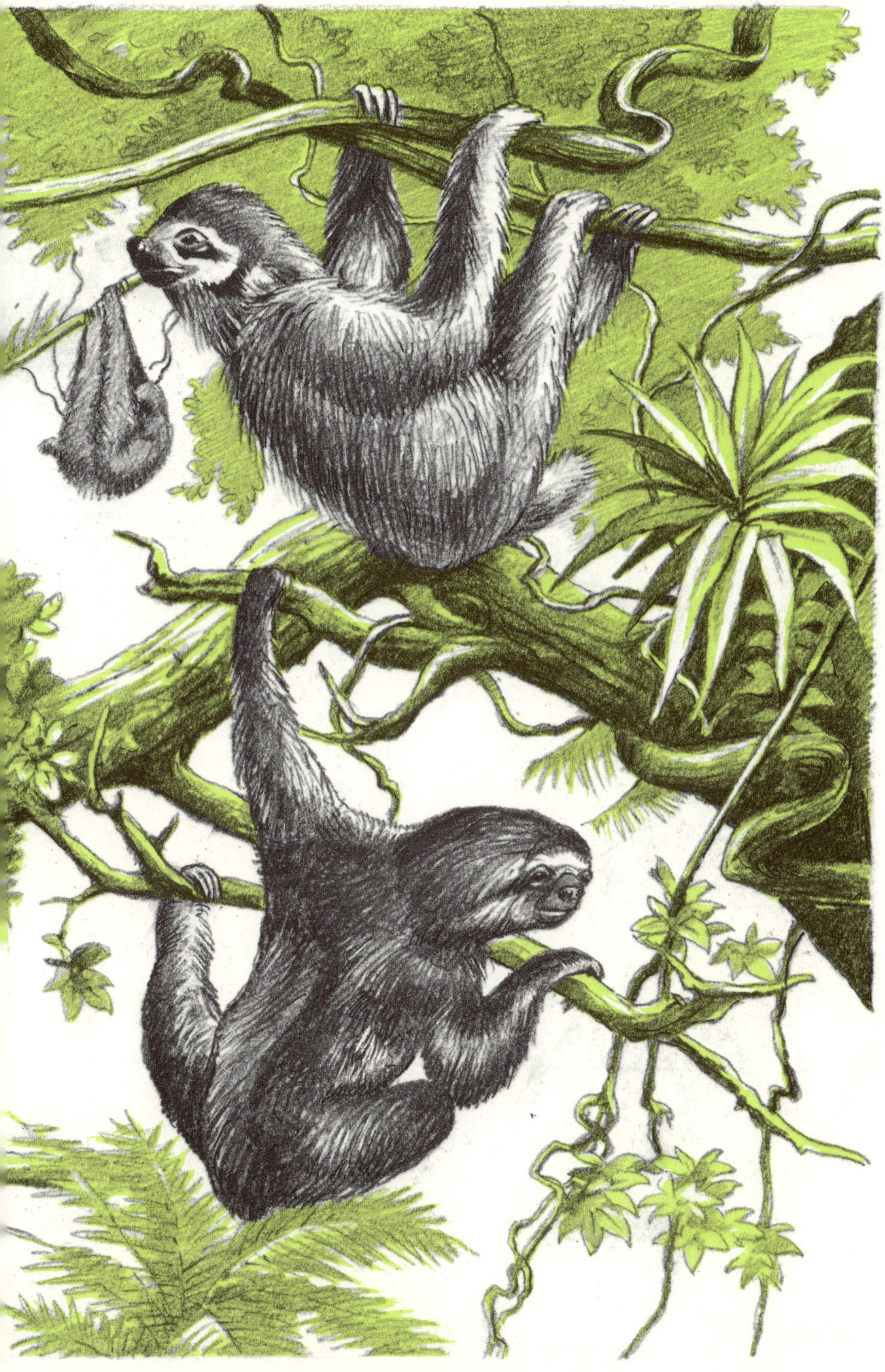

The Sloth never runs. When he moves at all, he moves very slowly. He moves so slowly that you might think it would be easy for the Jaguar to catch him.

It is not easy, though. The Sloth is the same color as the leaves of the trees, so it is hard to see him. Because he moves so slowly and makes so little noise, often the Jaguar does not even guess that he is there.

Another strange jungle animal is the Giant Armadillo. He wears a thick suit of armor. His thick suit of armor makes it hard for other animals to eat him.

The Giant Armadillo knows how to hide, too. He lives near the water where the ground is soft. He can dig in the soft ground with his claws and make a deep hole. That is where he hides when he thinks a big cat might be coming his way.

The Tapir is one of the biggest jungle animals in Latin America. He is about as big as a small car. He is so big that he looks as if he *must* eat other animals.

But he does not eat them. He eats only things like leaves and grass.

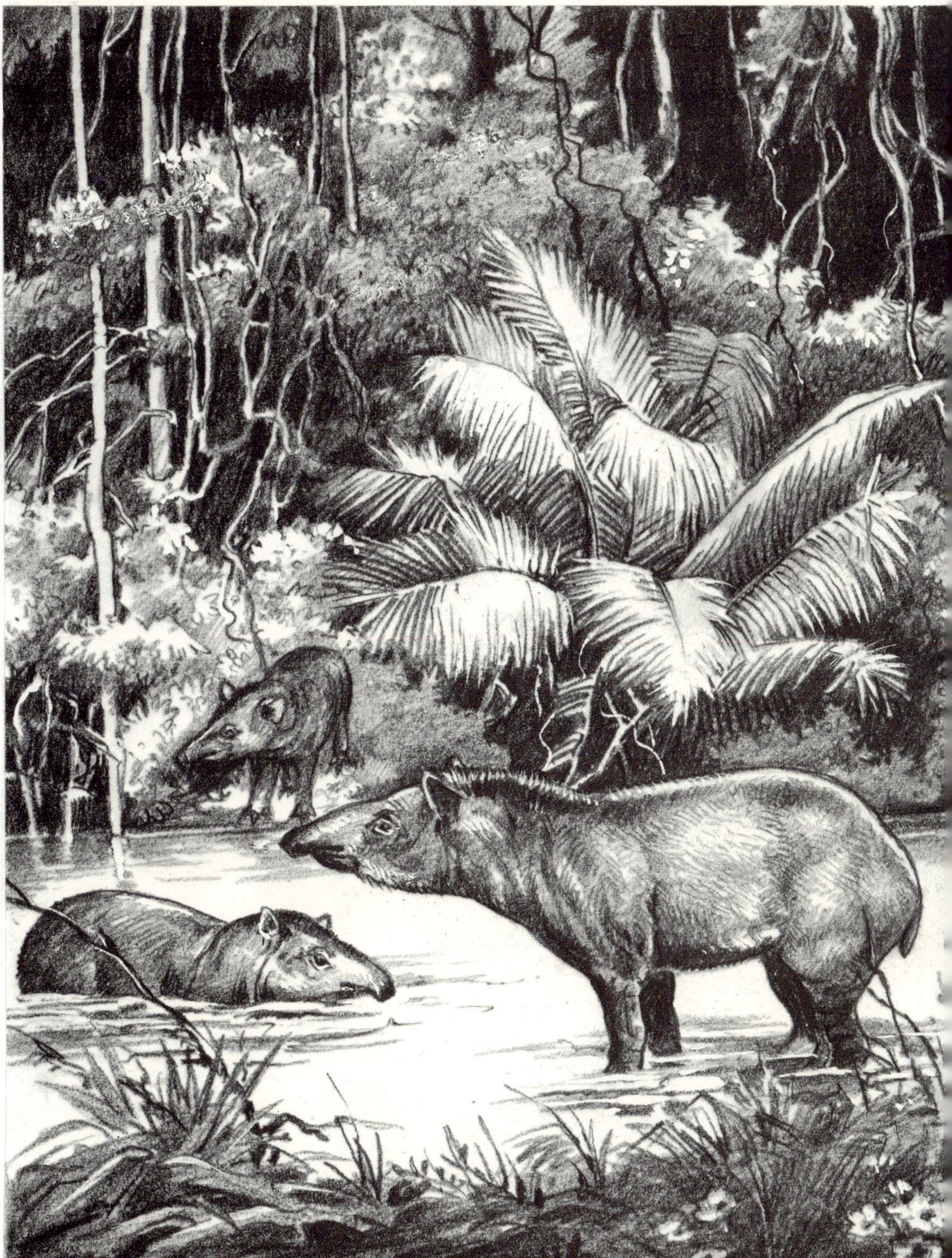

The shy Tapir likes to be alone, but sometimes at night a family of Tapirs will feed together.

If you find a baby Tapir, you can make a pet of him. Indian children in Latin America often have Tapir pets.

But they know another animal they would much rather have for a pet. They would much rather have the Capybara.

The Capybara is the biggest rodent in the world. He often grows to weigh more than two hundred pounds.

A wild Capybara likes to eat grass. A tame Capybara will eat other things. He will even eat peanuts out of your hand, if you should give him some.

A tame Capybara will follow you around the jungle, too. And he will come if you call his name.

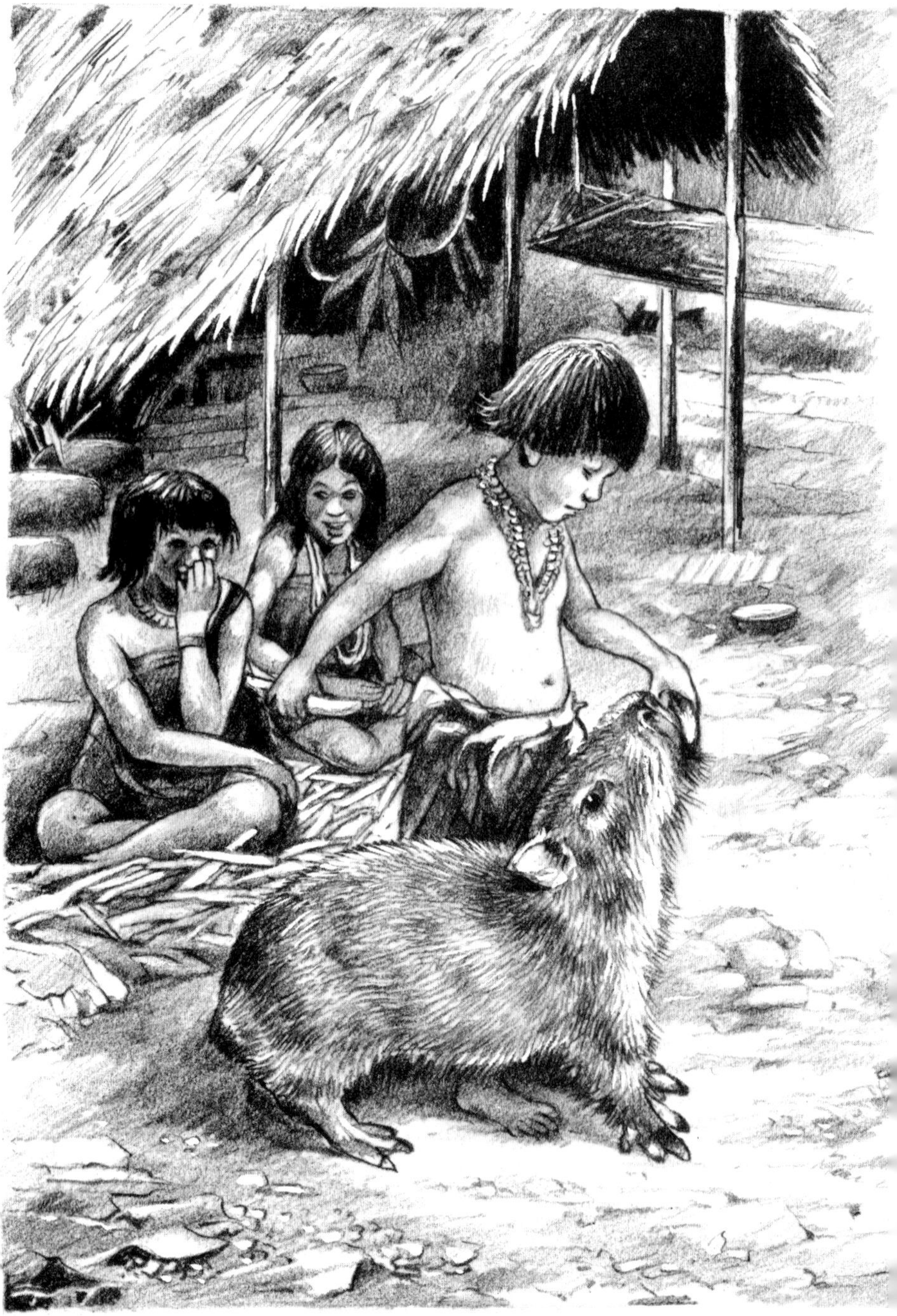

No wonder the Indian children of Latin America like to make a pet out of the Capybara — the biggest rodent in the world.

The lands to the south of us have many strange and wonderful animals. They have so many that no one can hope to see them all on a single trip.

That is why, if you want to see more of them, you must pay another visit to the Andes, the Pampas, and the jungles. For that is where you will find the amazing animals of Latin America.

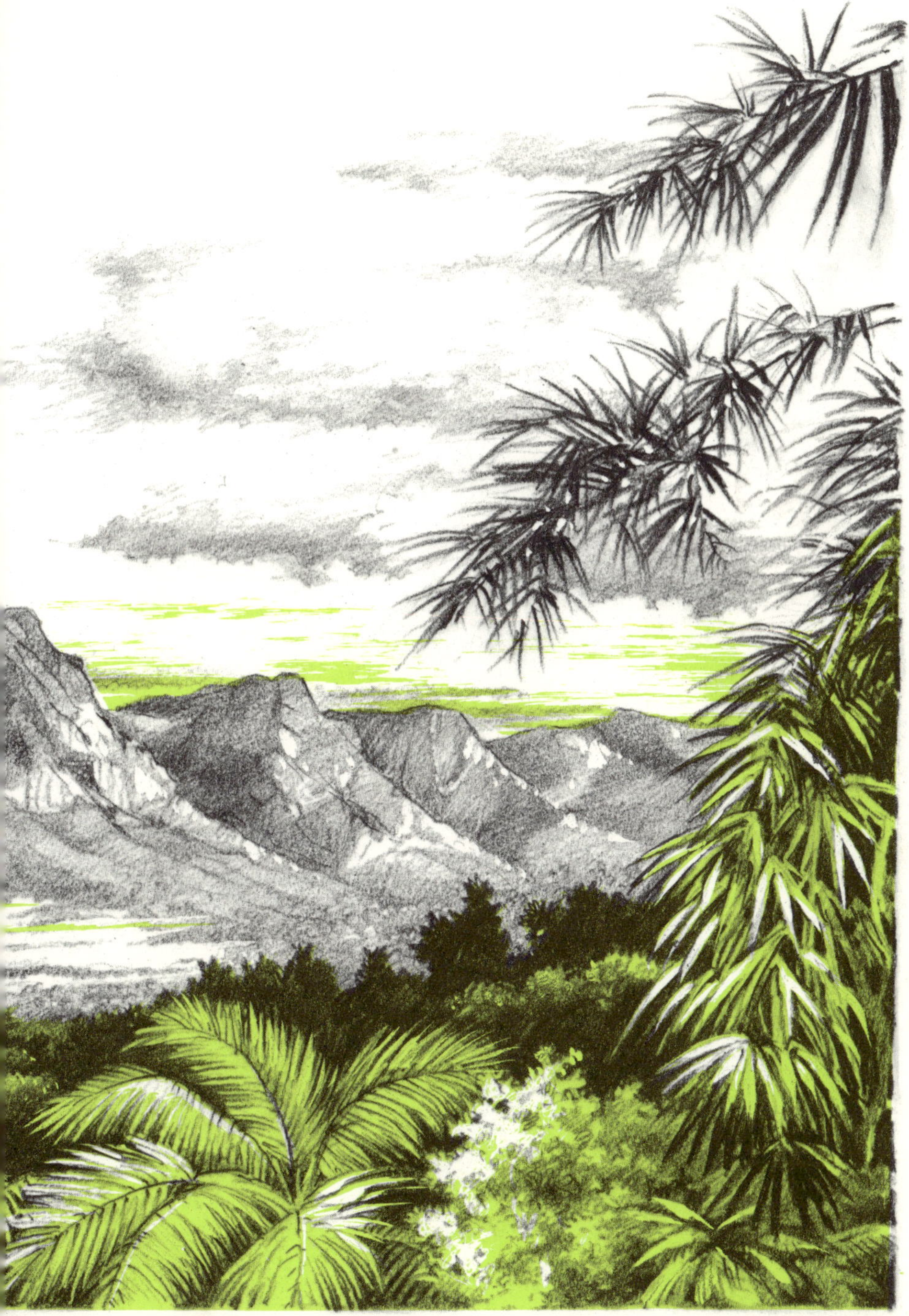

KEY WORDS

Andes Mountains	Jungle
Armor	Pampas
Claws	Plains
Domestic animal	Rodent
Indian	Snakes
Insects	Wool

The Animals:

Alpaca	Llama
Capybara	Pudu
Chinchilla	Puma
Coypu	Rhea
Giant Anteater	Sakiwinki
Giant Armadillo	Sloth
Howler Monkey	Tapir
Jaguar	Vizcacha

Selected Titles from Putnam's
SEE and READ Books

In the Time of the Dinosaurs
by William Wise • Illustrated by Lewis Zacks

The World of Giant Mammals
by William Wise • Illustrated by Lewis Zacks

Boy Who Lived in a Cave
by Estelle Friedman • Illustrated by Theresa Sherman

Monsters of the Ancient Seas
by William Wise • Illustrated by Joseph Sibal

Giant Birds and Monsters of the Air
by William Wise • Illustrated by Joseph Sibal

The Amazing Animals of Latin America
by William Wise • Illustrated by Joseph Sibal

The Author

WILLIAM WISE is the prizewinning author of more than a dozen books for young readers, including *In the Time of the Dinosaurs, The World of Giant Mammals, The Two Reigns of Tutankhamen*, which received a Boys' Club of America Junior Book Award Medal, *Monsters of the Ancient Seas*, and *Giant Birds and Monsters of the Air*. Mr. Wise's *Alexander Hamilton*, a Junior Literary Guild Selection, has been reprinted extensively by the United States Information Service. It has appeared in special Asian and South American editions and has been translated into Portuguese and Bengali.

The Artist

JOSEPH SIBAL is a distinguished natural history artist whose paintings have been reproduced in popular publications, such as *Life* magazine, and in semitechnical publications issued by museums. Mr. Sibal was born in Austria but came to New York City as a young boy and was educated there. He is the illustrator of *The Strange World of Dinosaurs, The Strange World of Reptiles, Monsters of the Ancient Seas*, and *Giant Birds and Monsters of the Air*.

PROPERTY OF 6842
FREDERICKSBURG CITY SCHOOLS

599   6842
Wis
    Wise
    The Amazing Animals of
    Latin America

Hugh Mercer School